INDIA'S WORLD

INDIA'S WORLD

{The Politics of Creativity in a Globalized Society}

Edited by
ARJUN APPADURAI
and ARIEN MACK
with an Introduction by
ARJUN APPADURAI

RAIN TREE
An imprint of Rupa Publications

Published in 2012
in RAIN TREE by Rupa Publications India Pvt. Ltd.
7/16, Ansari Road, Daryaganj,
New Delhi 110 002

Sales Centres:

Allahabad Bengaluru Chennai
Hyderabad Jaipur Kathmandu
Kolkata Mumbai

Printed in India by
Replika Press Pvt. Ltd.

Contents

Introduction

India today is, more than ever, important to understand. Its population stands at well over a billion people, second only to China. It is the most the successful continuous experiment in parliamentary democracy of all the nations that won their independence from colonial rule in the middle of the twentieth century. It was a vital member of the important group of nations that designated themselves as constituting a Non-Aligned Movement in 1956 at a major conference in Bandung, Indonesia. The other major nations in this group have had much more tortured histories. Tito's Yugoslavia fell apart in the early 1990s amid war, genocide, and ethnic cleansing, and is today a set of uncomfortable fragments. Nasser's Egypt is only this year coming out of five decades of military rule and may be assembling the basic pieces of a democratic culture. Sukarno's Indonesia experienced decades of military rule, which included major internal wars and political purges, particularly against local communists, and has struggled to establish a democratic system only since 1998, before which it was ruled by authoritarian military figures. Ghana has also had a checkered history since the mid-1950s, a stretch that has included long periods of authoritarian rule.

India has every reason to be proud of its continuous record of democratic governance, which (except for a brief period of National Emergency rule under Indira Gandhi during the late 1960s) has been characterized by a strong judiciary, an army that has remained tightly under civilian control, a large and professional civil service, and a vibrant, multi-linguistic press. But the country still has monumental problems, reflected in its dismal literacy rates, its severe levels of urban and rural poverty, and its poor infrastructure (especially in the areas of roads, sanitation, and transportation). Many of these challenges are condensed in India's public health statistics, which show shockingly high degrees of vulnerability to morbidity and mortality, especially among poor, rural, and socially disadvantaged communities. Thus the links between democracy and development in India have not been sturdy or reliable, and the country reveals at least one feature of social division that appears global in its reach, namely, the gap between the richest and poorest members of societies across the world.

India and China, because of their economic growth over the last decade, have special reasons to wonder whether that growth is the best route to justice and to equity, as in both cases the members of the professional, corporate, and political elites are vastly better off than the bottom 50 percent of their respective societies. In China, due to its authoritarian central government, this gap produces major worries about dissent, disharmony, and media freedom. In India, where dissent is much more rich and vocal, the problems of equity and inequality are not hidden from official or unofficial view, but nevertheless do not seem easily tractable to either market or state solutions.

SUCCESS AND FAILURE

India is today a world economic power with an annual growth rate in the range of 9.5% (which was recently adjusted to around 6.5% due to the current recession). It is also the world's largest democracy, with elections whose administration and execution constitute a miracle in their own right. Its constitution is secular and open to all faiths. This constitution is also oriented fundamentally to the inclusion and empowerment of those classes, castes, and regions which have historically been disadvantaged. These are indeed reasons for pride among India's ruling elite and many of its ordinary citizens.

India now aspires to economic domination in Asia and in the world. To these aspirations, it brings a long acquaintance with English, the energy of free enterprise, a highly skilled and innovative software industry, and some of the finest scientists and technologists in the world. Indian corporations have now gone global in a big way, with Indian media giants signing deals with Sony and DreamWorks, Indian auto manufacturers entering US and European markets, Indian engineering companies playing major roles in the modernization of the Gulf states and South East Asia, Indian software companies providing skilled workers to all the major industrial economies of the West, and Indian students entering the finest universities in the United States and Europe in record numbers.

Against these highly visible accomplishments, as I have already suggested, India has a great deal to be less proud of. Indian public health has yet to see the public health revolutions of the West, and India lags far behind China in most of the key numbers on morality, morbidity, and productivity. Waterborne diseases take a huge toll on children, in spite of major advances in treatment methods such as ORT (Oral Rehydration Therapy). In many areas of public health, Bangladesh is doing better than India. When we recall that India provides physicians to many of the hospitals and medical systems in the West and that Indian nurses are known globally for their skills and training, these facts are not just puzzling, they are scandalous.

Indian infrastructure, particularly in the areas of roads, electricity, and sanitation, is the major obstacle to foreign investors and manufacturers. Many Indian cities now have 6- and 7-star hotels, sophisticated flyovers, a surfeit of expensive automobiles, and an abundance of high-end housing and office development. Yet, every Indian city, without exception, is also a site of public filth, severely clogged traffic, damaged or non-existent pavements for pedestrians, vast areas of slum housing, and visible poverty that shocks even visitors from the poorest countries of the rest of the world. In the city of Mumbai, it sometimes takes 2 hours to go from the airport to South Mumbai, a distance of no more than 25 kilometers, this in spite of many flyovers and a major new sea-link between Bandra and Worli, which cuts driving time on this stretch by at least 30 minutes.

So we have in India a massive globalizing economy which has equally massive problems of poverty, inequality, and infrastructure. Many of the observations I have made so far are familiar to students of India. The authors who have contributed to this book also cast light on the numerous ways in which this paradox can be viewed. The question their contributions raise is how to understand the relationship between India's successes and its failures. In my view, they need to be understood together for they are intimately connected.

The essays in this volume cast light on the paradox of freedom without equity, though they were not commissioned with this question in mind. Ajit Balakrishnan tells us how India became a global giant in the IT industries and illuminates the preconditions for this fabled strand of India's rise as a global power. His essay deserves to be read in concert with Sabyasachi Bhattacharya's sobering essay on Indian science and the dangerous division between teaching and research in Indian science today. This pair of essays makes us ponder how weak science can coexist with innovative technology in the same developing society.

Mukulika Banerjee's rich description of Indian election culture shows us why Indian electoral turnout is remarkably high, despite major problems of transport, literacy, and poverty for many voters. The desire to be part of the national political process that the participants embody also shows up as part of the popular passion that surrounds the politics of Indian cricket. Cricket in India, as discussed by Boria Majumdar, is the richest part of the colonial heritage to animate Indian mass culture, and this popular interest has been transformed into a massive global commercial opportunity for the corporate world and the Indian state to share in the spoils of globalization today. Science and technology in India also have a dark side, as Lawrence Cohen demonstrates in his essay on the business of organ surgery in India, where high technology, commercialized medical entrepreneurs, and criminal mafias join to exploit the efforts of the semi-literate poor to benefit from advanced surgical technologies.

While the medicalized body is on sale in many Indian cities, the sexualized body brings out a deep strain of Puritanism, which, Wendy Doniger argues, is not, as is often suggested, a part of India's inheritance from Victorian England. Rather, this Puritanism is itself part of a long debate about sexuality, gender, and bodily revelation in Indic society and culture. The vehicles through which various debates about culture, politics, and morality are transmitted and transformed are to be found in India's rich literary tradition and media, which are the subjects of the essays by Ranjani Mazumdar, Sheldon Pollock, and Rajeswari Sunder Rajan. Pollock presents the depressing picture of a nation that is rapidly losing its links to its own classical heritage and at the same time beginning to lose the capacity to train the best writers, translators, and researchers both in the classical and the modern languages of India. What remains truly alive is the sphere of Indian writing in English, where, Sundar Rajan tells us, we can better understand the myriad ways in which, as Malcolm Muggeridge once said, "Indians are the last living Englishmen." Ranjani Mazumdar brings us full circle, in her essay on Bollywood cinema, to the ways in which terror, spectacle, and surveillance now form the bridge between urban violence and popular entertainment in India today.

The essays by Gopal Guru and Suvir Kaul return us to politics proper and to a world where cultural, religious, and ethnic identities are intimately caught up in national politics. Kaul's essay is a melancholic meditation on Kashmir, where India and Pakistan have co-conspired to create a cauldron of ethno-religious warfare in a valley long characterized by hybridity of every kind. Guru's essay reminds us of the dilemmas of India's large untouchable minority, which still strives against the grain for cultural dignity despite many successful legal and political changes that have occurred in the realm of affirmative action in India.

WHAT IS THE PROBLEM?

The first major structural fact that we need to understand about India (and this happens to be true of China as well), is that in the 60 years or more since India became an independent nation, the project of wealth creation has become radically unhinged from the project of poverty alleviation and social inclusion. India is now an unrelenting wealth-producing machine, where state policies and private enterprise have created a legal and economic framework in which the fetters to private enterprise and wealth accumulation have been radically weakened. The early socialist ideals of Nehru have mostly given way to the neo-liberal vision of the late Rajiv Gandhi and his heirs, who have a full-scale commitment to private wealth accumulation. The development state still exists in India, but it is mostly a vast rent-gathering apparatus which is there to assure that the poor are not in the way of massive capitalist development both in the rural and urban sectors.

The divorce between the developmental state (of the 1950s and 1960s) and the global corporatist state of the 1990s and the first decade of the twenty-first century, is the public expression of a deep transformation in the culture of the political classes in India and of the state in particular. This divorce is not the same as the classic tension between industrial capitalism and the regulatory state. It is, in fact, a change within the culture of the state itself and indeed of public politics in general. How are we to understand this change?

In my view, there are three primary factors which are also linked to one another. The first is corruption. The second is the "black economy" or the economy of untaxed and unrecorded wealth. The third is the thorough monetization of electoral politics by the first two. Together, these three factors have driven a deep wedge between the wealth-generating capacities of the Indian political classes and their obligation to commit public resources to the uplift of the vast majority of Indians who live in or near the conditions of abject poverty. How has this wedge been built and activated?

Corruption is now center stage in Indian politics. The remarkable rise of Anna Hazare in the past year and the national surge of middle-class support for his fasts and protests against corruption show that ordinary Indians understand that their politics is not simply tainted by corruption, but has, in fact, been hijacked by it. The recent all-out battle in the Parliament about the Lokpal Bill, which would have created an independent watchdog institution to root out corruption in the bureaucracy and the polity, showed us the vigor with which many politicians go a long way to make sure that corruption machine remains unchecked. Anna Hazare's movement is currently in trouble, beset by problems of political disunity and the failing health of its leader. But the corruption issue is now on the national agenda. Corruption is now the basic fuel of politics in India, rather than a hidden cost or shadow tax. Every week brings a new scam or illegal deal to light, involving businessmen, bureaucrats, and politicians moving sums of hundreds of millions of dollars, to buy favors in the largest auctions of corporate advantage in banking, information technology, real estate, and virtually every other area in which public monies are converted to private profit.

Corruption on such a scale could not exist with a huge black economy, which some scholars estimate to be twice as big as the official economy (in terms of taxed rupee incomes and wealth). The black economy operates, by definition, in the realm of cash, physical assets, and overseas bank accounts, outside the purview of the Indian banking and tax authorities (or the uncorrupt sectors of it). The black economy and political corruption now drive each other. Corruption needs vast stores of untraceable cash. Black money, in turn, requires large-sale corruption for its scale and flow to remain largely undetected and unregulated. These two forces are two sides of a money-machine that touches and taints every aspect of Indian life, from the Commonwealth Games to broadband spectra auctioning.

This combination of political corruption and black money wealth is what has destroyed Indian electoral politics and brought an unprecedented scale of crooks, criminals, and thugs into the public sphere in every state parliament in the nation, as well is in the national houses of Parliament. India has only a tiny handful of political leaders who remain personally uncorrupt, and among these, many are happy to turn a blind eye on the corruption of their cronies and associates. Elections throughout the nation run on black money channeled in illegal deals to buy votes, smear opponents, and buy media time and attention. There is a marked difference between this sort of monetizing of the democratic process, and, for example, the role of corporate lobbies in US politics. In India, except for a few high-end areas and market segments, corruption is not about influencing legislation by contributing the campaign funds of politicians. It is mostly about buying votes directly (usually in another wholesale form in vote banks), about buying media time and attention, and about buying political muscle at different levels to influence political action directly. This sort of corruption is primarily about affecting politics at the level of the voter rather than at the level of the legislator. This entire nexus of factors turns on the availability of vast stores of unaccounted-for (or "black" money). Why and how the Indian income tax authorities have proved impotent in checking this vast second economy is a problem that I cannot address in this brief essay.

The general criminalization of politics through the combined forces of black money and corruption at the executive rather than legislative level is also exacerbated by the strange role of the media in Indian politics. India's print press is huge (both in English and in all the vernacular languages). Indian television has hundreds of channels, also in multiple languages. By many criteria, the Indian press is dynamic, large, and effective in reach to ordinary citizens throughout the country. And in some sense, every Indian newspaper is filled with excellent investigative reporting about scams, illegal deals, political scandals, and tales of corporate chicanery. But this enormously vibrant media world still is better on rumor, gossip, scandal, and celebrity, than in its approach to politics. There is no well-developed sense of political or social criticism, which is the deep requirement of a vibrant public sphere. There is endless pitting of view against view, of voice against voice, of person against person, but there is not really a framework for measuring events against values without descending to the level of personality or gossip. Thus the media, which is in many ways relatively independent, vibrant, and far-reaching, lacks the deep capacity to serve as the basis for a thorough cleansing and reform of public politics.

WHAT IS TO BE DONE?

A collection like this can never claim to offer anything like a complete picture of India in the making. But it is not a random sampling either. Each essay points to the ways in which India builds on its deep cultural resources to construct its multiple modernities. Yet modernity brings its own troubles—to bodies, minds, and institutions. We might say, paraphrasing Tolstoy, that in a world of multiple modernities, every modern society is unhappy in its own way. India's achievements are not easy to disentangle from its unhappinesses.

It would be an act of arrogance for the authors—even in their collective wisdom—to offer any grand solution for the challenges India faces, as the engine of its global economy threatens to run free of the many wagons and coaches it needs to pull behind it, in a massively unequal society. Perhaps it would be better to ask what scholars, intellectuals, and publically-minded leaders in today's India might have to offer to the creation of a genuine public sphere of criticism, debate, and creativity, beyond the thrills and chills of the daily news cycle.

As scholars and critical intellectuals, we do have something to offer at this crossroads in India's history. We need to search our own hearts and minds to rethink the relationships between wealth and inclusion, growth and equity, success for some and survival for all. This is a task too important to be left to the politicians and the bureaucrats. It is even too important to be left to policy wonks and experts. It requires the full resources of an active debate about the optimal relationship between India's extraordinary cultural traditions, its remarkable relationship to the world economy, and its primary commitment to the goals of social inclusion and development. This is a collective task of criticism, debate, and reconstruction. To engage it, we need to think between our professional boundaries and outside our expert boxes. If we do, we have nothing to lose but our specialist chains, and India will surely be the better for it.

Mumbai   Arjun Appadurai
January 30, 2012

India's IT Industry: The End of the Beginning

Ajit Balakrishnan

T he Bombay skies were darker than usual that night in July 1991 when the procession of unmarked, heavily-armed vans sped toward the airport. The nation of more than a billion people was deep in slumber, little realizing the gravity of the situation. When the vans finally arrived at Bombay's airport they were flagged on to the tarmac, to the side of a chartered airplane. The armed men quickly transferred their cargo, 47 tons of gold, to the waiting airplane. Dark monsoon clouds were hovering as the plane took off on its way to London, where this gold would be transferred to the vaults of the Bank of England.

The surety of this 47 tons of gold was the only way the world's banks would provide credit to the Indian nation—credit badly needed for essential purchases to keep it going.

How had it come to this? What had happened to the promise that India's founding prime minister, Jawaharlal Nehru, had proclaimed in Parliament in New Delhi that fateful night in 1947, which had marked the birth of a new independent India? "At the stroke of the midnight hour, when the world sleeps, India will arise to life and freedom," Nehru had said. "India stands forth again, after long slumber and struggle, awake, vital, free, and independent"—words that every Indian schoolboy had been made to memorize.

The author thanks Barbara Pollock, Sougata Ray, and Nikhil Lakshman for comments on early drafts.

Now, a mere 44 years later, it looked as if that dream had turned into a nightmare. The country had foreign exchange that would cover just two weeks of imports. It was on the brink of default in its international financial obligations. Moody's, the American credit rating agency, had just put the country on credit watch. Would India now descend into chaos as desperate citizens hungry for food and essentials started rioting?

The year 1991 had been like no other. It started with the Gulf War, where US-led coalition forces pushed back Iraqi troops that had occupied oil-rich Kuwait. In March of that year, Georgia, the birthplace of Stalin, voted to leave the Soviet Union, further hastening the painful dismemberment of the Soviet state. In May, Rajiv Gandhi, the son and grandson of prime ministers and himself a prime minister until he lost the election in 1989, was assassinated while on the campaign trail. By July, Ukraine, Belarus, and Azerbaijan had also voted to leave the Soviet Union, and, as the world watched in astonishment, the Warsaw Pact itself was officially dissolved.

The Gulf War and the breakup of the Soviet Union had hit the Indian economy hard. India imported most of its oil from Iraq and Kuwait, often on long-term credit; these supplies were now halted. Oil prices had shot up by 65 percent, and had to be bought in the spot market and paid for in cash. Exports were hit because the Soviet Union, which had accounted for 20 percent of India's exports, had suspended purchases.

Things were no better in the United States. The economic expansion that began in 1981 had stalled by July 1990. By early 1991, the US economy was in a steep fall, made worse by the crisis in its savings and loan institutions.

It truly looked like India's dreams had come to an end on that night in July 1991. Yet, India pulled back from the brink and was soon growing at a brisk 9 percent or more annual rate; its foreign exchange reserves were bulging; and, in less than a decade's time, the country was being hailed as one of the emerging superpowers of the world and a major repository of the world's information technology expertise.

India's information technology (IT) industry is credited with playing a major role in this remarkable turnaround, and by 2007 the National

Association of Software and Service Companies (NASSCOM), the industry's trade body, was reporting annual software export revenues of $40 billion. The number of people directly employed in the industry was reported as exceeding 2 million, and those indirectly employed were as many as 7 million. The industry accounted by then for 5.2 percent of India's gross domestic product (GDP), and its annual expenditure in the domestic market was reported at $16 billion. This expenditure created multiplier effects in sectors that included housing construction, transport services, and household goods as young programmers set up homes.

What transformed this industry, which in 1990 had revenues of a mere $120 million and employed just 8,500 people (Heeks 1996)— numbers well behind tiny Ireland (at $185 million) and barely ahead of tinier Singapore (at $89 million)? What had, in less than a decade and a half, transformed India to world leader status and thereby helped to bring the country back from the brink of economic collapse?

Success, they say, has many fathers, and many different claimants have come forward. Proponents of the "market economy" say that the success of India's IT industry is an example of what energetic Indian entrepreneurs can achieve when the government of India steps aside. Reinforcing this view is India's business press, which frequently covers stories about "software millionaires"—not just the entrepreneurs and founders, but also rank-and-file employees of software companies who benefited handsomely from stock options.

Proponents of "globalization," such as *The New York Times* columnist Thomas Friedman in his book *The World Is Flat* (Friedman 2007), point to India's IT industry as an example of the kind of success that globalization brings: increased world trade that spreads prosperity around the world. Proponents of "privatization" point to the many decades of efforts by India's public sector IT companies that came to nothing until the private sector was "allowed" to participate in the IT industry. To them, this is proof that the government needs to privatize many other industries as well. Proponents of state activism point to the government initiatives that lie beneath the success: the zero-income tax status on export income that Indian IT companies enjoy, and the government-sponsored software technology parks where land and international telecom links were made available at subsidized prices.

But these views are probably like that old tale of the blind men of "Hindoostan," who, when asked to describe an elephant, said that it was like a wall, snake, spear, tree, fan, or rope, depending upon which part of the elephant each touched. The truth is that several different trends came together to create a perfect storm. Some of these threads go back in time; others are more recent, while still others have to do with the nature of computer software.

Central to the working of computing and software is the notion of the algorithm: a set of rules which, when applied to a defined input, will always result in a predictable output. For example, if the task at hand is to calculate the area of a rectangle, the algorithm is: "Take the length of the longer side and multiply that by the length of the shorter side and the resulting number is the area." The virtue of this algorithm is that once learned, it can be applied to any entity that is a rectangle. Computer programs are a series of such algorithms, and the job of programmers is to break any given problem into a series of algorithms that a computer is then programmed to compute.

The term "algorithm" is the Latinization of the name of a Persian mathematician, Muhammad ibn Musa al-Khwarizmi, who worked in Baghdad's House of Wisdom. His book, *On the Calculation with Hindu Numerals*, written in 825, was translated into Latin in the twelfth century as *Algoritme de Numero Indorum* (literally, "Al-Khwarizmi on the Hindu Art of Reckoning"). This book introduced a numeric decimal system composed of the numbers one to nine and zero. Any number, however large, can be expressed by combining these ten numbers. You could date the rise of India's IT industry to the twelfth century, when al-Khwarizmi's book was translated and made available to the Western world.

Or you could date it from February 2, 1835, when Lord Macaulay, while presiding over the Committee of Public Instruction of the British Colonial Government in Calcutta, cast his tiebreaking vote that confirmed the English language as the medium of instruction for higher education: half of the members were for pushing Sanskrit or Persian or Arabic as the medium of instruction in India; the other half for English. Since that date, practically all of India's higher education has been in English.

You could also date it from the day Mahatma Gandhi designed the flag of the Indian independence movement with a hand-spinning wheel as a motif. Gandhi intended this to be a daily reminder of the destitution felt by India's spinners and weavers because of mill-made yarn and cloth that flooded India, an outcome of the Industrial Revolution. Rather, it is often interpreted as a reminder of the disaster that fell on India because it "missed" the Industrial Revolution. Rajiv Gandhi, for example, in his first important speech after he became prime minister, said: "We missed out on the Industrial Revolution; we cannot afford to miss out on the computer revolution."

Or you could date it back to that day in June 1970, when IBM, which had until then provided software "free of charge" to customers who bought their hardware, was pressured by US anti-trust authorities to "unbundle" their software from their hardware offering, thereby giving birth to a software industry (Campbell-Kelly 2003).

Or you could date it from the time "programming languages" were invented. Until then, computing machines were instructed on what to do by a series of 0s and 1s (so-called machine code) that had to be painstakingly constructed. With the invention of programming languages, a single word of code—PRINT, for example—could generate several machine language instructions. This step not only saved programmers a lot of drudgery but also standardized a symbol system that could be taught to other programmers.

But you could date it from the financial profligacy of a succession of Indian governments in the 1980s as well, profligacy that created vast fiscal deficits that in turn led to steady annual depreciation of the Indian rupee against the US dollar, making Indian programmers look ever cheaper in US dollar terms. The financial profligacy was brought on by an attempt to buy political peace. Until the 1980s, industrialists, the rural rich, and the bureaucratic elite functioned according to a comfortable bargain, but land reforms and the Green Revolution in agriculture brought into the political arena a large group of middle peasants clamoring for free power and water, concessional credit, and subsidized fertilizers. Added to this clamor were the demands of the employees of the greatly expanded public sector for tax breaks for the salaried, and pressure from the rising middle class on the government for imported consumer electronics (Joshi 1994).

Or you could date it from when Adam Smith admiringly described a pin factory. "One man draws out a wire," he noted, "another straightens it, a third cuts it, a fourth points it, a fifth grinds it at the top to receive the head.... The important business of making a pin is in this manner divided into eighteen distinct operations performed by distinct hands." The benefits of partitioning an overall job into its subprocesses started off the outsourcing frame of mind.

Or you could date it from the time digitization made services tradable. Digitization converted service flows into stocks of information—for example, a legal brief that no longer needed to be delivered in person but could be sent as an email. The tradability of services further increased with the advent of low-cost, Internet-based telecommunication that made it possible for non-storable service flows such as customer care to be delivered from a distance (Dossani 2005).

The coming together of these disparate and independent threads: the mathematical heritage; an English-language higher-education system; the determination among the Indian elite that having "lost out" in the textile Industrial Revolution they could not afford to lose out in the Computer Revolution; the rise of teachable, standardized programming languages; a process view of work; the decline of the Indian rupee versus the US dollar; and the advent of digitization that made services tradable over long distances, is what created the setting for the emergence of the Indian IT industry. However, even as late as 1991, there was little to hint at how large the opportunity that lay ahead would be. That year, the Indian IT industry's exports were a meager $150 million and it employed just 6,500 programmers (Heeks 1996). The size of the median outsourced project to India at that time was just 150 man-months amounting to a few hundred thousand dollars (Arora et al. 2004).

If Indian policymakers were targeting the worldwide software services industry, so were other countries. The United Kingdom, for example, established an expert group that had produced a report with the title "Software—A Vital Key to UK Competitiveness" in as early as 1987. But the Indian software industry, by then, had some things going for it that set it apart from its international competitors. To start with, it had scale. By 1989, 350 colleges were turning out 10,000 computer graduates a year, and 100 more colleges were being certified by an activist government each year. And then there was the Indian diaspora: highly qualified graduates of elite institutions, such as the Indian Institutes of Technology and Indian Institutes of Management, perched in critical senior management positions in US and Canadian companies, quietly making the connections between their employers and software firms in India, founded in many cases by graduates from the same elite institutions. A study done by Harvard Business School points out that a fourth of the top-level customer contacts of Indian IT firm CEOs were from the Indian diaspora (Nanda et al. 2004).

Most critically, Indian programmers had the right skills, learned through large-scale government-sponsored computerization projects in the late 1980s, for the nationalized banking system and Indian Railways. Foresighted government policymakers had insisted that these applications be built using such technologies as the UNIX Operating System and Relational Database systems. This was fortuitous because the world was just then getting ready to make a paradigm change that would unleash an insatiable wave of demand for computer programmers well versed in UNIX and Relational Database Systems, the so-called client-server revolution that would mark the transition from giant mainframes to smaller, cheaper personal computers (PCs) and UNIX workstations. Until then, data and applications resided in large central mainframe computers. User requests for information were routed to centralized electronic document professionals (EDPs) who ran these requests on the mainframe and sent back answers in a few days, or even hours, to users. With the arrival of low-cost PCs and workstations, users were beginning to work on these requests themselves, so a large number of applications developed for mainframes now needed to be redone for these new platforms.

The surge in demand for programmers well versed in client-server technologies coincided with the dramatic devaluation of the rupee vis-à-vis the US dollar in 1991. An Indian programmer who used to cost, say, $4,000 per person, per month, now cost only half of that. Smart and entrepreneurial Indian software companies leapt at the opportunity to supply programmers with the requisite knowledge of such technologies, who were ready to travel to the United States to work on-site at the customers' offices. These simple "body-shopping" contracts allowed nascent Indian software companies to rapidly scale up revenue. All they needed to do was hire programmers and place them in clients' offices abroad. There were no demands on them to incur upfront capital investment on offices or computer hardware, or to take responsibility for completing projects in time.

This surge in demand for programmers from the client-server paradigm shift was barely being met by the early 1990s when a second wave arrived: the demand for programmers for Y2K (Year 2000) projects. Computer programs at that time denoted a year using only the last two numerals. Thus, 1993 was indicated simply as "93." There was a sudden realization that when the century turned in 2000, simple calculations, such as the age of a person, could now become problematic. Prior to the year 2000, a computer could subtract a year of birth ('43 for example) from the current year ('93) to give the correct result as "50." But once the current year was 2000 or later, the same calculation would go awry. For example, in 2003, subtracting '43 from '03 would produce an age result of -40. Millions of lines of code, especially in the heavily computerized banking and financial services industries in the United States, had to be rewritten to correct this, creating a demand for tens of thousands of programmers with rudimentary programming skills to comb through the code and make these simple changes. The Indian software industry was the only one in the world that could · provide these large numbers.

It has been estimated that Indian software companies earned $2.5 billion in the three years between 1996 and 1999 on Y2K assignments (Kumar 2001). Scrawny start-up software companies that rode this wave were very quickly turned into publicly listed, cash-rich companies employing thousands of programmers. More important, Y2K assignments introduced Indian software companies to a large variety of customers in the critical banking, insurance, and telecom industries in the United States and Europe. Smart Indian entrepreneurs used this once-in-a-lifetime opportunity to evolve their business designs. Work initially done on customer premises in the United States, Canada, and Europe was brought back in stages to be done in India. This made it cheaper for the customer since programmers' travel and living costs were eliminated—as well as more profitable for the Indian software company. By 2000, only half of all work was still being done on-site.

Indian software companies also wholeheartedly embraced international quality certifications, such as ISO (International Standards Organization) and CMM (Capability Maturity Model), providing strong signals to their customers about the quality of processes inside Indian companies. By 2005, more than 80 Indian companies had achieved CMM Level 5, the highest possible level, whereas there were no companies with similar certification in China, Latin America, or Eastern Europe; only a handful existed in Western Europe or North America.

The "offshore development center" was the industry's next business design innovation. This involved setting up a dedicated facility for a foreign client under an umbrella, multi-year contract. These contracts established "man-month" rates for time and material, thereby insulating the Indian company from many different types of risks (for example: 10 programmers working 5 months on a project = 10 x 5 = 50 man-months). The top Indian software companies soon operated multiple offshore development centers for multiple clients.

At this point, many international consulting companies, such as IBM and Accenture, set up wholly owned development centers in India to take advantage of cheap programming talent, thus adding another dimension to the industry. Soon IBM, Accenture, HP, Cap Gemini, and Oracle, among others, would boast of development centers employing tens of thousands of Indian programmers.

The demands of the world's computer services industry fit the Indian skill creation regime perfectly. Think of an industry that needed to add, every year, tens of thousands of perfunctorily educated fresh college graduates, with a functional knowledge of English, a rudimentary introduction to computer science concepts, ready to live as bachelors in shared apartments in unfamiliar cities in the West for months at a time, saving most of what they were paid, and willing to do all of this for $400 to $600 per month. This was the kind of demand that the Indian skill creation regime was perfectly suited to meet.

Countries take many different skill-building paths (Brown 2001). One path is characterized by Germany, which has a high-quality manufacturing sector that relies on high-quality scientific elite, a workforce with intermediate-level skills, and high levels of social trust, together with high average incomes and relative wage equality. Another model, exemplified by the United States and the United Kingdom, bases competitiveness on high levels of innovation and productivity in some high-tech manufacturing and services. This model also presents a skill formation system that is a polarized combination of a large number of low- or no-skill workers and a high-skills elite, which accepts a high level of income inequality between the two.

The Indian skills regime, on the other hand, has at its heart a small number of world-quality, state-subsidized, English-language-based higher technical and management educational institutions. Admission to these institutions is through a meritocratic entrance exam system, where fewer than 5 percent of applicants are selected. This tiny enclave coexists with an enormous number of privately funded educational institutions that play fast and loose with admission standards as well as with pedagogic quality. It was these latter private institutions that quickly responded to the surge in demand for engineering graduates during the sudden boom in the Indian IT industry. In a mere five years, between 1985 and 2000, the annual output of engineering graduates in India increased from 45,000 to 440,000, largely from these private institutions (Arora 2010). The mechanisms at work during this massive scale-up are best illustrated by the example of engineering education in Kerala state.

Until the mid-1990s, only approximately 4,500 students were admitted annually to engineering colleges in Kerala. At private-sector engineering colleges, roughly half of students admitted were on the basis of merit as judged by a Common Entrance Test (CET) conducted by the state; a fourth of the spots was reserved for affirmative action programs; and the final fourth was allotted based on financial donations the student was prepared to make. The students admitted based on merit and the affirmative action quota students were charged low fees as prescribed by the state government. There was no government price control on fees charged to students admitted under the management's discretionary quota. In the 1990s, encouraged by the demand from the IT industry, the annual intake of engineering colleges in Kerala grew from 4,500 to 18,000, with almost all of the increase coming from private engineering colleges.

It was soon discovered that of the 19,000 candidates who took the CET in a year, only 5,000 had scored even 10 percent in the mathematics section. If minimum marks of 30 percent had been prescribed for mathematics as a cutoff, fewer than 100 students out of the 19,000 would have qualified (Sivashankaran 2004). Faced with this discovery, the managements of the private engineering colleges, focused as they were on the profitability of their colleges, pressured the state government, first to relax the minimum score for admission and later, even remove the requirement, for the CET.

The Kerala data is by no means an exception, and thus it should come as no surprise that an all-India joint study by the Confederation of Indian Industry and the Boston Consulting Group in 2008 found that only about 20 percent of Indian graduates were "employable"—that is, with the requisite language, quantitative, and analytical skills that the Indian IT industry deemed necessary.

How is it that the Indian software industry was still able to move ahead in spite of the poor quality input of employees? The answer to this lies in the way the world software services industry is segmented.

There are two dimensions to this segmentation, according to a study by the Indian Institute of Management (IIM) Bangalore (Kumar et al. 2003). The first dimension is distinguished by the customer, of which there are three types: enterprises whose core business is not IT; software vendors; and intermediaries, such as IT consultants. The second dimension is characterized by a range of types of service provided. At one end are services that provide ideas and solutions aimed at generating a competitive advantage for the organizations that deploy them. At the other end are the services needed to operate and maintain IT infrastructure. Indian IT firms operate largely at the intersection of these two dimensions, providing customers whose core business is not IT with the services necessary to operate and maintain IT infrastructure. The critical factor for success in this segment, the authors point out, is the ability to deploy hundreds of programmers on short notice and manage them with high reliability.

The really successful Indian software companies are those that have responded to this pattern of demand and supply by building huge training centers, where tens of thousands of fresh college graduates can live and train at one time. In a way, these companies are trying to make up for a broken higher education system while simultaneously creating a barrier that prevents new software industry companies, whether in India or abroad, from entering the market.

Today, the range of services outsourced to Indian companies is staggering: research and development services in software, insurance claims processing, accounting, financial and credit analysis, tax preparation, data entry and conversion, transcription and translation services, customer interaction services, animation, engineering and design, website development and maintenance, remote education, market research, employee benefit, and payroll services—in all, about 800 different types of services.

The potential for the Indian IT industry looks immense. Much of the IT sector is deployed to improve the productivity of what economists call "producer services." These services include computer and data processing, personnel supply, management and business consulting, accounting and audit services, and engineering and architectural services. The contribution of "producer services" as a share of the GDP of both developed and developing economies is rapidly rising.

Many factors contribute to the growth of these services: increased government regulation, for example, drives up the need for more financial and legal compliance services; and the increasing complexity of work drives up demand for consulting services (Tschetter 1987). As Lou Gerstner, the chief executive officer of IBM in the late 1990s, who led its transition from a failed hardware manufacturer to a leader in software services, points out, "I have never seen a business with such a capacity for self-renewal. Every time the [computer] industry moves in a new direction, the IT services opportunity is re-invented" (Gerstner 2002).

As the worldwide demand for IT services spirals upward, Indian policymakers are clearly central in determining whether India wins or loses this opportunity. The outcome will be determined by how they can improve the skills regime in India. The current regime, as we have seen, produces large numbers of graduates with token skills. Employers select 2 to 5 percent of the applicant pool and then spend 6 to 12 months training them to give them the requisite skills.

The obstacles to changing this clearly wasteful skills regime are formidable and probably constrained by centuries-old social prejudices in India. Take, for example, the ongoing struggle to legislate and enforce free and compulsory education in India. The parliamentary bill providing for this was just passed in 2009, some 60 years after Independence, but the rule-making and budget-allocating process to implement the bill are still under discussion. This may sound surprising in a country where so much public discourse is devoted to doing well in the emerging knowledge economy.

Myron Weiner (1991), who studied this paradox, says that the Indian elite has historically had no self-interest in enforcing free and compulsory primary education, unlike the elite, for example, in Germany and the United States. In Germany the pressure came during the late nineteenth century, when the elite felt that keeping children at school would protect them from the influence of the emerging socialist movement as well as provide a healthy group for conscription to the army. In the United States, the drive for free and compulsory education was driven by the desire of the elite that the stream of incoming immigrants be homogenized into an English-speaking American society. In China, the major expansion of primary education came during the Cultural Revolution, a period during which the state saw education as an instrument for creating an ideologically committed population. In India, the elite sees no similar benefit; their own children are well taken care of largely through a private education school system.

There are also some painful lessons from Indian history about trying to build an industry based on low labor cost. In the seventeenth century, Bengal, a province of India, by itself annually exported 85 million pounds of hand-spun textile yarn at a time when Britain, as the next largest exporter, did only a fraction of that amount. Then a series of inventions in Britain, starting with the spinning jenny, machines like Crompton's Mule, and the famous inventions of the first Industrial Revolution, changed all that. In a few decades the British spinning industry had completely wiped out Bengal's, causing widespread destitution. Robert Allen (2009) has convincingly demonstrated that the simple reason for the non-adoption of the spinning jenny in India was that wages in India were so low compared to the cost of capital that the Indian spinner would have seen a negative return of 7 percent had he invested in one. This is a cautionary tale from Indian history for policymakers trying to build a whole industry on low labor costs.

In another lesson from history, the young Mohandas Gandhi, arriving back in India in 1916, a virtual unknown to his countrymen after his stints in England and South Africa, went to the aid of indigo growers in the Champaran district of Bihar in eastern India in their battle for better financial terms from the British landowners there. As every Indian schoolboy has been taught, Gandhi succeeded in obtaining better financial terms for the indigo growers using his non-violent method. He became a nationally known figure because of this and, with the success of Champaran behind him, went on to take charge of the floundering independence movement and ultimately led India to independence.

But this story has another side. The plight of the indigo-growing peasant of Champaran was only in a small way due to the bad behavior of the British landowners. The larger issue was the precipitous fall in world indigo prices because the Germans had found a way to produce the dye synthetically from coal tar. The synthesis of indigo in turn led German scientists to understand the nature of the chemical bond and ultimately brought them to dominance in the world chemical and pharmaceutical industry for decades. One can only wonder what trajectory the Indian industry would have taken if Gandhi had commandeered Indian chemists and sought to solve the Champaran indigo problem through scientific innovation, rather than seeing it as a problem of the peasants not being paid a fair wage for their efforts.

There is some evidence that what we have seen so far in IT is only its early labor-saving aspects, and real applications may yet lie ahead of us. Scientists working at Siemens in the United States report a machine-learning-based software tool that enables non-experts to detect colon polyps with 96 percent accuracy, a rate better and many times faster than expensively trained radiologists. In another example, scientists at the University of Wisconsin in Madison report building another machine-learning-based software tool that uses images from fine needle aspiration and correctly diagnoses breast cancer. These kinds of IT applications may revolutionize the way healthcare is delivered by bringing down costs and making it more widely available, but would require IT personnel who are products of a high skills regime.

It is tempting to conclude that India's challenge with quality education is a continuation of a centuries-old tradition, where only children of the Brahmin, Kshatriya, and Vaishya castes, who comprise about 15 percent of the population, were considered "educable," as pointed out by Nigel Crooke (1996). However, there might be more complex issues here because we see the quality problem in education even in Kerala state, where social prejudice issues of this kind are minimal and a 100 percent literacy rate has been achieved for some years now.

One of the challenges India's educational policymakers face is that the IT services revolution has reinforced the role of English in India and thus favors only those with access to English education, leaving behind the large number of students who attend the state-owned school system, where the medium of instruction is not English.

Also, the challenge of creating a skills regime that produces a large proportion of the population with high skills does not seem to be unique to India; reports such as *A Nation at Risk* (US Department of Education 1983), *Bankrupt Education* (Sommer 1994) from Canada, and *The Academy in Crisis* (Emberley 1994) from the United Kingdom indicate that many other countries are grappling with similar issues.

We can get some insights about how to approach the educational quality challenge from the work of educational researchers who believe that the real value of education is to give students the ability to "transfer learning" (Haskell 2000)—to apply what is learned in one context to solving a similar problem posed in another context or even to completely new situations. Transfer of learning is what is happening whenever you say a problem "is like" or "is equivalent to" or "is the same as" or "resembles" or "is comparable to." This kind of reasoning is evidence of the skills of mental abstraction, generalization, induction, and logical inference, all of which are the hallmarks of true, high-quality education.

Most innovation happens by using such skills. Take for example Peter Chen's account (Chen 2002) of how his native Chinese culture inspired him to think of the Entity-Relationship model, a seminal concept in computer science that offers a true breakthrough in how to view data. In Chinese, he says, the pictographs for the sun and moon are placed next to each other to form the character for "brightness" because both the sun and the moon have the ability to reflect. The Entity-Relationship model in computer science similarly combines properties of individual entities to create new ones. Chen had transferred his learning of how Chinese pictographs are combined to the completely new realm of computer science.

Unfortunately, attempts to teach such transfer of learning skills by using the classic structured drills in the basics does not seem to do the job. Nor have efforts in which students are given unstructured free reign for self-discovery succeeded.

In India's elementary education system, this challenge is doubled because children who come from homes where they are the first to go to school must negotiate not only the challenges of transfer of learning skills but of learning in English, a language they are likely to encounter only in school and not in their home environment.

In the search for a solution to this pedagogic problem, scholars such as Clayton Christensen (2008) believe the answer lies in delivering student-centric learning. In this scheme, students learn each subject in a manner that is consistent with their type of intelligence and learning style. Unfortunately, the current education system in every country in the world is organized into value chains—just as manufacturing and mass retail are organized. In such industries, materials (in this case, students) are input, some material is transformed by subjecting it to standardized processes (standard textbooks and standard teaching methods) and output to the next stage (a higher class) if the student performs adequately in standardized tests. In the current business design of education, each part of this process—standard curricula, standard textbooks, and standardized tests—have scale economics and, hence, are difficult to customize.

What is needed is a business design for education in which we acknowledge that students learn in many different ways, have a different mix of linguistic, mathematical, and visual "intelligences," and learn at different paces. Delivering this kind of individualized learning on a mass scale and at a reasonable cost requires extensive use of IT: online media that exploits video, audio, and interactive elements. To do this on the scale that India faces is mind-boggling. There are 4 million schools and 20,000 colleges in the country and, in the next 15 years, 345 million Indians will turn 18 and seek to enter the job market. Maybe the struggle to find enough high-skills employees with high transfer of learning skills will prompt a breakthrough in how students are truly educated.

The future success of the Indian IT industry may lie in its ability to make the transition from being a provider of low-cost programming services, but this is not going to be easy. First, the generation of middle managers who now dominate the industry are those whose core skills so far have been to hire and quickly deploy ever-increasing numbers of programmers. Will they now be able to oversee a new business design where the yardstick by which they are measured is not how quickly they can ramp up manpower, but how they make do with decreasing numbers of programmers per dollar of revenue? And can the industry make this fundamental transition in a period when many of the founding CEOs who drove this dynamic industry are now in their 60s and starting to retire?

In many ways these steps represent the end of one era and the beginning of another, where the quality of people matters more than anything else. In the process of making this transition, the Indian IT industry may also pioneer solutions to India's giant-scale education challenge and mark the end of an old education era and the beginning of a new one, just as it led India's economic rise after that dark night in July 1991.

REFERENCES

Allen, Robert. "The Industrial Revolution in Miniature: The Spinning Jenny in Britain, France and India." *Journal of Economic History* 69 (2009): 901-927.

Arora, Ashish, and Alphonsa Gambardella. "The Globalization of the Software Industry." Working Paper 10538, National Bureau of Economic Research, 2004.

Arora, Ashish and Surendra K. Bagde. "Human Capital and the Indian Software Industry." Working Paper 16167, National Bureau of Economic Research, 2010.

Brown, Phillip. *High Skills: Globalization, Competitiveness, and Skill Formation.* New York: Oxford University Press, 2001.

Campbell-Kelly, Martin. *From Airline Reservations to Sonic the Hedgehog.* Cambridge: MIT Press, 2003.

Chen, Peter. *Entity-Relationship Modeling: Historical Events, Future Trends, and Lessons Learned.* New York: Springer Verlag, 2002.

Christensen, Clayton, Michael Horn, and Curtis Johnson. *Disrupting Class.* New York: McGraw-Hill, 2008.

Crooke, Nigel, ed. *The Transmission of Knowledge in South Asia: Essays on Education, Religion, History, and Politics.* New York: Oxford University Press, 1996.

Dossani, Rafiq. "Globalization and the Offshoring of Services: The Case of India." *Brookings Trade Forum* (2005): 241-267.

Emberley, Peter, and Walter Newell. *Bankrupt Education: The Decline of Liberal Education in Canada.* Toronto: University of Toronto Press, 1994.

Friedman, Thomas. *The World Is Flat: A Brief History of the Twenty-first Century.* New York: Farrar, Strauss, Giroux, 2007.

Gerstner, Louis. *Who Says Elephants Can't Dance.* London: HarperCollins, 2002.

Haskell, Robert. *Transfer of Learning: Cognition, Instruction and Reasoning.* New York: Academic Press, 2000.

Heeks, Richard. *India's Software Industry: State Policy, Liberalization and Industrial Development.* Thousand Oaks, Calif.: Sage Publications, 1996.

Joshi, Vijay, and I. M. D. Little, eds. *India: Macroeconomics and Political Economy, 1964-91.* New York: Oxford University Press, 1994.

Kumar, K., and R. T. Krishnan. *Growth Challenges of Software SMITs: A Strategic Analysis. IIMB Management Review* 15 (2003): 112-118.

Kumar, Nagesh. "Indian Software Industry Development." *Economic and Political Weekly,* November 10, 2001.

Nanda, Ramana, and Tarun Khanna. "Diasporas and Domestic Entrepreneurs: Evidence from the Indian Software Industry." Working Paper 08-003, Harvard Business School, 2004.

NASSCOM. <www.nasscom.in>.

Sivashankaran, C. J. "An Investigation into the Wastage in Engineering Colleges in Kerala." Project Report, Integrated Rural Technology Centre, Mundur, Palakkad, 2004.

Sommer, John, ed. *The Academy in Crisis: The Political Economy of Higher Education*. New Brunswick, NJ: Transaction Press, 1994.

Tschetter, John. "Producer Services Industries: Why Are They Growing So Rapidly?" *Monthly Labor Review* 110 (December 1987): 31-40.

US Department of Education. *A Nation at Risk*. Washington DC, 1983.

Weiner, Myron. *The Child and the State in India*. Princeton: Princeton University Press, 1991.

Crisis in the Classics

Sheldon Pollock

In October 2004, after an electoral sweep in the spring parliamentary elections brought it unaccustomed influence over the ruling coalition in Delhi, the Dravida Munnetra Kazhagam (DMK), the Dravidianist party of the state of Tamil Nadu, demanded that the United Progressive Alliance declare Tamil a classical language—which it did, apparently the first such declaration by a national government in recorded history. Sanskrit was soon granted classical status, without external pressure, but the floodgates were now open to other language activists to seek classical status as well, and they proceeded with passion to petition the central government on behalf of Kannada (2006), Telugu (2007), and Malayalam (2009).[1]

This is not the classical language debate India should be having, however; there is something other than status to worry about—and to worry about deeply.

At the time of independence in 1947, India was home to scholars whose historical and philological expertise made them the peer of any in the world. They were the heirs of the longest continuous multicultural literary tradition in the world, and produced editions, and literary and historical studies, of texts in Apabhramsha, Assamese, Bangla, Brajbhasha, Gujarati, Kannada, Malayalam, Marathi, Oriya, Persian,

I would like to thank Robert Goldman and Pratap Bhanu Mehta for criticisms and suggestions, as well as audiences at the Indian Academy of Sciences in Bangalore, the University of Texas at Austin, the School of Oriental and African Studies in London, the University of Calicut, and St. Stephen's College in Delhi, where I presented earlier versions of this essay.

Prakrit, Sanskrit, Tamil, Telugu, Urdu—the list could go on because the list of Indian languages goes on—that are still used today. Two generations later their works have not been replaced, not because they are irreplaceable—it is in the nature of scholarship that later knowledge should supersede earlier—but because there is no one capable of replacing them. And this is a sign of what people should be worrying about: if Indian education and scholarship continue along their current trajectory, the number of citizens capable of reading and understanding the texts and documents of the classical era—or precolonial or premodern or pre-1800 era, all equivalent terms for my purposes here—will very soon approach a statistical zero. India is about to become the only major world culture whose literary patrimony, and indeed history, are in the custodianship of scholars outside the country: in Berkeley, Chicago, and New York; Oxford, Paris, and Vienna. This would not be healthy either for India or for the rest of the world that cares about India.

Admittedly, there are a lot of problems in the world. Very big problems, like global warming, AIDS, unequal power, and vast poverty; intermediate problems like terror, especially terror in South Asia, or the periodic financial upheavals of global capitalism; smaller-scale problems, like the political transformation of India in the postcolonial period, with the astonishing rise and acceptance of new and shocking forms of communal irrationality and violence. Then there are very small problems like the potential disappearance in India of classical textual knowledge. Michel Foucault drew a distinction between universal intellectuals, masters of truth and justice who occupy themselves with the big, bigger, and biggest problems; and specific intellectuals, who work in a particular sector of society and speak to the small-scale issues constitutive of that sector. These may be distinct forms of intellectual engagement, but they are not opposed; on the contrary, there is something of a fractal relationship between the two. The very small problem I will deal with in this essay contains a very big question indeed, about what it means to be fully and richly human.

Four questions immediately present themselves by the assertions I make above. Is the hypothesis of a looming collapse of classical knowledge in India actually valid? If this knowledge is indeed threatened with extinction, and we are witnessing something more than the chronic crisis that humanists have been trumpeting since there were humanists, how is it to be explained? The third question—perhaps the first for some—is why anyone should care. Many people are entirely unconvinced that the past should not simply be allowed to pass away. Explaining clearly why it should not is an obligation that classicists do not usually rush to discharge. Last, but alas least answerable, is what if anything can be done about the situation in India—about the fate, as I once named more generally, of a soft science in a hard world? (Pollock 2009)

IS THERE A CRISIS IN THE CLASSICS IN INDIA TODAY?

Legitimate research problems should be empirically answerable, and at present this one is only partly so. Not only is the question of the vitality of classical knowledge complex but data on higher education in India are woefully inadequate to answer it. There is no systematic database or accurate metric to enable us to move beyond the subjective and actually measure the severity of this problem, or indeed, almost any problem of knowledge production in the social sciences and the humanities. Accordingly, my account will be largely personal and anecdotal, and limited in its truth value by the limits of one person's experience—though these experiences are real and have a certain heuristic value.

The Indian case is extreme, but for comparative purposes it is worth looking at the bigger picture. I began worrying about the situation in India more than a decade ago but started lecturing on it only in the past few years, and during this period the situation for the humanities in general and classical studies in particular has grown more dire almost globally. Every week, it seems a new book is published on the corporatization of the university, the commodification of education, the technologization and scientization of all knowledge, and the concomitant denigration and, increasingly, discontinuation of humanities programs.

Recent statistical studies for the United States unequivocally reveal a decline in both absolute and relative support for research in humanistic scholarship that has been described, perhaps optimistically, as "dangerous." The national budget for humanistic studies in the United

States in general dropped from more than $400 million in 1979 to less than $150 million in the past two years. Humanities faculty have grown far more slowly than any other area; in fact, relative to other disciplines, they have not grown at all (14 percent of the professoriate has been the steady figure for the past decade), and the number of full-time positions has shrunk dramatically to just over half in the same period. The humanities currently produce the lowest number of PhDs of all fields—8 percent, a 45 percent drop since the 1970s—and these figures include the bloated discipline of history. Only a tiny fraction of that 8 percent are PhDs in classical studies, even according to the broadest definition, "global premodern language-based studies": the total of non-English language and literature PhDs in relationship to all PhDs (and this includes modern as well as premodern) dropped by two-thirds from the mid-1970s to the present (Brinkley 2009).[2] In short, the population of scholars in the United States responsible for understanding and transmitting a large segment of historical human culture stands in an almost exact inverse proportion to its object.

A look at classical Indian studies in Western Europe offers a good sense of the state of affairs. In the past 30 years, Dutch Indology, the heir of a great tradition, has been decimated, losing all but 2 of 20 positions. In Germany during the same period, at least 11 professorships have been lost entirely or converted to modern South Asian social science; Indian philological studies in Berlin, whose birth (in 1821) was virtually simultaneous with the birth of the university, is expected to be closed in the near future. At Cambridge and Edinburgh, long-standing professorships have been replaced by low-level lectureships, and even these are threatened with elimination. The situation at the College de France today is indicative of the larger picture beyond Indian studies. The current Indologist will not be replaced when he retires in a few years, something that has already happened with classical Arabic, Chinese, and Semitic. Speaking of the latter, a recent position paper on philology in Europe notes that scholarship in Syriac—the language that forms the most important link between classical European and Islamic culture—has virtually died (Ahmed et al. 2010).

The endangerment of classical studies is thus clearly a global problem, and it is perhaps only because India has so much more to lose than other cultures that it seems to have lost so much more. Let me give a few examples, starting with Sanskrit, first because it had been the most widely cultivated of the traditionally identified classical languages of India, but also because it is the tradition I know best.

I was recently asked to contribute to a centenary volume on D. D. Kosambi, one of the most interesting and influential of classical studies scholars in the immediate post-Independence period. Kosambi combined strong philological skills with a richly developed theoretical approach to his subject matter. But perhaps the most remarkable realization I had in thinking about his work is not why he used this method or defended that theory, but rather why, since his time India has produced not a single scholar with an equivalent combination of skills (Pollock 2008). Indeed, there have been no successors to any of the pre-Independence generation of Sanskrit scholars, the sort who mastered their discipline and thought conceptually about it and wrote for an international audience: S. N. Dasgupta, S. K. De, Mysore Hiriyanna, P. V. Kane, S. Radhakrishnan, Venkata Raghavan, C. Kunhan Raja, V. S. Sukthankar are the first in a long and distinguished list from across India (I leave aside the loss of the great tradition of pandit learning, which is now virtually extinct). There have been no major Sanskrit projects in India since the completion of the critical edition of the *Ramayana* at Baroda more than 30 years ago. All the great classical series (such as Anandasrama, Trivandrum, Gaekwad, Madras) have been more or less discontinued, and as a result the manuscripts in those collections are no longer being published. Indeed, there have been few new Indian editions of complex Sanskrit texts at all from among the scores of important manuscripts that lie unpublished in archives. In the area of hermeneutics (*Mimamsa*), for example, I know of no one in India today capable of editing works like those edited just a generation ago by P. N. Pattabhirama Sastry or S. Subrahmanya Sastry. (The same holds for many other areas of classical studies; with the death of A. N. Upadhye in 1975 and H. C. Bhayani in 2000, the editing of Prakrit and Apabhramsha works seems to have died too.) I have not encountered a single PhD dissertation on Sanskrit in India—and I have seen many—worthy of publication by a Western university press.

The situation is no different in the other classical languages, as I learned in the late 1990s when I organized a project on the histories of South Asian literary cultures (Pollock 2003). Our core group of colleagues was looking for others to join us who possessed a deep historical understanding of a regional language, conceptual skills, and the capacity to communicate their knowledge effectively. We were able to locate only four qualified scholars in India, and identified no one for a host of languages, including Assamese, Marathi, Newari, Oriya, and Panjabi.

If anything, the situation has deteriorated since. Two years ago the Indian Institute for Advanced Study, Shimla, organized a conference to explore precisely the topic of this essay. The conveners were seeking university-based professors of pre-1800 Indian literary studies who had a record of strong scholarship. They sent out dozens of letters to Indian and Western scholars seeking recommendations. Let me review a few of the profoundly disheartening responses.

An Indian colleague working in North America who knows the Indian scene intimately confirmed my own worst suspicions about Sanskrit. When it was suggested to him how difficult it seemed to find an academic Sanskritist in India who fit the bill he replied, "The remark saddens me deeply, but I have to accept its truth." He could provide just three names in all of India, only one of whom worked on literature.

Three prominent scholars of Bengali history and culture together could offer only a single suggestion. As one wrote, "The picture is depressing, no question. I can't think of anyone in Kolkata doing interesting work on Bharatchandra or even Ramprasad Sen [two celebrated eighteenth-century authors]. The better-known stuff is all by older scholars." A wide-ranging historian from Chennai wrote almost the same thing about Tamil literary studies: Finding that type of person is "a difficult question," he wrote. "I can think of only two scholars, and one of these can communicate only in Tamil." A colleague from the United States with 30 years' experience in Maharashtra offered two names in reply but added, "I have to say I have not heard of or read any of these people's work in premodern Marathi literature. The really good people, in my experience, are retired or dead, or never got a university job." Perhaps the most knowledgeable American scholar of Malayalam wrote: "Sorry to say, I don't really know anyone working in premodern Malayalam literature in universities in India. It's always been a disappointingly unpopular field in Kerala. I've had to be self-taught, working with one very knowledgeable, very old retired linguist, and the occasional odd pandit-types." For Panjabi, the organizers heard from an eminent Indian scholar teaching in the United States who had just returned from a sabbatical year in Punjab:

> Although painful to see the absence of Panjabi in *Literary Cultures in History*, I knew that it would not have been easy to find some one to do the relevant piece. The situation does not seem to have changed much in the past decade. For a complex set of reasons, the present generation of scholars in the Punjab is more interested in the post-1850 period and there is no one presently teaching there who could meet the criterion laid out in your note. I am just back from the Punjab. The three names that come to mind are all retired faculty.

I could go on with responses received about other languages, including the national language, Hindi, whose classical idiom (known as *riti*), we learned, is currently taught at neither of the great universities of Delhi (the true analogy would be no one teaching Corneille, Racine, and Molière in Paris). But let me end this jeremiad with India's second great cosmopolitan language: Persian. A colleague contacted about the conference offered in reply a rather poignant Urdu proverb: *padhen fars, beechen tel—ye dekho qudrat ke khel* (He studied Persian but now sells oil—look at the game destiny plays). The history of the interpretation of this proverb recapitulates the crisis that I am trying to capture, for it migrated 50 years ago from describing the unjust fate of a scholar of learning, to its current sense of lamenting the economic fate awaiting anyone foolish enough to opt for Persian as a main university subject. The names of only four active scholars in all of India could be suggested, and it was not clear what even they were doing. Just consider that *diwan*s of some of the greatest Indo-Persian poets such as Fayzi and Bedil remain unpublished to this day, and when new works are brought out, it is typically from Teheran, not Delhi or Hyderabad.

Let me say again that the people whom the Indian Institute for Advanced Study, Shimla, contacted are both Indians and American academics who have worked in India for years. It may be that there are strong scholars who were overlooked—but if so, it would be an almost equally sad and instructive commentary on the lack of communication between Indian and Western classical scholars. The truth, I fear, is that there are few left to communicate with.

Consider these additional facts. There are no major centers in India for training in classical studies: all the important and serious research institutes are devoted to the social sciences (Madras Institute for Development Studies; Centre for Social Studies, Surat; Centre for Studies in Social Sciences, Calcutta; Centre for the Study of Developing Societies and the Centre for Policy Research, both Delhi). An exception was the Centre for Excellence in Classical Languages at the Central Institute of Indian Languages (CIIL)—or could have been. But the center never did anything, so far as I can tell, and in 2009, as a result of the classical languages mania mentioned at the start of this essay, it transformed itself into the Central Institute of Classical Tamil. The fate of this new center offers a revealing gloss on the state's role in the crisis of the classics. An official at CIIL told me the following:

> For you and me, readying scholars who could devote their lives to classical studies may be important, but for the players in national and regional politics, this fact (of recognition of Tamil as a classical language) is viewed as an achievement that must be fully utilized [read: the political goals of this decision must be achieved]. The reason for this shift is to tell the people of Tamil Nadu that the fruits of the union government's decision on declaration of Tamil as a classical language—on par with Sanskrit—has finally come to Tamil Nadu with creation of a Central Institute of Classical Tamil there. Now their problem is that they need to appoint people to run it and give it a direction, and they are unable to find a truly capable linguist and a scholar. . . . [In addition] the political decision to find a person amenable to the political elite and also acceptable to Tamil scholars is not easy to resolve.

There are many other symptoms of crisis besides the institutional void. There exist no Indian scholarly journals devoted to classical studies that have an international stature. None of the once-great publications— *Annals of the Bhandarkar Oriental Research Institute*; *Bombay Branch of the Royal Asiatic Society*; *Indian Historical Review*; *Journal of the Asiatic Society of Bengal*; *Journal of the Oriental Institute, Baroda*; *Journal of Oriental Research, Madras*—are any longer thought of as obligatory reading or as suitable venues for international contributions. India-based classical scholars rarely publish in major Western humanities journals, and never publish, so far as I can see, in Western university presses. Indeed, it is rare to find their publications in the best presses in India (Oxford University Press Delhi, for example, or Permanent Black). Equally rare is it to find Indian postgraduates enrolling in doctoral programs in the United States who have serious training in classical studies; students with good skills in a modern Indian language can be found, to be sure, but they invariably lack access to the classical past.

Every datum I can find, then, and every measure I can use, indicates that the tradition of scholarship on precolonial texts has decayed in the last 50 years almost to the point of extinction.

IF THERE IS A CRISIS, WHAT HAS CAUSED IT?

If evidence shows that there is indeed a crisis in the classics in India, it also suggests that the crisis is largely a post-Independence phenomenon. Why has this come about? I am decidedly no expert in modern Indian history in general, let alone educational history in particular: I have only some very general hypotheses to propose.

One could argue that the process of decay has roots that reach back far beyond Independence, with the disqualification of traditional learning in the Western-style universities established in 1857 in Bombay, Calcutta, and Madras, where only those with MA degrees were permitted to teach. The kinds of classical skills that could have been institutionalized and hence preserved and reproduced were arguably precluded from the very start of Westernized university education.

And yet, some structures of education and of philological sentiment were clearly in place up to 1947 to produce the great scholars I mentioned earlier, and who graced virtually every Indian literary tradition. Conditions must have since changed, that fundamentally altered the rules of the game. One factor was no doubt the nationalist movement in the first half of the twentieth century, and the transition to linguistic states in the second. Both were a spur to historical-philological studies (just as was the case in nineteenth-century Europe). But as both objectives were achieved, the quest for origins—a concomitant of much interest in the classics, however deplorable—may have lost its raison d'être.

To be sure, there were larger tendencies at work, with far more discernible impact. Even non-modernists like myself know about Nehruvian materialism, and, later, slash-and-burn globalization, where, as many have pointed out, high dams became the new temples, and the image of Lakshmi, goddess of wealth, replaced that of Sarasvati, goddess of learning. The outcome for education of Nehruvian state initiatives has been a concentration on science and technology at the expense of virtually all other forms of knowledge. Any reasonably careful reader of the reports of the (recently disbanded) National Knowledge Commission, which was charged with recommending long-range solutions to India's higher education deficit, cannot fail to register the utter indifference with which the humanities in general and premodern studies in particular have been treated.

The problem of the domination of science and technology in India hardly differs from that in the United States, or Europe, for that matter, as the Browne Report on higher education in the UK makes clear (Browne 2010).[3] But the fact is that Indian university degree programs in the humanities, let alone the classics, rarely get the best students (as we in the United States often do) except in the case of the indomitably dedicated anomaly. In large part this may be because there are so few life chances, as a result of the factors earlier mentioned. But there is a dialectical rhythm here: the low-esteem jobs for classicists ensure that only weaker students will pursue such careers, which further lowers the profession's esteem.

To some degree, non-Brahminism and Islamophobia, two widespread (and perversely complementary) early twentieth-century ethnochauvinist movements in the south and the north, respectively, have worked to further weaken classical studies already weak from the sociological changes just noted. It is not necessary to deny that non-Brahminism had its justification as a movement for social transformation, or that it created a new context of respect for the Dravidian past, to recognize at the same time that it seriously damaged the foundations of classical study. You cannot read classical south Indian languages (or for that matter classical north Indian languages) without strong skills in Sanskrit, but a false equation of the language and Brahminism turned the study of Sanskrit into an object of derision, if not shame. Contradictorily, today Sanskrit, as part of the "three-language formula," can be taken to fulfill a school requirement, but I have never encountered a single student who thereby developed competence in the language. Obligatory Sanskrit in middle school is a complete failure and has done nothing to improve children's education, let alone secure a future for classical studies.

The case of Persian is hardly different. Before 1947, all school students of Urdu in the United Provinces were required to take one year of Persian or Arabic. Not only was that requirement abandoned after 1947, but it became almost impossible to study Persian in secondary school. As C. M. Naim recounts:

> I don't think the situation was so drastic for Persian before 1947, at least not in U.P., where I grew up. Every high school had a Persian and Arabic teacher, just as they had a Sanskrit teacher, for under the colonial rule the education syllabus required one year of a "classical" language relevant to the pupil's mother-tongue. Since mine was Urdu, I had to choose between Persian and Arabic. I chose Persian, while two of my closest friends chose Arabic. Our two teachers were Muslim, but I recall my Persian class even then had one or two Hindu students too. All that disappeared after 1947; students were given no choice—they had to study Hindi and Sanskrit. If their parents wished to have them study Urdu, the parents had to find at least 29 more parents wishing the same, then petition to the government to provide a teacher. The Persian and Arabic *maulavis* were quickly retired or forced to teach other subjects to younger children (Naim ms.).

The impact on classical studies of such nativist movements was redoubled at the end of the twentieth century by vulgar anti-Orientalism. The original Orientalist critique was salutary in its day (as was the critique of the imperialist foundations of anthropology, to take only that example from elsewhere among the disciplines), but in later times and in lesser minds this critique was guilty of grotesque excesses. Those who could not or would not try to understand the past wound up either stipulating the very enterprise to be conceptually impossible—colonialism, we were told, imposed an epistemic barrier whose untranscendability was somehow known a priori—or condemning it as inevitably reactionary. It took years before a serious history of colonialism was understood to presuppose a serious history of precolonialism, but by then the greater part of a generation of scholars was lost to the study of historical languages.

Some colleagues in India have suggested that the erosion of classical studies may be connected with the policy of reservations. It was the case, or so they told me, that reservation quotas required of an Indian Institute of Science or Indian Institute of Technology could be passed on down the line, with the result that—to take an almost farcical example—the Maharaja's Sanskrit College in Mysore, when I was living there in the mid-1990s, had a Vedic Sanskrit post reserved for a Scheduled Caste (formerly, untouchable) scholar. But, generally speaking, most people with adequately working brains understand that merit is randomly distributed among castes and classes, and good institutions can create good scholars, whatever their origins (see Mehta 2006 for one of the best brief statements). The problem is "good institutions."

A counterintuitive but potentially consequential factor in the erosion of classical language skills lies in the erosion of English language skills. There is little question that, as a result of state policy, as in West Bengal or Tamil Nadu, linguistic pride in many parts of the country, or postcolonial rejection everywhere else (Gandhi's *Hind Swaraj* providing an astonishing charter; see Parel 1997: 100-101)—the capacity to communicate in English has decayed dramatically among classical, and indeed most other, scholars in India since Independence.[4] As a result, Indian classicists are almost entirely shut out of the international community of scholarship and show little substantive understanding of what is being done in classical studies outside of India, or even in India itself.

The erosion of English would not loom so large if, by way of compensation, the Indian translation industry were remotely functional. I cannot examine this topic here in any depth—or the ironic, post-Independence reversal of nineteenth-century translation initiatives such as those at Benares Sanskrit College into Sanskrit (Dodson 2007), or Delhi College into Urdu (Minault 1999), or across the Bombay-Pune region into Marathi (Naregal 2002)—but consider just the case of translation into Hindi. I and the colleagues I polled must surely be mistaken but none of us could identify a single article, let alone monograph, on classical Indian studies written in English that has been translated into Hindi in post-Independence India—or indeed, on any topic in South Asian studies, however broadly appealing. There is no *Provincializing Europe* in Hindi, no *The Nation and Its Fragments,* none of the works of Bernard Cohn, not even Gayatri Spivak's "Can the Subaltern Speak?"[5] If Indian scholars are not reading English and not reading translations of English in Indian languages, they cannot participate in the global scholarly community and thus cannot secure whatever support, intellectual or material, that the community might have to offer.[6]

Add to this mix, as noted earlier, the larger forces at work globally. Some of these are old, since corporatization, commodification, and technologization have been part of university life in the United States, for example, for more than a century. (In 1891, Andrew Carnegie congratulated graduates of a business college for being "fully occupied in obtaining a knowledge of shorthand and typewriting" rather than wasting time "upon dead languages" [Donoghue 2008: 4]; just one representative quote from a litany of philistinism in Donoghue's book.)

Some are very new, however, like the rise of a post-literate society and the death of reading as a result, not of a sociological but of a physiological transformation, as the circuitry in our brains, some suggest, is being remapped by digital devices. I certainly have sometimes felt an unfamiliar sense of having to drag "my wayward brain back to the text. The deep reading that used to come naturally has become a struggle" (Carr 2010: 5-6).[7] A reading style that prioritizes efficiency and immediacy militates against developing the habit of "slow reading," as Nietzsche called it, upon which literary, especially classical literary, studies depends.

Among this scattershot array of factors behind the crisis in classical studies in India, from the structure of the nineteenth-century university to the erosion of reading with the rise of the Internet, at least some have to be consequential to some degree. But it really does not matter what caused the crisis if no one believes it is a crisis worth caring about.

WHO CARES?

Why should we care at all about the fate of the classics in India? What is lost if that particular competence is lost? Competencies are lost all the time—cultures are dying everywhere. Fifty years ago Erich Auerbach, the great philologist of Western literature, raised the same specter of crisis for Europe, describing the loss of philology as "an impoverishment for which there can be no possible compensation." And yet he seemed to assume that it was those alone who already appreciated philology who could understand how grievous the loss would be ("only those who have not totally sustained this loss would be aware of privation") (Auerbach 1969: 5). It is admittedly no easy task to preach to the unconverted. I want to try, however, proceeding by way of a brief reflection on the idea of the "classic" itself, which might lead us toward the beginning of an answer to the question of why anyone should care.

I have been using "classic" in the context of India to refer to any and all literature written before c. 1800.[8] That moment did mark a profound transformation: colonialism would not only eventually render the literary past unreadable to most Indians, it would remake the literature of India according to its own image (whatever indigenization would eventually occur). It is this rupture, for me, that defines the classical.

For virtually everyone who has written on the "classic" in the West, from C. A. Sainte-Beuve's "Qu'est-ce qu'un classique?" (1850) to T. S. Eliot's "What is a Classic?" (1944) through "The Example of the Classical" in Hans-Georg Gadamer's *Truth and Method* (1996 [1960]) to Frank Kermode's *The Classic* (1975), it has been the supposed capacity for universalization that grounds the category. The classic, as Sainte-Beuve famously put it, uncovers "a certain moral truth that is not equivocal" and recaptures "a certain eternal passion in the heart where all seemed known and discovered"; it is "effortlessly contemporaneous with all ages," possessed as it is of a "universal morality" (1895:44-45, 52). For Kermode, the classic possesses "intrinsic qualities that endure," it is "more or less immediately relevant," with a "perpetual contemporaneity" (1975: 45, 15-16). Gadamer, too, thinks of the classic as "a kind of timeless present that is contemporaneous with every other present" (1996: 288). Eliot demands of the classic maturity, amplitude, catholicity, nonprovinciality, comprehensiveness, and, yet again, "universality" (Eliot 1975 [1945]:116, 128).[9] While J. M. Coetzee, in his rereading of Eliot's essay, memorably describes him as "a man with the magical enterprise of redefining the world around *himself*," that, I submit, is precisely what each one of our authors does in defining "classic." It's just that Eliot's un-self-awareness allows a particularly bright light to shine on the specious universalism inherent in the very idea of the classic.

I follow an entirely different logic, abandoning the "normative significance" of "classical" and the subjectivism and illegitimate generalization of the present that such normativity always smuggles in.[10] To me "classic" means precisely the opposite of what my predecessors understood: a work is classical by reason of its resistance to contemporaneity and supposed universality, by reason of its capacity to indicate human particularity and difference in that past epoch. The classic is not what tells me about shared humanity—or, more truthfully put, what lets me recognize myself as already present in the past, what nourishes in me the illusion that everything has been like me and has existed only to prepare the way for me. Instead, the classic is what gives access to radically different forms of human consciousness for any given generation of readers, and thereby expands for them the range of possibilities of what it means to be a human being.[11]

Let me turn now to why classical studies, in my—no doubt for some, perverse—sense of "classical," are important. I do this by distinguishing four different human ends they serve, a sort of *chaturvarga*, if you will, the classical Four Ends of Man. Classical studies 1) promote real pedagogy, especially and perhaps unexpectedly radical pedagogy;

2) stimulate care for memory and help shape a usable sense of the past, preserving memory from those who would abuse it, and open the past to responsible critique; 3) enable us to acquire new "tools for living"; 4) make possible an encounter with the enduring beauty and intellectual excitement created by the vast labor of several thousand years of human consciousness.

There is a general pedagogical importance of the classics attaching to the study of language as such. Here I can agree with Gadamer that "Language is not just one of man's possessions in the world; rather, on it depends the fact that man has a world at all.... Man's being-in-the-world is primordially linguistic" (440). We learn to know the world and to know ourselves by learning language, and learning a non-modern language is, however counterintuitively, the most profound way to come to know one's own.

This general aspect of pedagogy in the classics—of understanding human being as mediated by language—is complemented by, perhaps inseparable from, a particular, political aspect of such pedagogy. It can be argued—and, as I read him, Antonio Gramsci tried to argue—that in the era of the capitalist and corporatist university, the most radical education is the most radically noninstrumental. This is not simple contrariety. The discipline of learning a non-modern language and learning it well is at once personally transformative and (in the widest sense of the term) politically oppositional: "Pupils did not learn Latin and Greek in order to speak them, to become waiters, interpreters or commercial letter writers," Gramsci reflected; rather, they studied in order to learn not a particular vocational skill but, first, the discipline of work as such rather than this or that particular job, and second, the possibility of acting in the world in a disinterested, even anti-profit manner (Gramsci 1986: 37-40; Entwistle 1979: 170-172; Borg and Mayo 2003). Moreover, teaching students to confront the difficult and the non-instrumental, teaching them the patience to listen to unfamiliar voices and to continue to listen until they make sense—to teach slow reading in a fast world—is one way of teaching them, as Gramsci suggested, to think for themselves. And nothing is quite so radical a political act as that.

This discipline of making sense of texts, which I have been talking about all along here, is what used to be called—and what I hope will one day again be called, with pride—philology. Philology is central to all reading, whether that of a Sangam poet or a Dalit novelist, though it seems to confront us as a methodological issue in direct proportion to the distance in time and space that separates us from the text. We naïvely think the contemporary text transparently accessible, but making sense of it always requires philology, which becomes more effective the more present it is to our consciousness. Learning a classical language renders philology permanently present; it enables us to read with sustained discipline, teaching us above all to distinguish and balance the three core domains of meaning: the author's, the tradition's, and, most important, our own.

The philology of texts leads, thus, to a philology of life, whose first if fragmentary theorist was Nietzsche: "Philology is, in a general sense...the capacity for absorbing facts without interpreting them falsely, and without losing caution, patience and subtlety in the effort to understand them...whether one be dealing with books, with newspaper reports, with the most fateful events or with weather statistics—not to mention the 'salvation of the soul'" (Nietzsche 1980, 6: 233). I don't claim the salvation of our souls depends on the salvation of classical philology, but some portion of our humanity might well.

The capacity to shape memory likewise has two aspects for me, one general, concerning the value of memory as such, and one particular, concerning the critique of memory.

If you question the study of the classics you inevitably question the value of history as such, since the two (as Vico was the first to understand) are inseparable—or put more pertinently to the present, the classics are significant to the same degree that history as such is significant. That significance is, to be sure, not unproblematic for many, starting again with Nietzsche. But even for Nietzsche, it is only the beast that lives unhistorically. If you argue for an "ethics of forgetting" you might as well argue for an ethics of unconsciousness; if you lose memory you lose all sense of self (or indeed, your mind, as the *Bhagavad Gita* puts it, *smritibhramshad buddhinashah*: "from loss of memory comes the destruction of the mind").

India is well on the way to losing its memory, and not just losing it—since in fact the past never passes away—but surrendering it to the abusers of memory. If classical scholars in India or elsewhere cede control of memory, it will be left to the delusions and the ravings of the anti-historians, who, almost in lockstep with the loss of classical knowledge over the past generation, have moved ever closer, if incredibly so, to a credible place at the center of public discourse in India.

The second, more particular aspect of memory, is again oppositional. When I talk about the memory cultivated by classical studies I mean to include the capacity made available for critiquing the past. We may unhesitatingly grant the premise that classical culture, Sanskrit for example, offers at one and the same time a record of civilization and a record of barbarism, of extraordinary inequality and other social poisons. Once we all agree on the toxicity of this discourse, however, there will be contestation over how to overcome it. In my view, you do not transcend inequality, to the degree that it is a conceptual category taking some of its force from traditional discourse, by outlawing the authors and burning the discourses, or indeed by trying to forget them; you transcend inequality by mastering and overmastering those discourses through study and critique. You cannot simply go around a tradition to overcome it, if that is what you wish to do; you must go through it. You only transform a dominant culture by outsmarting it. That, I believe, is precisely what some of India's most disruptive thinkers, such as Dr. Ambedkar, sought to do, though they were not as successful as they might have been had they had access to all the tools of a critical philology necessary to the task.

The third end, recovering "tools for living" from the past, means recovering possibilities of other ways of being in the world that have been lost or that we have falsely come to believe are impossible, thanks to the amnesia enforced by the insistent universalizations of Western modernity. It was for me a transformative life experience to have been able to glimpse, in my study of classical Kannada and Sanskrit literature, the existence of practices now deemed unthinkable: a voluntary cosmopolitanism as opposed to the familiar compulsory one, a vernacularity of accommodation instead of the usual vernacularity of necessity, ways that globalism and localism could beneficially coexist (Pollock 2006). The possibilities for imagining a different future are sometimes made available by discovering a different past.

From all this you will understand my impatience with the ignorant and self-crippling attack on the classics by a shallow post-Orientalism and postcolonialism on the one hand, and the criminal attempt at its appropriation by the alphabet soup of indigenist forces (RSS, BJP, VHP, DMK, et cetera)[12] on the other. Of all the historical literary cultures of India, it is Sanskrit that has most fatefully been caught between two benighted armies, the lumpen saffron right and the anti-Brahmin infantile left. It is shocking and painful to recognize how debased is the level of public discourse on Sanskrit these days, politicized in the most ignorant fashion. I have already explained the role I believe critique must play. But there are vast areas of Sanskrit and other classical literatures and forms of knowledge that have enduring beauty and intellectual excitement, and that cannot be simply reduced to some sort of false consciousness that must be overcome. This was precisely what Marx grasped in that all-too-brief remark in the *Grundrisse*: "But the difficulty lies not in understanding that the Greek arts and epic are bound up with certain forms of social development"—that is, slave-holding, Asian-hating, women-oppressing forms; "the difficulty is that they still afford us artistic pleasure" (Marx 1973: 111). And not just pleasure: studying the assembled record of 3,000 years of Indian thinking, thinking of the very highest order, is not merely a pleasure or a duty we owe the dead—though it is both those things, too—but a unique, and uniquely fulfilling, way of tracing the genealogy of our contemporary selves, whether you are Indian or not. If we lose the ability to read these texts of the past we lose something essential to us that we can find nowhere else.

What I have been suggesting by my account of pedagogy, memory, tools for living, and beauty is that the study of the classics is crucial to an enriched human life, but also that that study needs to be reinvented under the sign of what we might name *critical classicism*. How did we lose the radical potential of this form of thought? How did we wind up so completely ceding the classics to an often vicious conservatism of the present? Even today the simpleminded argument continues to be made that "to love old art is to honor old arrangements" (Gropnik 2008).[13] But Marx and Gramsci stand as evidence to the contrary, and so too does a contemporary Indian thinker like the late D. R. Nagaraj, a true heir of Ambedkar, who went from a childhood as an indentured weaver outside of Bangalore to an adulthood as a scholar and cultural activist who strove tirelessly to master Old Kannada and Sanskrit and write at once critically and appreciatively about both (Nagaraj 2010). Critical classicism is thus a legacy to be recovered, but also an obligation to be discharged and a resource to be cherished.

WHAT IS TO BE DONE?

If there is a crisis, and if we have some sense of the complex of factors that caused it, and if we see good reason to address the crisis because the classics are important to our lives—if there is pain (*duhkha*), a source of pain (*duhkhasamudaya*), the need and possibility to end pain (*duhkhanirodha*)—then what is the way?

This is where I am weakest, I am sorry to say, for I am no Buddha. At the end of the day, the vortex of the market may suck us all down. Here and in so many areas both good and bad, postcolonial India, with its various crises including the classics, may constitute not an anomaly but the world's future: no longer in the waiting room of history but history's guest of honor. (And the problem may really be far larger than I can see. Indian learning as such may be on the line: the historical arc of creative Indian science, for example—the age of Meghnad Saha, S. N. Bose, and C. V. Raman—shadows classical studies.)[14] Still, we cannot have come this far simply to throw up our hands.

I long thought the solution to the crisis in the classics was governmental—it used to be clear that when India is convinced of something's importance it can do something important about it—and I accordingly promoted the idea of an Indian Institute of Classical Studies, along the lines of the Indian Institutes of Science, Technology, Management, and now Information Technology. This would have to be a place where the realistic assessment of Dipesh Chakrabarty is realistically acknowledged:

> It is a shame, isn't it? But why will bright people invest in learning difficult languages and literatures if it is going to hurt their life-chances? What India needs is real elitist streaming in education, so

that some people, chosen on very strict criteria, are allowed to pursue philological studies but be compensated at such a high level that their life-chances and those of their children are not compromised. We are talking of diverting brains from technological studies. This can't happen without real incentives. The incentives on the other side are much, much higher (Chakrabarty, n. d.).

I have more recently thought that the solution might be a demonstration department of philology in one of the new universities—Nalanda University (a pan-Asian affair), SAARC's South Asian University (a regional affair), or Vedanta University (a private affair)—and I actually sketched out the design of such a department at the request of the Nalanda Mentor Group Advisory Council. But the plan came to nothing, as Nalanda itself seems to have come close to nothing, SAARC is headed by an economist (enough said) and Vedanta U. may never be realized. As for the new state universities called for under the Eleventh Plan—which Pratap Bhanu Mehta characterized as "a strategy for *university buildings*, not for *building universities*" (Mehta 2008)—I fear there is little hope. Consider the new humanities initiative for the IITs, whose frivolity an Indian newspaper captured with its headline, "IITs to go artsy, to offer courses in music, architecture, performing arts" (*Indian Express* 2009). Why on earth are the IITs competing in areas that are already strong and where the skills produced are eminently marketable? Can no one understand the importance of supporting those critical, yet fragile because unmarketable, forms of knowledge such as the historical and textual? Nor do I see the point of the competition announced by the government of Tamil Nadu, the "Kalaignar M. Karunanidhi Classical Tamil Award," which carried an award of 1 million rupees, an 80-gram gold medal bearing the likeness of Karunanidhi (then chief minister), and a five-metal statue of Thiruvalluvar (author of the *Tirukkural*). What good are awards if there is no one trained to compete for them?

It would be worth exploring in more detail than I am capable of the comparison to contemporary China, where the state is—uniquely in the world at present—investing vast resources in classical studies.[15] But for India, I am no longer so sure that the central government is the solution rather than the problem. Having had considerable experience with *sarkari* institutions (the term used effectively to dismiss the "government" to which the word refers), especially in the past few years, I have grown increasingly convinced that the dead hand of the state would likely wind up perverting any such initiative. It is hard to disagree with Bruno Latour, who argued recently that "there is no more urgent task than removing from the production of knowledge the double stranglehold of the state and the market" (Latour 2008), but also hard to see how to do it. Perhaps the enlightened private sector can offer a way forward—the founding of the Murty Classical Library of India through an endowment from an Indian family is one stellar example—or cooperative arrangements between private Indian actors and the international community of classical programs, pressed though these themselves may be for essential resources.[16]

Solve this problem we must, however. Let me end by stating things as plainly as I can. India is confronting a calamitous endangerment of its classic knowledge, and India today may have reached the point the rest of the world will reach tomorrow. This form of knowledge, under the sign of a critical classicism, must be recovered and strengthened not for the mere satisfaction of those outside of India who cultivate the study of its past, but for the good of the people of India themselves. I may not have ready to hand an institutional solution to the crisis in the classics, but I remain hopeful that one can be found. Achieving this solution will require a collective public conversation on the problem—and the conversation must be insistent and loud.

NOTES

1. The articles from *The Hindu* newspaper cited in the references chart something of the history of this burlesque, which deserves a full study; for now see Venkatachalapathy (2009).
2. See the Humanities Resource Center Online, the "Humanities Indicators" (http://www.humanitiesindicators.org/humanitiesData.aspx). Brinkley notes that the National Endowment for Humanities budget today is one-third less than 30 years ago, while academic humanities receive only 13 percent of that budget.

3. For Browne, the value of knowledge will henceforth be judged by students in terms of "the employment returns from their courses." "What universities teach," as one commentator summarizes, "will henceforth be determined by their anticipation of consumer demand." (Collini 2010).

4. Admittedly, the capacity for, and interest in, participation in international scholarship was unevenly spread across classical studies in pre-independence India. Many Sanskrit scholars named earlier did take part; but perhaps for obvious reasons very few scholars of classical Kannada or Hindi did, world-class though they were.

5. The translation of Hindi or other Indian-language scholarship or thought (beyond belles lettres) into English, which is almost nonexistent, is an important related problem.

6. Hindi-language publishers have recently begun to bring out more scholarship in translation, but this is largely Western history or theory (Hobsbaum, Marc Bloch, Voloshinov). The Indian Languages Programme at the Centre for the Study of Developing Societies translates into Hindi English-language works of *Indian* social scientists. Incidentally, the National Knowledge Commission recognized that "the current facilities for translation are inadequate and less than socially optimal.... Therefore some amount of public intervention is crucial to encourage the translation industry" (see http://www.knowledgecommission.gov.in/focus/translation.asp).

7. For others Carr's worries are "merely" about a particular form of cultural death. The net isn't making us stupid, it has simply unmasked Tolstoy as the bore he is: "Too long and not so interesting" (Shirky 2008).

8. I say "written" but have no desire to insist on the question of literacy. But subaltern opponents to the classics should understand that the history of written culture in India is in part the history of dominated communities seizing the power to write themselves into the historical record (think of Raidas, for example, or Tukaram or Eluttacchan). Moreover, a commitment to literate literature does not preclude a commitment to oral literature, with its own specific methods of study and theories of its conditions of possibility.

9. It is in keeping with Eliot's provincialism disguised as cosmopolitanism that such universality could only be expression in Latin, "the universal

means of communication between peoples of all tongues and cultures"
(1975: 130).

10. How else could one possibly think oneself capable of identifying the
particular stage of the development of humanity that produced "the
perfect form of the human"? And what can "perfect form of the human"
possibly mean? See Gadamer (1996 [1960]): 285-286.

11. I reserve for another occasion explaining the Rankean foundation of my
argument here, and only note that even a secularist can take seriously
his argument that "*Jede Epoche ist unmittelbar zu Gott*" (every age is
immediate to God) (Ranke 1971 [1854]: 59-60).

12. That is, Rashtriya Swayamsevak Sangh (National Volunteer Organization);
Bharatiya Janata Party (Indian People's Party); Vishva Hindu Parishad
(World Hindu Council).

13. "His love of poetry and music and art," the author says further of John
Stuart Mill, "also led him toward conservative thought. Aesthetes always
bend to the right."

14. Pratap Mehta has seen this larger dimension, and for science research in
particular calls my attention to Prathap (2004).

15. According to Stephen Owen,

> The state has spent and continues to spend huge sums
> supporting students, scholarly projects and scholars. The
> quality of philological work is not universally good, but
> where it is good, it is very good indeed.... Virtually every
> printed book... since the eleventh century has been at least
> photo-reprinted, and available in digital form—sometimes
> free online. This is clearly in the interest of the state,
> teaching national culture. There are issues about what is
> done with the material, but the texts and scholarly skills
> are definitely preserved—not quite in the old way—but
> preserved (private communication).

A recent visit I made to the Institute for Advanced Studies in the
Humanities at Fudan University in Shanghai bore all this out.

16. See <www.murtyclassicallibraryofindia.com>. Note also the "Campaign
for Classics in the Twenty-first Century" (http://apaclassics. org/index.
php/support_the_APA/campaign_for_classics), an unprecedented
initiative of the American Philological Association, which is at once a
symptom of the crisis and a model response to it.

REFERENCES

Ahmed, Manan, Islam Dayeh, Angelika Neuwirth, Nicolai Sinai. "Zukunftsphilologie: Revisiting the Canons of Textual Scholarship." Berlin: Forum Transregionale Studien, n.d. [2010].

Auerbach, Erich. "Philology and Weltliteratur." *The Centennial Review* 13 (1969): 1-17.

Borg, Carmel, and Peter Mayo. "Gramsci and the Unitarian School: Paradoxes and Possibilities." *Gramsci and Education*. Eds. C. Borg et al. Lanham, Md.: Rowman and Littlefield, 2003.

Brinkley, Alan. "The Landscape of Humanities Research and Funding." Humanities Indicators Prototype, American Academy of Arts and Sciences, 2009.

Carr, Nicholas. *The Shallows: What the Internet is Doing to Our Brains.* New York: Norton, 2010.

Chakrabarty, Dipesh. Personal communication.

Coetzee, J. M. *Stranger Shores: Literary Essays 1986-1999.* New York: Viking, 2001.

Collini, Stefan. "Browne's Gamble." *London Review of Books* (November 2010): 23-25.

Dodson, Michael. *Orientalism, Empire, and National Culture: India, 1770-1880.* Basingstoke and New York: Palgrave Macmillan, 2007.

Donoghue, Frank. *The Last Professors: The Corporate University and the Fate of the Humanities.* New York: Fordham University Press, 2008.

Eliot, T. S. "What is a Classic?" *Selected Prose.* Ed. Frank Kermode. New York: Harcourt, 1975 (1945).

Entwistle, Harold. *Antonio Gramsci: Conservative Schooling for Radical Politics.* London: Routledge and Kegan Paul, 1979.

Gadamer, Hans-Georg. *Truth and Method.* New York: Continuum, 1996 (1960).

Gramsci, Antonio. *Selections from the Prison Notebooks.* London: International Publishers, 1971.

"Grant Classical Language Status to Telugu: YSR." *The Hindu*, February 19, 2008.

Gropnik, Adam. "Right Again: The Passions of John Stuart Mill." *The New Yorker*, October 6, 2008.

Khajane, Muralidhara. "Classical Tag Is a Reward for Kannada: Javare Gowda." *The Hindu,* November 1, 2008.

Latour, Bruno. "Autonomie, que de crimes on commet en ton nom!" *Le Monde,* February 25, 2009.

Marx, Karl. *Outline of the Critique of Political Economy (Grundrisse).* London: Penguin, 1973.

Mehta, Pratap Bhanu. "Democracy, Disagreement and Merit." *Economic and Political Weekly,* June 17, 2006: 2425-2427.

———. "Obstacles to a New Revolution." *Seminar* 590 (2008): 44-49.

Minault, Gail. "Delhi College and Urdu." *Annual of Urdu Studies* 14 (1999): 119-134.

Naim, C. M. ms. "A Note on Persian."

Nair, C. Gouridasan. "Classical Language Status: Kerala to Lay Claim." *The Hindu,* November 10, 2008.

Nagaraj, D. R. *The Flaming Feet and Other Essays: The Dalit Movement in India.* Ed. Prithvi Datta Chandra Shobhi. New Delhi: Permanent Black, 2010.

Naregal, Veena. *Language Politics, Elites and the Public Sphere: Western India Under Colonialism.* London: Anthem, 2002.

Nietzsche, Friedrich. *Sämtliche Werke: Kritische Studienausgabe.* Eds. Giorgio Colli and Mazzino Montinari. 15 vols. Munich, 1980.

Parel, Anthony J. *Gandhi: Hind Swaraj and Other Writings.* Cambridge: Cambridge University Press, 1997.

Pollock, Sheldon. *The Language of the Gods in the World of Men: Sanskrit, Culture, and Power in Premodern India.* Berkeley: University of California Press, 2006.

———. "Towards a Political Philology: D. D. Kosambi and Sanskrit." *Economic and Political Weekly* (D. D. Kosambi Centenary Volume), July 26, 2008: 52-59.

———. "Future Philology? The Fate of a Soft Science in a Hard World." *The Fate of the Disciplines.* Eds. James Chandler and Arnold Davidson. *Critical Inquiry* 35:4 (2009): 931-61.

Pollock, Sheldon, ed. *Literary Cultures in History: Reconstructions from South Asia.* Berkeley: University of California Press, 2003.

Prathap, Gangan. "Indian Science Slows Down: The Decline of Open-ended Research." *Current Science* 86:6 (2004): 768-769.

Ranke, Leopold von. *Über die Epochen der neueren Geschichte*. Munich: Oldenbourg, 1971 (1854).

Rao, K. N. Venkatasubba. "Kannada Likely to Get Classical Tag." *The Hindu*, October 4, 2006.

Sainte-Beuve, C. A. "Qu'est-ce qu'un classique"? *Selected Essays*. Ed. J. R. Effinger. Boston: Ginn, 1896 (1850).

"Sanskrit to Be Declared Classical Language." *The Hindu*, October 28, 2005.

Shirkey, Clay. "Why Abundance Is Good: A Reply to Nick Carr." *Encyclopaedia Britannica Blog*, July 17, 2008 <http://www.britannica.com/blogs/2008/07/why-abundance-is-good-a-reply-to-nick-carr/>.

Venkatachalapathy, A. R. "The 'Classical' Language Issue." *Economic and Political Weekly*, January 10, 2009, 13-15.

From Kama to Karma: The Resurgence of Puritanism in Contemporary India

Wendy Doniger

A pervasive and often violent moral policing has taken over parts of the Indian world today. A typical instance of this occurred in 2007 when Chandramohan Srilamantula, a 23-year-old student of fine arts at the Maharaja Sayajirao University of Baroda (in Vadodara, Gujarat), mounted an exhibition for other students and staff. He had previously received awards for his work, including the forty-ninth Lalit Kala Akademi National Exhibition award in 2006; later he won first prize in the 2009 Bhopal Biennale. In the 2007 exhibition, one painting depicted a crucified Christ with explicit genitals and a toilet beneath the cross; another, was of a nude Durga using a trident (the weapon of the god Shiva) to kill a baby issuing from her womb.

Christian leaders lodged protests against the first painting, and a group of activists from the VHP (Vishva Hindu Parishad, "World Hindu Council") and the BJP (Bharatiya Janata Party, "National People's Party") vandalized the exhibition and roughed up Chandramohan (Valsan 2007). They were led by Niraj Jain, who has been known to brandish a revolver and once threw eggs at the Gujarat education minister for including them in school midday meals (Dharker 2007). The police stood by and then arrested not the vandals but the artist. (He was later released.) When the acting dean of the Faculty of Fine Arts, Shivraj Panikkar, refused to close down the exhibition, the vice-chancellor,

Manoj Soni, suspended him. Panikkar, stating that he feared for his life, went into hiding. Students and spokespersons of the Indian art community held protests throughout India, claiming that the closing of the exhibition was a direct assault on the rights of freedom of expression.

In commenting on this event, the well-known editor, columnist, and critic Anil Dharker remarked:

> What has made the artists come together in protest is that this attack isn't an isolated one, but one more in a series now increasing in both frequency and wantonness.... The Mumbai Police stood by when Shiv Sainiks attacked cinema theatres showing a Deepa Mehta film.... Recently, the Mumbai cops did some moral policing of their own, arresting young couples found in "compromising positions" (policespeak for young men and women having their arms around each other) (Dharker 2007).

Dharker went on to list several more instances, but even these few are representative of broad patterns of attacks by various Hindutva groups, whose members are known as Hindutvadis.[1] Some Hindutvadis forced Deepa Mehta to leave Varanasi, where she was making a film about the mistreatment of widows in Varanasi (*Water* 2005); on January 30, 2000, "fundamentalist thugs" from the BJP (a coalition of Rashtriya Swayamsevak Sangh [RSS, "National Corps of Volunteers"]), VHP, and others, together with Uttar Pradesh government officials destroyed the film sets and later threatened the cast and crew; on February 6, 2000, the state of Uttar Pradesh ordered a suspension of production, and Mehta finished the film in Sri Lanka (Philips 2000). Other BJP groups stopped the screening of films starring actors such as Shah Rukh Khan (who had expressed admiration for Pakistani cricketers) and Aamir Khan (who had supported Medha Patkar, a famous woman social activist) (Dharker 2007).

The protest against Chandramohan Srilamantula was one of a number of campaigns against artists and writers who linked Hindu deities with sexuality. In 1996, Hindutvadis began terrorizing M. F. Husain for his paintings of naked Hindu goddesses. In 2006, after death threats and legal cases, the 91-year-old Husain, whom many regarded as India's greatest living artist, was forced into exile in Dubai. The

Mumbai policing of young couples that Dharker mentioned is matched by equally outrageous attacks on young "pub-crawling" Indian women in Mangalore, and by regular efforts to attack stores and restaurants that celebrate Valentine's Day (on the grounds that it is a Western corruption of Indian values). The Hindutvadis often blame Western influence on the people they censor, while, ironically, many of the Hindutvadis' own actions closely resemble censoring frenzies in the United States. But the Indian incidents are better seen as part of a separate logic of Hindu Puritanism, which has a long history of its own.

THE EARLY HISTORY OF HINDU EROTICISM AND ASCETICISM

When a group of students and artists at Baroda University attempted to stage a protest demonstration for Chandramohan at the Faculty of Fine Arts, they organized an exhibition of photographs taken from the explicitly erotic sculptures that adorn the temples at Khajuraho, in Madhya Pradesh (Bordewekar 2007: 62). In choosing Khajuraho, they were making an implicit historical statement: the art heritage of India is rich in erotic themes, of which the images on the Khajuraho temples (built between 900 and 1100 CE) are a famous example. What happened to that tradition? How did India get from there to the scandal in Baroda?

Erotic religious imagery is as old as Hinduism. The earliest Hindu sacred text, the *Rig Veda* (c. 1500 BCE), revels in the language of both pleasure and fertility. The Upanishads, which followed a few centuries later, analogized the Vedic oblation of butter into the fire to the act of sexual procreation (*Brihadaranyaka Upanishad* 6.2.13, 6.4.3). The worshipper in a sexual embrace with his wife imagines each part of the act as a part of the ritual of the oblation, while presumably anyone making the offering into the fire could also imagine each action as its sexual parallel. Sensuality continued to keep its foot in the door of the house of religion throughout the history of India.

But the Upanishads also introduced into India the concept of two paths: one, the path of family life, society, and children, the other, the path of renunciation, solitary meditation, and asceticism. And although asceticism always remained alive and well in India, householders continued to obey the command to be fruitful and multiply. The tension between the two paths, the violent, sacrificial, materialistic, and sensual path of worldliness on the one hand, and the non-violent, vegetarian, ascetic, and spiritual path of renunciation, on the other, was sometimes expressed as the balance between bourgeois householders and homeless seekers, or between traditions that regarded *karma*—the accumulated record of good and bad deeds—as a good or a bad thing, respectively.

The tension remains in the Tantras, a large body of texts composed between about 650 and 1800 CE that proposed strikingly transgressive ritual actions, violating all the taboos of conventional Hinduism, such as drinking wine and menstrual blood, eating meat, and engaging in sexual activity with forbidden women. These Tantras thus collapsed the Upanishadic metaphor, saying that the ritual sexual act is not just *like* a ritual (as it is in the Upanishads) but *is itself* a ritual, the equivalent of making an offering into the fire. But other Tantras, situated within the anti-erotic tradition of Hinduism, insisted that the ritual instructions were never intended to be followed literally, but were purely symbolic. They argued that "wine" really meant a meditational nectar, that "flesh" meant the tongue of the practitioner, and that the sexual act stood for "the supreme essence." (White 2003: 220) This was a very early form of censorship, and a very mild form, for it merely proposed an alternative, anti-erotic interpretation of the text but did not attempt to muzzle the other, erotic interpretation.

And so the two paths of Tantra, meditation and ritual action, lived side by side, sometimes coexisting in a single worshipper, sometimes within a group—as, for instance, in some texts that say beginners actually do the ritual, while advanced practitioners just meditate. The split-level connotations were present from the start. Given the attention that Indian literary theory pays to double meanings, to words and indeed whole literary works that simultaneously mean two different things (Bronner 2010), it seems wise to assume that the Tantrics were capable of walking and chewing imaginary gum at the same time.

The erotic tradition continued to thrive in Hinduism. Many poems to gods in the medieval devotional tradition of *bhakti* imagine the god as a lover, often an unfaithful lover, and depict the relationship with all the sensual details of good erotic poetry. The poet Kshetrayya, who may have lived in the mid-seventeenth century and who worshipped a form of the god Krishna, imagined a courtesan speaking to her customer who is both her lover and her god. Kshetrayya's songs survived among courtesans and were performed by male Brahmin dancers who played female roles. His poems deal with such down-to-earth matters as a woman's concern to find a drug or a magic potion to abort the child that she conceived from her lover—the king, the god, and her customer (Ramanujan 1994: 117-18).

THE KAMASUTRA

In addition to these religious texts that incorporated eroticism, there were more worldly texts that treated the erotic *tout court*, of which the *Kamasutra*, composed in north India, probably in the third century CE, is the most famous. The two words in its title mean "desire/love/pleasure/sex" (*kama*) and "a treatise" (*sutra*). Virtually nothing is known about the author, Vatsyayana, other than his name and what we learn from this text. There is nothing remotely like it even now, and for its time it was astonishingly sophisticated; it was already well known in India when the Europeans were still swinging from trees, culturally (and sexually) speaking. The *Kamasutra*'s ideas about gender are surprisingly modern, and its stereotypes of feminine and masculine natures are unexpectedly subtle. It also reveals attitudes to women's education and sexual freedom, and views of homosexual acts that are strikingly more liberal than those of other texts in ancient India—or, in many cases, in contemporary India.

Vatsyayana dismisses with one or two short verses the possibility that the purpose of the sexual act is to produce children; one of the things that make sex for human beings different from sex for animals, he points out, is the fact that human women, unlike animals, have sex even when they are not in their fertile period (*Kamasutra* [KS] 2.2.20). Given the enormous emphasis that the traditional texts of Hindu religious law (*dharma*) place on having sex *only* to produce children, the *Kamasutra*'s attitude here is extraordinary. It is also extraordinary in assuming that women would, and should, know this text:

A woman should study the Kamasutra and its subsidiary arts before she reaches the prime of her youth, and she should continue when she has been given away, if her husband wishes it. Scholars say: "Since females cannot grasp texts, it is useless to teach women this text." Vatsyayana says: But women understand the practice, and the practice is based on the text. This applies beyond this specific subject of the *Kamasutra*, for throughout the world, in all subjects, there are only a few people who know the text, but the practice is within the range of everyone. And a text, however far removed, is the ultimate source of the practice. "Grammar is a science," people say. Yet the sacrificial priests, who are no grammarians, know how to gloss the words in the sacrificial prayers. "Astronomy is a science," they say. But ordinary people perform the rituals on the days when the skies are auspicious. And people know how to ride horses and elephants without studying the texts about horses and elephants. In the same way, even citizens far away from the king do not step across the moral line that he sets. The case of women learning the *Kamasutra* is like those examples. And there are also women whose understanding has been sharpened by the text: courtesans and the daughters of kings and state ministers. (*KS* 1.3.1-11)

Vatsyayana is also a strong advocate for women's sexual pleasure. He tells us that a woman who does not experience the pleasures of love may hate her man and leave him for another (*KS* 3.2.35,4.2.31-5). If, as the context suggests, this woman is married, the casual manner in which Vatsyayana suggests that she leave her husband is in sharp contrast to the position assumed by the *Laws of Manu*, the most famous of the textbooks of *dharma*, composed a few centuries before the *Kamasutra*: "A virtuous wife should constantly serve her husband like a god, even if he behaves badly, freely indulges his lust, and is devoid of any good qualities" (Manu 5.154). Vatsyayana also presents an argument in favor of female orgasm far more subtle than views that prevailed in Europe until very recently indeed, and certainly worlds above the attitudes of his predecessors, whose cockamamie ideas he quotes. Vatsyayana also knew about the G-spot (named after the German gynecologist Ernst Graefenberg): "When her eyes roll when she feels him in certain spots, he presses her in just those spots" (*KS* 2.8.16). He also tells the man how to recognize when a woman has reached a climax—or, perhaps, if we assume (as I think we should) that the text is intended for women, too, he is telling the woman how to fake it (*KS* 2.8.17). And he argues that the woman has seed just like a man and therefore, by implication, contributes an equal portion to the child; that women have orgasms just like men; and in fact that the woman must have an orgasm in order to become pregnant, presumably in order to release her seed. He concludes: "Therefore the woman should be treated in such a way that she achieves her sexual climax first" (*KS* 2.1.23-30). Clearly he is, at least here, on the side of the angels.

Some parts of the book were evidently designed to be used by women. Book Three devotes one episode to advice to virgins trying to get husbands (*KS* 3.4.36-47), and Book Four consists of instructions for wives. Book Six is said to have been commissioned by the courtesans of Pataliputra, presumably for their own use (*KS* 1.1.11). The earliest extant commentator, Yashodhara, writing in the thirteenth century, tells us how this happened:

> A Brahmin named Dattaka learned all the arts and sciences in a short time. One day he had the idea of learning the finest ways of the world, best known by courtesans. And so he went to the courtesans every day, and learned so well that they asked *him* to instruct *them*: "Teach us how to give pleasure to men." But another quite plausible story is also widely believed: Dattaka once touched (the god) Shiva with his foot in the course of a festival to bless a pregnant woman, and Shiva cursed him to become a woman; after a while he persuaded Shiva to rescind the curse and let him become a man again, and because of that double knowledge he made the separate book. But if the author of the *Kamasutra* had known that he had such double knowledge, then he would have said, "Dattaka, who knew both flavors, made this book" (*KS* 1.1.11).

It is an inspired move on the part of the commentator to make the author of this text a bisexual like the Greek Teiresias (queen for a day, king for a day), who "tastes both flavors," or, as we would say, swings both ways or bats for both teams. (The Arabic expression is "he eats both pomegranates and figs," and the British, "oysters and snails.") Yet this is also a move that greatly mitigates the strong female agency in the text: where Vatsyayana tells us that women had this text made, the commentator tells us that an extraordinary man knew more about the courtesans' art than they knew themselves. During the millennium that separates the text from the commentary, the control of women by men increased dramatically in India, and this erosion of their status is reflected in the transition from the text's statement that women commissioned the text to the commentary's statement that a man did it better than they could do it.

Most extraordinary is Vatsyayana's attitude to people who engage in homosexual acts. Classical Hinduism is in general significantly silent on the subject of homoeroticism, but Hindu mythology does drop hints from which we can excavate a pretty virulent homophobia. The *dharma* textbooks, too, either ignore or stigmatize homosexual activity. Male homoerotic activity was punished, albeit mildly: a ritual bath (Manu 11.174) or the payment of a small fine (Kautilya 3.18.4) was often a sufficient atonement.

The Sanskrit word *kliba* has traditionally been translated as "eunuch" but almost certainly did not mean "eunuch." The political textbook called the *Arthashastra*, on which the *Kamasutra* modeled itself in many ways, uses another term (*varsha-dhara*, "rain-holder," that is, celibate) to designate what may have been eunuchs—that is, men intentionally castrated, particularly in order to serve as guardians in the royal harem (Kautilya 1960, 1.21.1-2). Men were castrated in punishment for various crimes in ancient India (and animals were gelded to control them), but such men were not employed as eunuchs. "*Kliba*," rather, includes a wide range of meanings under the general rubric of "a man who does not act the way a man should act," a man who fails to be a man, a defective male, a male suffering from distortion and Lacanian lack. It is a catch-all term that traditional Hindus coined to indicate a man who was in their terms sexually dysfunctional (or in ours, sexually challenged), including someone who was sterile, impotent, castrated, a transvestite, a man who had oral sex with other men, who had anal sex, a man with mutilated or defective sexual organs, a hermaphrodite, or, finally, a man who produced only female children. Often, it has the vaguely pejorative force of "wimp" or, more literally, "limp-dick." Thus, when the incarnate god Krishna wishes to stir the martial instincts of the conscience-stricken human hero Arjuna, he says to him, "Stop being a *kliba*!" (*Bhagavad Gita* 2.3). (A similarly broad definition of sodomy, even broader than the one still on the books in several American states, prevailed during the Renaissance, a definition that included masturbating, sex in the wrong orifice, bestiality, and sex between Christian and Jew) (Bray 1990).

The *Kamasutra* departs from the *dharma* view of homosexuality in significant ways. It does not use the pejorative term *kliba* at all, but speaks instead of a "third nature" (*tritiya prakriti*, a term that first appears a few centuries earlier, in the great Sanskrit epic, the *Mahabharata*) or perhaps a "third sexuality" or "third gender" in the sense of sexual behavior:

> There are two sorts of third nature, in the form of a woman and in the form of a man. The one in the form of a woman imitates a woman's dress, chatter, grace, emotions, delicacy, timidity, innocence, frailty, and bashfulness. The act that is [generally] done in the sexual organ is done in her mouth, and they call that "oral sex." She gets her sexual pleasure and erotic arousal as well as her livelihood from this, living as a courtesan. That is the person of the third nature in the form of a woman (*KS* 2.9.1-5).

The *Kamasutra* says nothing more about this cross-dressing male, with his stereotypical female gender behavior, but it discusses the fellatio technique of the closeted man of the third nature in considerable sensual detail, in the longest consecutive passage in the text describing a physical act, and with what might even be called gusto:

> The one in the form of a man, however, conceals her desire when she wants a man and makes her living as a masseur. As she massages the man, she caresses his two thighs with her limbs, as if she were embracing him. Then she becomes more boldly intimate and familiar…, pretending to tease him about how easily he becomes excited and laughing at him. If the man does not urge her on, even when he has given this clear sign and even when it is obvious that he

is aroused, she makes advances to him on her own. If the man urges her to go on, she argues with him and only unwillingly continues (*KS* 2.9.6-11).

And so forth, and so on. This is a remarkably explicit analysis of the mentality of the closet, the extended double entendre of an act that is cleverly designed to appear sexually innocent to a man who does not want, or does not want to admit that he wants, a homosexual encounter, but is an explicit invitation to a man who is willing to admit his desire for such an encounter. And a massage is a massage in the *Kamasutra*: "Some people think that massaging is also a kind of close embrace, because it involves touching. But Vatsyayana says: No. For a massage takes place at a particular time set aside, has a different use, and is not enjoyed by both partners in the same way" (*KS* 2.2. 27-8). Or is it? Consider this: "But when a woman who is giving the man a massage makes sure he has understood her signals and rests her face on his thighs as if she had no desire but was overcome by sleep, and then kisses his thighs, that is called a kiss 'making advances.'" (*KS* 2.3. 31) And this: "'Gooseflesh' is made when nails of medium length are brought close together and moved over the chin, breasts, or lower lip, so lightly that they leave no line but by the mere touch cause the thrill of gooseflesh and make a sound as they strike one another. A man can do this to the woman he wants, in the course of massaging her body" (*KS* 2.4.12-13).

One passage suggests that some people, cited when Vatsyayana warns the bridegroom not to be too shy with his shy bride, disapprove of men of the third nature: "[Certain scholars] say, 'If the girl sees that the man has not spoken a word for three nights, like a pillar, she will be discouraged and will despise him, as if he were someone of the third nature'" (*KS* 3.2.3). So judgmentalism appears to creep in after all. But when we look closer we see that the people who make this judgment are the "scholars" with whom Vatsyayana almost always disagrees, as he does here, for he goes on to remark: "Vatsyayana says: He begins to entice her and win her trust, but he still remains sexually continent. When he entices her he does not force her in any way, for women are like flowers, and need to be enticed very tenderly. If they are taken by force by men who have not yet won their trust they become women who hate sex. Therefore he wins her over with gentle persuasion" (*KS* 3.2.4-6). This is the sort of man whom the wrong sort of scholar, but not Vatsyayana, might fear that some people might stigmatize as someone of the third nature.

Men of the third nature are always designated by the pronoun "she," basically because the word "nature" is feminine in Sanskrit (as it, and most abstract nouns, are also in Latin and Greek). Indeed, the idea of a third gender, rather than a binary division, may come from the basic habit of Indo-European languages to assign three genders—neuter as well as masculine and feminine—to all nouns. Yet the very use of the word "third"—which clearly implies a previous "first" and "second"—demonstrates that Vatsyayana is thinking primarily in binary, more precisely dialectic, terms that would have satisfied Hegel or Claude Lévi-Strauss: two opposed terms modified by a third. Vatsyayana actually analogizes men and women to grammatical terms, in the discussion of gender stereotypes, which does not take account of the third nature at all: "By his physical nature, the man is the active agent (the subject) and the young woman is the passive locus (the locative case, in which the action takes place)" (*KS* 2.1.26). (The object is the sexual act.) But there is another, better reason why Vatsyayana uses the female pronoun for a person of the third nature, and that is because of her perceived gender: he lists the third nature among *women* who can be lovers (*KS* 1.5.27). This use of the pronoun "she" can also be seen as an anticipation of the practices of some cross-dressing gay men of our day.

What about homoerotic women? Vatsyayana is unique in the literature of the period in describing lesbian activity. He does this at the beginning of the chapter about the harem, in a brief passage about what he calls "Oriental customs" (*KS* 5.6.2-4). (The use of the term "Oriental" or "Eastern" for what Vatsyayana regards as a disreputable lesbian practice in what was soon to be a colonized part of the Gupta Empire—indeed, the Eastern part—suggests that "Orientalism" began not with the British but with the Orientals themselves.) These women use dildos, as well as bulbs, roots, or fruits that have the form of the male organ, and statues of men that have distinct sexual characteristics. But they engage in sexual acts with one another only in the absence of men, as we sometimes say of men in prison, or English boys in posh boarding schools, not through the kind of personal choice that drives a man of the third nature: "The women of the harem cannot meet men, because they are carefully guarded; and since they have only one husband shared by many women in common, they are not satisfied. Therefore they give pleasure to one another with the following techniques" (*KS* 5.6.2). Yashodhara's commentary on this passage makes this explicit, and also helpfully suggests the particular vegetables that one might employ: "By imagining a man, they experience a heightened emotion that gives extreme satisfaction. These things have a form just like the male sexual organ: the bulbs of arrow-root, plantain and so forth; the roots of coconut palms, bread fruit, and so forth; and the fruits of the bottle-gourd, cucumber, and so forth." One can imagine little gardens of plantain and cucumber being cultivated within the inner rooms of the palace, the harem.

The *Kamasutra* makes only one brief reference to women who may have chosen women as sexual partners in preference to men: the text says that a girl may lose her virginity with a girlfriend or a servant girl, and the commentator specifies that "They take her virginity by using a finger" (*KS* 7.1.20). The *dharma* text of Manu says that a woman who corrupts a virgin will be punished by having two of her fingers cut off (Manu 8.369-70), a hint of what Manu—like Yashodhara—thinks lesbians do in bed. Vatsyayana never refers to women of this type as people of a "third nature," but the commentator's belief that the children produced when the woman is on top might be "a little boy and little girl with reversed natures" (*KS* 2.8.41) refers to the view that the "reverse" intercourse of parents might wreak embryonic damage, resulting in the reversed gender behavior of the third nature—significantly, for a girl as well as a boy, the female type not spelled out by the text's discussion of the "third nature."

In addition to male and female homosexual acts, a few oblique, passing remarks suggest bisexuality. The female messenger who is sent to praise the man in the presence of the woman he is wooing may have had bisexual behavior in mind when, praising the man's charm, she says, according to the commentator, "He has such luck in love that he was desired even by a man" (*KS* 5.4.15). And two verses describe men who engage in oral sex not by profession, like the men of the "third nature," but out of love:

Even young men, servants
who wear polished earrings,
indulge in oral sex
only with certain men.
And, in the same way, certain men-about-town
who care for one another's welfare
and have established trust
do this service for one another (*KS* 2.9.35-36).

These men, who seem bound to one another by discriminating affection rather than promiscuous passion, are called "men about town," *nagarakas*, the term used to designate the heterosexual heroes of the *Kamasutra*. In striking contrast with men of the third nature, always designated by the pronoun "she," these men are described with nouns and pronouns that unambiguously designate males. Perhaps, then, they are bisexuals. The commentator on the *Kamasutra*, as we have seen, even makes Dattaka, the author of the part of the text commissioned by the courtesans, a serial bisexual (*KS* 1.1.11).

Thus it is possible for us to excavate several alternative sexualities latent in the text's somewhat fuzzy boundaries between homoeroticism and heteroeroticism. But we must admit that we find these alternatives in the Sanskrit original carry meanings that have value for us, only if we transcend, if not totally disregard, the original context. Were we to remain within the strict bounds of the historical situation, we could not notice the voices speaking against their moment in history, perhaps even against their author. Only by asking our own questions, which the author may not have considered at all, can we see that his text does contain many answers to them, fortuitously embedded in other questions and answers that were more meaningful to him. This reading suggests various ways in which the *Kamasutra*'s implicit claim to sexual totality might be opened out into a vision of gender infinity.

The *Kamasutra* was a revolutionary document, for women and for people of the "third nature." It exerted a profound influence on subsequent Indian literature, particularly in court life and in the privileged, classless society that it describes at great length. But, at the same time, the *dharma* texts with their deep suspicion of women and eroticism retained their stranglehold on much of Hindu society. And then came the British.

SIR RICHARD BURTON'S VERSION OF THE KAMASUTRA

The *Kamasutra* plays almost no role at all in the sexual consciousness of contemporary Indians, and one reason for this is that it is known, in both India and Europe, almost entirely through the flawed English translation by Sir Richard Francis Burton, published in 1883. Burton did for the *Kamasutra* what Max Müller did for the *Rig Veda* during this same period; his translation had a profound effect upon literature across Europe and America. Burton's main contribution was the courage and determination to publish the work at all; he was the Larry Flynt of his day. To get around the censorship laws, Burton set up an imaginary publishing house, The Kama Shastra Society of London and Benares, with printers said to be in Benares or Cosmopoli. (The title page read: "The Kama Sutra of Vatsyayana, Translated from the Sanscrit. In Seven Parts, with Preface, Introduction and Concluding Remarks. Cosmopoli: 1883: for the Kama Shastra Society of London and Benares, and for private circulation only.") Even though it was not legally published in England and the United States until 1962, the Burton *Kamasutra*, soon after its publication in 1883, became "one of the most pirated books in the English language," constantly reprinted, often with a new preface to justify the new edition, sometimes without any attribution to Burton (Brodie 1967: 358). It is free (at first poached from the illegal editions, then long out of copyright) and recognizable as what people think the *Kamasutra* should be. Indeed, it is quite a wonderful text: great fun to read, extraordinarily bold and frank for its time, and in many places a fairly approximate representation of the Sanskrit original. It remains precious, like Edward Fitzgerald's *Rubaiyat*, as a monument of English literature, though not much closer to Vatsyayana than Fitzgerald was to Omar Khayyam. For the Sanskrit text often simply does not say what Burton says it says.

Moreover, it is not even the work of the man who is known as its author, Sir Richard Francis Burton. It was far more the work of Forster Fitzgerald ("Bunny") Arbuthnot, whose name appears on the title page with Burton's only in some editions, though Burton later referred to the *Kamasutra* translation as "Arbuthnot's Vatsyayana" (Archer 1963: 36). But the translation owed even more to two Indian scholars whose names do not appear on the title page at all: Bhagavanlal Indrajit and Shivaram Parashuram Bhide. (There is a pre-postcolonial irony in the fact that Arbuthnot later tried to get the censors off his trail by stating, in 1885, a half-truth that he almost certainly regarded as a lie: that the translation was done entirely by Indian pandits) (Brodie 1967: 357). It really should, therefore, be known as the Indrajit-Bhide-Arbuthnot-Burton translation, but since Burton was by far the most famous member of the team, it has always been called the Burton translation.

In many ways, it should be called the Burton mistranslation. W. H. Auden put it bluntly: "thus, squalid beery Burton stands / for shoddy thinking of all brands" (Auden 2007: 225). Consider the G-spot. Vatsyayana quotes a predecessor who said, "This is the secret of young women" (*KS* 2.8.1) and, indeed, it remained a secret in Europe. It is not widely recognized that the *Kamasutra* knows this secret, and that is because Burton missed the G-spot. His translation of the relevant passage reads like this: "While a man is doing to the woman what he likes best during congress, he should always make a point of pressing those parts of her body on which she turns her eyes" (Burton 1962: 121). Where did Burton go wrong? He was following the commentator, who first gives a correct gloss of the crucial verb ("the pleasure of that touch makes her eyes whirl around in a circle") but then goes on to suggest several alternative glosses of that same verb, just as he had told an alternative story about Dattaka and the courtesans:

> This remains secret because women do not make it known. There is some argument about this. Some people say that whatever place the woman *looks at,* either specifically or vaguely, that is the place where he should press her. Others say that, if she looks at many places, he should press her in one place after another. Or, whatever place she looks at very hard is the place where he should press her very hard (*KS* 2.8.1).

By following this part of the commentary, Burton has missed one point of the passage (how to locate the G-spot), and by inserting, gratuitously, the phrase "what he likes best" ("while a man is doing to the woman what he likes best during congress"), he has totally missed the larger point: the importance of learning how to do what the woman likes best. As for Burton's use of the term "congress," I always wonder, "Where is the Senate, and where the House of Representatives?"

The Burton translation also robs women of their voices, turning direct quotes into indirect quotes, thus losing the force of the dialogue that animates the work and erasing the vivid presence of the many women who speak in the *Kamasutra*, replacing these voices with reported speech rephrased by a man. Thus, where the text says that, when a man is striking a woman, "She uses words like "Stop!" or "Let me go!" or "Enough!" or "Mother!" (*KS* 2.7.20), Burton translates it like this: "She continually utters words expressive of prohibition, sufficiency, or desire of liberation." Moreover, when the text says that this may happen "When a man [is] in the throes of passion," and "If a man tries to force his kisses and so forth on her," Burton says it happens "When the woman is not accustomed to striking," reversing the genders and reversing the point (Burton 1962: 117-18).

Burton also erodes women's agency by mistranslating or erasing some passages in which women have strong privileges. Take this passage (here translated more or less literally): "Mildly offended by the man's infidelities, she does not accuse him too much, but she scolds him with abusive language when he is alone or among friends. She does not, however, use love-sorcery worked with roots, for, Gonardiya says, 'Nothing destroys trust like that.'" (*KS* 4.1.19-21).

Burton renders it: "In the event of any misconduct on the part of her husband, she should not blame him excessively, though she be a little displeased. She should not use abusive language toward him, but rebuke him with conciliatory words, whether he be in the company of friends or alone. Moreover, she should not be a scold, for, says Gonardiya, 'There is no cause of dislike on the part of a husband so great as this characteristic in a wife.'" (Burton 1962: 160).

What is wrong with this picture? In the first place, Burton mistranslated the word for "love-sorcery worked with roots" (*mulakarika*), which he renders as "she should not be a scold" (though elsewhere he correctly translates *mulakarika*). Second, "misconduct" is not so much a mistranslation as an error of judgment, for the word in question (*apacara*) does have the general meaning of "misconduct," but in an erotic context it usually takes on the more specific meaning of "infidelity," a choice that is supported both by the remedy that the text suggests (and rejects)—love-magic—and by the commentator's gloss (*aparadha*). But the most serious problem is the word "not" that Burton gratuitously adds and that negates the wife's right to use abusive language against her straying husband, a denial only somewhat qualified by the added phrase "rebuke him with conciliatory words." Was this an innocent error or does it reflect a sexist bias? We cannot know.

More significantly, Burton's translation misses the entire point about same-sex eroticism because he renders "third nature" as "eunuch" (the usual mistranslation of *kliba*) throughout. He also leaves out, entirely, the line that includes the "third nature" in the list of women who are sexually available (*KS* 1.5.27). Why did Burton make such an error? Probably he used the word "eunuch" in its broader sense: to designate not a guardian in the harem but a man who had been castrated for one reason or another. It is possible that Burton confused the men of the third nature with the Hijras, castrated transvestites who function as male prostitutes in India today, and are often called "eunuchs" (Nanda 1960). The Hijras do correspond rather closely to the first type of third nature, the cross-dressing female type that is dismissed after just a sentence or two, but not to the second type, the closeted male type, to which Vatsyayana devotes so much attention. Burton had written about the Hijras in the notes to his translation of the *Arabian Nights,* but there is no evidence of their existence at the time of the *Kamasutra.* Why, then, did he not recognize the text's reference to sexually "entire" men who happened to prefer having (oral) sex with other men? Did he read the text as implying that this was the only option available to them due to some sort of genital malfunction? Did he confuse the third sex with *kliba*s, the elastic category that includes both castrated men and homosexual men? There is no question about his knowledge of homosexuality, both in the *Arabian Nights* and in the India of his day; he had undertaken a study of male brothels, staffed by "boys and eunuchs" (Archer 1963: 17), in Karachi in 1845 (Brodie 1967: 369). His famous "Terminal Essay" to the *Arabian Nights*, published in 1885, includes an 18,000-word essay entitled "Pederasty" (later republished in his collection of essays, *The Erotic Traveller*) that was one of the first serious treatments of the subject in English, though he called it "the vice, the abuse, pathological love" and stated that Hindus held the practice in abhorrence (Brodie 1967: 370). No, Burton's "eunuchs" are, rather, a matter of "Orientalism": the depiction of "Orientals" as simultaneously oversexed and feminized. The word "eunuch" was bandied about loosely in British writings about the Orient, conveying a vague sense of sexual excess, cruelty, and impotence, and it infected Burton's translation of the *Kamasutra*, too.

DETUMESCENCE UNDER THE BRITISH

Though many of the British in India, particularly at the start, in the eighteenth century, appreciated all forms of Hindu culture, including its eroticism, British scholars of India remained largely ignorant of the *Kamasutra*. (Sir Monier Monier-Williams, who composed, in 1899, the great Sanskrit-English dictionary still used by most scholars, lists Vatsyayana but not the *Kamasutra* as potential sources and seldom, if ever, cites a word from that text in his lexicon.) And the puritanical Protestant ministers who evangelized India after 1813 loathed the eroticism of the temples, the temple dancers, and the amatory excesses of the god Krishna. A Supreme Court ruling from 1862 states that "Krishna...the love hero, the husband of 16,000 princesses...tinges the whole system (of Hinduism) with the strain of carnal sensualism, of strange, transcendental lewdness" (Bombay 1962: 213). These were, after all, the Victorians, who were not amused by the copulating couples on the walls of the temples of Khajuraho. The officers and missionaries under the British Raj despised all forms of what they regarded as Oriental excess, all those arms, all those heads, all those wives. The fraction of Hinduism that appealed to Protestant, evangelical tastes at all was firmly grounded in the other path of Hinduism, the philosophical, renunciant path.

Scholars have noted a pattern in which colonized people take on the mask that the colonizer creates in the image of the colonized, mimicking the colonizer's perception of the colonized (Nandy 1983). Many highly-placed Hindus so admired their colonizers that, in a kind of colonial and religious Stockholm syndrome, they swallowed the Protestant line themselves, and not only gained a new appreciation of those aspects of Hinduism that the British approved of (the *Gita*, the Upanishads), but became ashamed of those aspects that the British scorned (erotic sculptures on temples, temple dancers). Following the British lead, these Hindus largely wrote off the dominant strain of Hinduism that celebrated the passions of the gods.

The highly Anglicized Indian elite developed new forms of Hinduism heavily influenced by British Protestantism. The key figure in this movement was Rammohan Roy (1772-1833), whose religion combined monistic elements of Hinduism and Islam (he had studied the Qu'ran as well as the Vedas and the Upanishads) and, later, eighteenth-century Deism (belief in a transcendent Creator God reached through reason), Unitarianism (belief in God's essential oneness), and the ideas of the Freemasons (a secret fraternity that espoused some Deistic concepts). His beliefs were further fueled by his realization that the colonial government viewed Hindu customs alternately with abhorrence (Vedic polytheism) and fascination (Vedantic, or Upanishadic, monism), and by his desire to rebut the scathing critiques of the missionaries. Rammohan Roy formulated a new Hinduism, called the Brahmo Samaj ("Assembly of God"), which extracted the Sufism from Islam, the Vedanta from Hinduism, and Unitarianism from Christianity. He gave educated Hindus a basis on which they could justify their religion to an Indian consciousness increasingly influenced by Western values.

Rammohan Roy's most influential successor was Swami Vivekananda (1862-1902), who carried a form of Neo-Vedanta to America. In 1883 (the same year that Richard Burton published the first English translation of the *Kamasutra*), a Brahmo Samaj leader named Protap Chunder Mozoomdar visited America, initiating the Hindu mission movement there (Mullick 2010). In 1893, at the World's Parliament of Religions, Vivekananda brought Vedanta to Chicago. Vivekananda's Hinduism jettisoned much of the worldly and erotic path of Hindu polytheism (doctrines, dogmas, rituals, books, oral traditions, and temples) in order to extract a universal essence of "spirituality." He influenced Hindus far beyond the bounds of the Brahmo Samaj, inspiring the form of Neo-Vedanta called Sanatana Dharma (Eternal or Universal Dharma) embraced by many Hindus to this day. Sanatana Dharma is the banner of Hindutva, which presides over the censorship of art, film, literature, and social behavior.

The British, even after 1947, continued to shackle Indian freedom of expression through the Film Censor Board, which, from the early 1950s, implemented a policy basis that had roots among the Raj administrators (who had worried more about sedition than about sex). The Film Censor Board's concern for visual pedagogy, nationalism, and publicity broadcast a shadow that extended over Indian visual arts and literature as well as film.

Hindu attitudes toward sexuality were further confused by the very public, and very contradictory, sexuality of the man who was one of the most important Hindus of the twentieth century, Mahatma Gandhi. Gandhi's insistence on celibacy among his disciples caused difficulty for some of them, as did his habit of sleeping beside girls young enough to be called jailbait in the United States, to test and/or prove his own celibate control. His practice drew not so much upon the Upanishadic and Vaishnava ascetic traditions, which were the source of many of Gandhi's practices, as upon the hydraulic Tantric techniques of internalizing power, indeed creating quasi-magical powers, by first stirring up the sexual energies and then withholding semen. Gandhi was a one-man model of the perennial Hindu attempt to deal with sexuality by driving with one foot on the accelerator and one foot on the brake.

In the nineteenth and twentieth centuries, liberal Indian intellectuals, who noticed the shift in attitudes to Hinduism's erotic past from appreciation to embarrassment, tended to explain contemporary Hindu prudery in terms of power and patronage from the past. As James McConnachie summarized this attitude, "Erotic literature had been the creation of poets and princes, the argument ran, and as 'lascivious' Hindu despots had given way to 'fanatical' Mughal overlords, the patronage on which erotic literature depended had withered and died" (McConnachie 2007: 197-8). V. S. Naipaul in his book, *Half A Life*, offers his own, rather jaded, version of this accusation:

> [I]n our culture there is no seduction. Our marriages are arranged. There is no art of sex. Some of the boys here talk to me of the Kama Sutra. Nobody talked about that at home. It was an upper-caste text, but I don't believe my poor father, brahmin though he is, ever looked at a copy. That philosophical-practical way of dealing with sex belongs to our past, and that world was ravaged and destroyed by the Muslims (Naipaul 2002: 110).

And then (the twisted, chauvinist argument goes), then came the British missionaries, adding insult to injury. Thus nationalists blamed India's sexual conservatism on "an unholy combination of imposed Muslim religiosity and imported British 'Victorianism'" (McConnachie 2007: 197-8).

There is some truth in that general historical argument, but it has three serious flaws. First, as for the Mughals, it ignores the enthusiasm for the erotic arts on the part of such Muslims as the Lodi dynasty in the sixteenth century, who commissioned one of the last great works of Sanskrit eroticism, the *Ananga Ranga* (McConnachie 2007: 55, 57), and the Mughals, who had textbooks of Hindu erotic arts and religious texts translated from Sanskrit to Persian and illustrated with Persian painting techniques. The nationalists dismissed all of this, ungenerously, as "the last, valedictory flourishing of a tragically deracinated tradition." Second, blaming the British for Hindu prudery allows the very real memory of missionary puritainism and the racist snobbery of the Raj club culture to overpower the equally important role of other sorts of Brits in the rediscovery of India's erotic heritage (McConnachie 2007: 197-8). Most of all, blaming the Muslims and the British ignores the history of native Hindu anti-eroticism. For, as we have seen, India had its own homegrown traditions of prudery in opposition to its own sensuality.

THE FALL OF KAMA AND THE RISE OF KARMA

An adolescent girl in Vikram Chandra's story, "Kama," says, "Sister Carmina didn't want to tell us. It's the *Kama Sutra*, which she says isn't in the library. But Gisela's parents have a copy which they think is hidden away on the top of their shelf. We looked it up there." And the adult to whom she tells this says, "You put that book back where you found it. And don't read any more" (Chandra 1997: 126). In India today, people will often give a copy of the *Kamasutra* as a wedding present, to demonstrate their open-mindedness and sophistication, but most people will merely sneak a surreptitious look at it in someone else's house.

And on the public scene, "a Hindu-nationalist Health Minister can insist that the 'Indian traditions' of abstinence and fidelity are more effective barriers against HIV than condoms; and...the 1860 Penal Code [still in effect] defines all extramarital sex as criminal" (McConnachie 2007: 228). These are the Hindus, in India but also increasingly in the American diaspora, who advocate a sanitized, "spiritual" form of Hinduism (and, in India, a nationalist and anti-Muslim form). For such Hindus, the problem is not (as it was for some liberal Indian intellectuals) how to explain how India lost its appreciation of eroticism but, on the contrary, how to maintain that Hinduism was always the pure-minded, anti-erotic, ascetic tradition that it became, for many upper-class Hindus, in the nineteenth century. One way to make this argument was to swing to the other side of the pendulum and blame the British not for *suppressing* Indian eroticism but for *causing* it. Under Nehru, the Indian government passed a penal code of sexual repression, Article 377, which prohibits "sexual relations against nature with a man, woman, or animal, whether the intercourse is anal or oral." Nehru insisted that "such vices in India were due to Western influence" (McConnachie 2007: 209). The irony is that in aping the Muslim and British scorn for Indian sexuality, contemporary Hindus who favor censorship are surrendering their own identity, letting foreign ideas about Hinduism (and Protestant fundamentalist ideas about censorship) triumph over and drive out native Hindu ideas about and pride in their own religion and in the diversity and tolerance that have always characterized the world of the mind in Hinduism. Among the other bad habits they picked up from the West, from seeds sown, perhaps, during colonization but flowering only in the more recent contacts with American imperialism, was the habit of censorship. Never before has the old tension between the erotic and ascetic strains of Hinduism taken the form of one path telling the other path that it has no right to exist.

But the India of the ancient erotic past is not so easily stamped out. In 2009 Article 377 was revised to exclude adult consensual acts. Even in the nineteenth century, most Hindus on the path that celebrated the earthier aspects of life did not even know that the Anglophone Hindus regarded them as either beneath contempt or entirely nonexistent. They went on worshipping their gods, singing their songs, telling their stories. And now they live on in "a reported two-thirds of young adults who would have casual, pre-marital sex before an arranged marriage" (McConnachie 2007: 229), and who, since 1991, can buy condoms called *KamaSutra*. Clearly the attempt to transform the culture of the *Kamasutra* into what many people, Hindus and non-Hindus alike, mistakenly refer to as the *Karmasutra* (presumably a Vedantic text about reincarnation) has not succeeded.

NOTES

1. It seems to me it would be far simpler just to add a single "t" to the abstract term, Hindutva, on the model of the way that people involved in bureaucracy are called bureaucrats, and call these Hindus, Hindutvats.

REFERENCES

Archer, William G. "Preface." *Kama Sutra*. London: George Allen and Unwin, 1963.

Auden, W. H. *Collected Poems*. New York: Random House, 2007.

Bombay (Presidency). Supreme Court. *Report of the Maharaj Libel Case: And of the Bhattia Conspiracy Case*. Bombay: Bombay Gazette Press, 1862.

Bordewekar, Sandhya. Interview with Shivaji K. Panikkar and Chandramohan. *Art India* 12:3 (2007): 61-67.

Bray, Alan. *Homosexuality in Renaissance England*. New York: Columbia University Press, 1996.

Brihadaranyaka Upanishad. Early Upanishads. Ed. and Trans. Patrick Olivelle. New York: Oxford University Press, 1998.

Brodie, Fawn M. *The Devil Drives: A Life of Sir Richard Burton.* New York: Ballantine, 1967.

Bronner, Yigal. *Extreme Poetry: The South Asian Movement of Simultaneous Narration.* New York: Columbia University Press, 2010.

Burton, Sir Richard Francis. *The Kama Sutra of Vatsyayana: The Classic Hindu Treatise on Love and Social Conduct.* New York: E. P. Dutton, 1962.

Chandra, Vikram. *Love and Longing in Bombay.* Boston: Little, Brown and Company, 1997.

Dharker, Anil. "Beauty And the Beast: Baroda Episode Underscores Threat to Creative Expression." *Mainstream* 45:23 (May 25, 2007).

Kautilya. *Arthashastra.* Ed. and Trans. R. P. Kangle. Vol. 1: Text. Vol. 2: Translation. Bombay: University of Bombay, 1960.

Manu, *Laws of Manu.* Trans. Wendy Doniger with Brian K. Smith. Harmondsworth: Penguin Classics, 1991.

McConnachie, James. *The Book of Love: In Search of the Kamasutra.* London: Atlantic, 2007.

Mullick, Sunrit. *The First Hindu Mission to America. The Pioneering Visits of Protap Chunder Mozoomdar.* New Delhi: Northern Book Centre, 2010.

Nanda, Serena. *Neither Man Nor Woman: The Hijras of India.* Belmont, Calif.: Wadsworth, 1990.

Nandy, Ashis. *The Intimate Enemy: Loss and Recovery of Self under Colonialism.* Delhi: Oxford University Press, 1983.

Naipaul, V. S. *Half a Life.* New York: Vintage Books, 2002.

Philips, Richard, and Waruna Alahakoon. "Hindu Chauvinists Block Filming of Deepa Mehta's *Water.*" *World Socialist Web Site*, February 12, 2000 <http://www.wsws.org/articles/2000/feb2000/film-f12.shtml>.

Ramanujan, A. K., V. Narayana Rao, and David Shulman. *When God is a Customer.* Berkeley: University of California Press, 1994.

Valsan, Binoy. "Baroda Art Student's Work Stirs Up Religious Controversy." *Rediff India Abroad*, May 10, 2007.

Vatsyayana. *The Kamasutra of Vatsyayana.* Trans. Wendy Doniger and Sudhir Kakar. London and New York: Oxford World Classics, 2002.

White, David. *Kiss of the Yogini: "Tantric Sex" in its South Asian Contexts.* Chicago: University of Chicago Press, 2003.

Elections as Communitas

Mukulika Banerjee

I ndia presents an interesting puzzle for the story of democracy in the
contemporary world. It has maintained a consistent record of being
governed by democratically elected governments; the voter turnout
at elections has remained stable, averaging 60 percent; and elections
have become fairer and freer over a 60-year period. It has done this
despite widespread international misgivings about its future at the time
of its inception, which—in tune with intellectual orthodoxies—held
that a largely illiterate electorate and an economically weak country
could not be trusted with the responsibility of democracy. Further,
the size of India's electorate is vast, exceeding the combined number
of all voters in North America, Australia, and Europe. To conduct a
national election of this scale would challenge any country, not only
a poor and infrastructurally weak one such as India. And indeed, on
other indicators, India's record has been wanting. Despite internationally
celebrated economic growth rates its illiteracy and infant mortality
rates, food insecurity, and the gap between rich and poor continue to
remain at unhealthily high levels. Yet, when it comes to elections, the

I wish to thank Geert de Neve, Grace Carsten, Mekhala Krishnamurthy, Badri
Narayan, Satendra Kumar, Roseena Nasir, Priyadarshini Singh, Mahshweta Jani,
Dolonchampa Chakrabarty, Goldy George, Deepu Sebastian, Vanita Falcao, and
Abhay Datar for their collaboration on the Comparative Electoral Ethnographies
project during the 2009 elections, on which data for this paper is based. I wish to
thank the UK Economic and Social Research Council for funding this research project
and Arjun Appadurai, John Dunn, Chris Fuller, Jonathan Spencer, and Yogendra
Yadav for inspiration and comments.

country seems to pull it off every time, holding them according to impeccable standards, and with an electorate that seems to participate with energy and enthusiasm. So far, ethnographic and survey research in India has shown that of those who did not vote in an election, only a quarter chose to do so out of lack of interest or apathy (NES Survey 2009). For people who know that the material conditions of life are unlikely to improve much from one election to the next, and for whom voting is not compulsory, it seems inexplicable that they continue to participate in an electoral process whose essential function is to bring seemingly ineffectual political parties to power.

So the puzzle is: Why are Indian voters enthusiastic about elections? If they knew better, would they prefer to stay at home and turn their backs on the process as their counterparts in other democracies increasingly do? Are Indian voters naïve and gullible, or have they simply run out of options? Do they turn out to vote because they are forced to do through coercion and incentives, or because, as a largely illiterate population, they do not know any better? Do Indian voters not share any of the cynicism and apathy of the electorates of other democracies? Or is their understanding of the electoral process a wholly different one? In this essay, on the basis of ethnographic data from the 2009 national elections, I shall provide some answers to solve this puzzle posed by Indian democracy.[1]

As we know, most electoral analysts tend to concentrate on who people vote for and what will make parties win. Indeed, which party people vote for and answering the "Who will win?" question provides the drama on election nights. It is no different in India, and given the various political parties and agendas, voters have a wide range to choose from. Such analyses have shown the role of vote banks, electoral corruption, and caste politics in determining electoral results. By comparison, the "Why people vote?" question is asked less often in analysis of elections, and the relationship between the two questions is rarely probed—that is to say, the question of whether *why* people vote has anything to do with *who* they vote for. Instead, the powerful and corrupt electoral forces are seen to achieve their purpose without according agency to the subjects of their coercion. The question of *why* people vote has agitated the study of politics generally for the latter half of the twentieth century onward. It is a question that political scientists and economists alike have asked of political behavior, looking to rational choice and game theories, among others, to provide the answers. In the Indian case, it gains even more importance than usual due to the contradictions that it brings to light.

RATIONALITY

In the discussion of why (should) people vote, one dominant aspect is the question of the rationality of participation in a mass activity in which a single action would go unnoticed. Given that national election results are rarely decided by a single vote, why do people bother to cast an individual vote that is highly unlikely to make a difference? This question has been posed, for instance, in exploring the idea of "free riding," according to which in a large cooperative activity, it is more rational for people to simply take a free ride on the actions of others rather than act themselves. Those who support the free-riding theory would claim that, given the outlay of effort and time—say, the effort of going to cast your vote or to support trade union activity—in return for an indeterminate result, it makes more rational sense to stay home than go to the polling station. This person might assume that because everyone else will make the effort, his or her own single abstention would go unnoticed. Of course, despite a decision to abstain, one would still benefit from the results of the collective activity, such as a stable government or better wages negotiated by the union, but that is precisely the point of free riding.

Critics of such a theory point out that in cases of cooperative activity having thresholds—that is, the point at which the balance can tip in favor of one side or the other (for example, election results, but perhaps not trade union activity), there is nothing rational about free riding. In fact, they would argue, it is entirely rational for one to cast an individual vote because that vote could be the one to tip the balance beyond the 50-50 mark in support of one candidate over the other, or could be one of the votes that makes up the winning margin. To consider irrational those individuals cooperating in a collective activity, as the free-riding theorists would argue, is therefore incorrect. And because such participation is rational, the argument goes, it is unnecessary to add moral strictures about duty or citizenship to the impulse for cooperation (Tuck 2008). If people vote, it is not because they feel any moral pressure but because it is entirely rational to do so. Voters who do not vote could therefore be said to be acting in an irrational manner.

Clearly, Indian voters are on the side of the critics of free riding because they vote. What is less obvious is whether their motivations stem from the rational impulse or an alternative perspective. One possible answer is provided by a well-known story in India.

Once upon a time, a king suggested holding a feast for his people. He said he would provide the main courses, but asked everyone to help with the dessert. It was to be a rice pudding, for which he would supply the rice and sugar, but he requested that everyone contribute one cup of milk each. This was agreed and, accordingly, on the appointed day, a large copper vessel was suspended over a fire in the center of the village. There was one man, known for his miserliness, who told himself that he could not be bothered to share his own milk and instead took along a cup of water. As he emptied the cup into the boiling vat he told himself, "No one will notice that the milk is slightly thinner as a result. It is only one cup of water after all!" At the end of the evening, when everyone had filled their bellies with the delicacies that the royal kitchen had provided and it was time for dessert, the vat was uncovered in eager anticipation of this rarely enjoyed luxury. But as the cover came off, lo and behold! The vat was full of boiling... *water*! Everyone had had the same idea as the miser and had contributed water instead of milk to the vat.

Like all stories, the details vary slightly in each telling, but the basic message is the same: the importance of not cheating in a collective activity because, ultimately, the people would themselves be the losers. The parallels with politics and democracy are of course immediately plain: our individual vote is like our cup of milk, which on its own could never make pudding. But by adding it to several other cups of milk, we could collect a lot of milk and create something rare and luxurious, which we can then enjoy together. To ask us why we vote is to ask why we contribute milk rather than water to the vat. After all, it is a small contribution: one cup of milk, one day of our lives when we have to rearrange things a bit and make arrangements to visit the polling station. Don't we do this in order to get something special? The story of the rice pudding, like all moral fables, is an example of how people come to understand the importance of ethical behavior and why cheating leads to anomie. That is why all over the world, most people do not steal; they do their bit and make the world work. It also provides an obvious critique of free riding and is based on a nuanced notion of rationality. It points out implicitly that the free-riding theory is premised on the assumption that only a small section of the population can afford to be free riders.

As with any example of a collective effort, such as applause after a concert or saying "amen" during a church service—actions that are premised on each individual doing her bit to make up the final result—one or a few people abstaining from participating does not alter the overall effect. Even with a few abstentions, there would still be an audible applause or the hum of "amen" being spoken. But, on the other hand, if *every* individual decided to abstain, the overall effect would be radically altered and would result in total silence, the equivalent of the vat of boiling water. The story of the rice pudding therefore demonstrates the limits of free riding. It also raises the question that if free riding works only when a few decide to abstain, on what basis would an individual make the decision to free ride? How would she know that others do not have the same intention? For free riding assumes the participation of others. But this is impossible to ascertain for any single individual, just as it was impossible for the miser to know that everyone else in the village would have the same thought as him.

But in India, a simple system makes it possible to ascertain just that. In an Indian polling booth, when a voter has his or her name ticked off the electoral register and just before he or she casts a vote on the voting machine, the base of the nail and cuticle on the left index finger is marked with a short vertical line in indelible black ink. While this is done to avoid fraud, it also makes it easy to identify a person who has voted on election day and for several days afterward. It has therefore become customary for people to "check out" others to see if they have voted or not. There is no scope for lying, because if you have voted the proof is for all to see; there are no exceptions.

Photo credit: Dixie

The coveted black mark

The free-riding theorists might argue that this makes the job of the free rider easier. Unlike the pudding pot, where people could not lift the lid to check if there was any milk in it, on an Indian election day one can quite easily estimate whether enough people have voted to make the election viable and for them to free ride.

In practice, however, it does not seem to work this way. Instead, the mark on someone else's finger seems to make the potential free rider do the exact opposite: it compels him or her to vote. The black line does more than avoid fraud; it also creates peer pressure and civic pride. On election day, not to have a black line on your finger leads to endless questions from others about why you have not voted, when you intend to go to the booth, solicitous offers of help to make it possible, and so on. Not to have the black line on your finger the following day can lead to criticism, more questioning, isolation, avoidance, and stigma, for a marked finger has come to symbolize good citizenship, responsibility, and commitment.[2] There is thus no quiet way to hide one's abstention in an Indian election: not to have voted becomes a visible statement vulnerable to scrutiny by all. The black mark thus metaphorically renders the cup in the story transparent—everyone can tell whether you have contributed milk or water. The social censure that Indian citizens face for not having voted is therefore simply not worth the free ride. In such contexts free riding becomes too costly, and it is simply more rational to make the effort to vote rather than face the knock-on effects afterward.[3]

CYNICISM

Another frequently cited reason for the rise of voter apathy in democracies is increasing cynicism with politics. It is argued that this is so because people are skeptical about politicians. Moreover, because of the narrowing ideological distance between political parties, and the greater role of corporations and international markets in determining governance agendas at the expense of the opinions of voters, they do not bother to vote anymore. But avid Indian voters also share this skepticism about politicians, and their verdict is unequivocally damning. Not only are politicians seen as venal and corrupt, their politics itself is seen to be corrupting. A common saying to describe this is *jey jayey Lonka shey hoye rabon*: one who goes to hell becomes the devil. In contemporary democratic India, the word *rajniti* is used in common parlance to refer to the corrupt, violent, and immoral world of the powerful, who try to buy votes to fill their own bellies. And yet, despite this popular understanding of *rajniti* as demonic, rather than voter apathy we find voting alacrity. Clearly, something different is going on among Indian voters who continue to vote despite their cynical views about politicians.

One reason for this commitment to electoral participation is that the Indian electorate chooses not to throw the baby out with the bath water; that is to say, the corrupt world of *rajniti* is not allowed to exhaust all meanings of the political. Instead, people recognize another vast domain of politics that is distinct and complementary to it: the activity called *politics*.[4] *Politics* is an umbrella term to describe a range of popular activities such as agitation, mobilization, and struggle, including student politics, ecological movements, land rights agitations, the women's movement, and so on. When people say something is political they mean it might be tricky, it involves negotiation with power or powerful actors, and requires careful balancing of interests.

While *rajniti* is what remote, privileged, and powerful people in immaculate clothes do, the leaders of *politics* tend to be a bit more weatherbeaten, darker skinned, and drawn from among the less privileged sections of society. It is this domain of politics that has led to the democratic upsurge since the 1990s that witnessed the entry of unlikely actors drawn from among the most underprivileged castes of India into electoral competition.[5] No wonder some scholars have dubbed this democratic upsurge of popular politics "a silent revolution" (Jaffrelot 2003). While Indian voters are cynical about politicians in power, they also recognize that an electoral system allows for the entry of new players into the democratic arena.

Further, there exists a third realm of politics that is available to everyone: the politics of participation and citizenship. The very act of voting, for a large proportion of the electorate, is performative of *uber* democratic ideals: political equality (when each person is genuinely equal to another), popular sovereignty (a moment when each individual matters—*ek din ka sultan* is how people put it in Hindi), and citizenship (when people have a chance to perform their rights and duties). By turning up to vote, queuing patiently at polling stations, exercising their choice, and wearing their blackened fingers as a badge of honor, they demonstrate their belief and participation in the most demotic acts of democracy, which continues to flourish despite the demonic politicians.

It is important to recognize that the clarity of such a vision of democratic politics focused on ordinary people and their citizenship does not suddenly dawn on people's minds on election day. Rather, it is instilled over a period of several weeks through people's experience of the election campaign, the performance of the Election Commission of India, and the track record of India's past elections. It is during this period that the virtues and vices of politicians, the diabolical nature of high politics, the excesses of electoral corruption, and the ultimate sameness of what is on offer are discussed. But these discussions are held *alongside* those on the importance of casting one's vote and of resisting political pressure by utilizing the secret ballot to fulfil an important duty. These reflections make the contradictions between the demonic and demotic apparent and lead people to reflect and debate, rather than merely resign themselves to the situation.

ELECTION CAMPAIGNS: THE GREAT LEVELLER

Elections bring a special temporality to the country. Institutionally, the Election Commission of India introduces what is known as the "Model Code of Conduct" on all political parties from the time that an election is announced. Thus, in the weeks when nominations are filed, names of the contesting candidates are confirmed, and the election campaign is conducted, behavior is governed by the conventions of the Model Code of Conduct. Under this code, all parties are expected to behave in moderation and are open to constant scrutiny by the millions of officials who are drafted in to work for the Election Commission across the country. These officials, who are drafted for election duty, are usually on the payroll of the government of India as schoolteachers, administrative officers, and so on. Once elections are declared, incumbent governments are forbidden from offering schemes and loans that might act as electoral incentives; the administration is expected to perform efficiently; and the power of the Election Commission supersedes the powers of all institutions of government.[6]

The constitutional backing of the Election Commission's sphere of jurisdiction implies that it can function above political or state interference. All political parties, including those that form the incumbent government, have to defer to its authority, as do all levels of the state's administration. As a result, candidates can be disqualified, partisan bureaucrats and police officers transferred away from their domains of influence, and parties fined for violating the norms of the Model Code of Conduct. Elections thus witness the unusual sight of nervous and vigilant political parties, an efficient administration, and ordinary people empowered in their role as Election Commission officials. This extraordinary "election time" thus forms a period of liminality during which the ordinary rules of national life are suspended and replaced by a more orderly, albeit upside-down, world. Unlike other carnivalesque festivals, such as Holi, when anti-structure prevails (see Marriott 1971 for an example), elections bring with them a reversal that can be characterized as "hyper-structure"—when things were far *more* structured and efficient than otherwise. The country is suspended in

Photo credit: Dixie

Polling officials depart on election duty

a high pitch of excitement as campaigns gather momentum and every inch of public space is taken over by a visual and aural display. Posters, pamphlets, banners, and bunting displaying the symbols of political parties and their colors line streets and buildings; loud hailers roam the streets exhorting people to vote for a particular candidate, and new businesses spring up to cater to the needs of the new publics that are created during the campaign. A huge proportion of the Indian electorate attends large public rallies and street corner meetings, and political parties see the influx of a young, energetic task force that aspires to get noticed for its hard work during a campaign. During an election in India, the country is therefore transformed into a large fairground, and it is impossible to miss the occurrence of what is clearly the largest public festival in the country.

During this time, the privileged world of *rajniti* intersects with those of ordinary voters and the politics of vote banks, caste politics, clientism, and electoral corruption that are an inextricable part of power politics come into play. But the need to woo voters also causes a strange levelling effect. Laundered clothes of elite politicians are sullied by dusty campaign journeys; their well-groomed and arrogant heads are bent low to enter the humble dwellings of voters; and their hands seem perpetually folded in their plea for votes. People are of course aware of the hypocrisy of such gestures, but nevertheless delight in the sheer visual effect of the reversal. Just as the classic anthropological studies of ritual reveal, this time of *communitas* lies betwixt and between periods of social time, and thereby heightens the contrast between the everyday and the extraordinary.

Such reversals are therefore also inherently unstable and so bring with them the threat of danger, of radical possibilities, and violence. This increased criminalization of politics has been noted by all observers of Indian politics and indicates the limits to India's electoral record. And, in an effort to counter this trend in *rajniti,* there was also a sort of popular Model Code of Conduct, a basic decorum on how ordinary people conducted themselves during an election. On the whole, people were polite to campaigners who appeared on their doorstep even when they did not support the campaigners' candidate. Workers from different parties shared space when required to, supporters of different parties attended each other's political meetings, and election officials were polite to voters. In the state of Uttar Pradesh, for instance, in a village full of diverse political alliances, Bharatiya Janata Party (BJP) supporters in May 2009 were seen to be attending Samajwadi Party (SP) meetings even though it was unlikely that they would vote for them. Similarly, in the southern state Tamil Nadu, where the two local rivals, the All India Anna Dravida Munnetra Kazhagam (AIADMK) and the Dravida Munnetra Kazagham (DMK), were in electoral alliances with the national rivals, the Communist Party of India (Marxist) (CPI[M]) and the Congress, people did not allow the rivalry of the bigger parties to further intensify the local rivalry. This accommodation was fairly extraordinary, given the otherwise high levels of adrenalin and excitement and vast amounts of money involved in the elections.

A number of factors might help explain this ethos of civility in a climate of fierce competition. First, as we have noted above, there are several institutional restraints that are placed on conduct in public life through the implementation of the Model Code of Conduct by the Election Commission of India, whose powers are over and above the world of demonic political interference. This forces the players who have the most at stake in the electoral game—politicians and political parties—to conduct their campaigns according to established rules.

The threat of fines and, worse still, disqualification, that take place routinely are severe restraints.

Second, the capillary nature of the Election Commission's organization and its 2-million-strong workforce means that observers acting on its behalf are present everywhere. As these officials are drawn from local populations of schoolteachers and clerks, it is difficult to identify their presence, and this causes further nervous self-regulation on the part of political actors. That these officials report directly to the Election Commission of India (ECI) rather than the local administration gives their authority the teeth that most other regulatory bodies lack. Further, 24-hour media channels ensure that no incident, especially those that invite the attention of the ECI, goes unreported, not least because controversies always sell, and politicians are keen to avoid any adverse publicity.

At the local level, the importance of politeness stems perhaps from an instinctive desire for survival as much as from norms of civility. Elections, after all, are temporary affairs, and when all is said and done, people still need to live together. While people may be divided by political loyalties during elections, they nevertheless need to live with these political differences. Thus, there is respect alongside the recognition of political differences. Further, when it comes to political meetings held in the village, everyone attends regardless of political allegiance, because the norms of village sociality override political divisions. This does not mean for one moment that political loyalties are weak or meaningless; if anything, it is their unshakable allegiances that allow people to be accommodating in order to put up a united front in the presence of outsiders.

Alongside politics, other allegiances based on religion or kinship also continue to exist. This fact was made starkly visible in a village in eastern Uttar Pradesh, where one could see each household flying the colors of the party they supported, whether the blue of the Bahujan Samaj Party (BSP), the saffron of the BJP, or another party's colors. To a certain extent these party divisions coincided with caste membership, so it was possible to guess the caste membership of the household by looking at the color of the flags they were flying. But each household also displayed a second set of identical flags: that of the religious sect of Guru Jaigurudev, who had a wide and diverse following in that area. The cross-cutting ties of religion clearly put political divisions in perspective.

In the Tamil Nadu village there was another factor at work. Every election brought with it a new configuration of alliances between national and local parties, which led parties that had been in opposite camps in one election to ally with each other in the next. While party leaders made these calculations with abstract electoral arithmetic in mind, at the ground level it meant that real people were either pitted against each other or thrown together in alliance. As a result, friendships were tested, neighbors alienated from each other, and families divided. People learned to treat these alliances with pragmatism, not allowing them to intrude into personal relationships.

The *communitas* of election time thus brought with it an effervescence that marked it as a special time. The various materials of the campaign transformed the physical landscape of the country from its drab everyday character into a festive one, and the social landscape too was transformed as the codes of exaggerated civility among ordinary people sought to challenge the depravity of the political classes. Election time therefore ushered in at least the possibility of the demotic, providing a challenge to the demonic in politics, a possibility that was otherwise absent in everyday time.

ELECTION DAY

During the national elections in 2009, as in all other elections, the momentum and extraordinariness of the campaign finally sublimated on election day, when the spirit of *communitas* suffused through all aspects of the day's events. As we shall see in this section, voters reported how each detail contributed to their decision of whether or not to vote. The journey to the polling station, the way in which queues were managed, how polling officials treated the voters, the accessibility of the voting process, the simplicity of the procedure—all were important factors in determining individual participation. The overwhelming responsibility for this process is of course that of the Election Commission of India, which has to pull off the largest human exercise imaginable every time it conducts national elections in India. The electorate has nearly 715 million voters, 1 million voting machines, nearly 7 million polling stations, and 543 constituencies in a country of enormous linguistic, cultural, and physical variety. 2 million people serve as officials to conduct the elections and the results are declared within less than 12 hours of the final vote being cast, and with negligible instances of recounts. In a country where much smaller events have been tainted with scandal and inefficiency, it is indeed extraordinary that the Election Commission delivers such an exceptional performance every time. It should therefore come as no surprise that Indian citizens rank the Election Commission of India highest among all public institutions (NES survey).

At least part of this credibility might lie in the technology of voting in Indian elections as it has evolved into the twenty-first century. In particular, a number of measures, such as the introduction of electronic voting machines (EVMs), the use of party symbols against the name of each party, and the location of the ballot box away from the gaze of polling officials, have all made voting attractive for illiterate and literate voters alike. And the Election Commission attempts to make adjustments to its arrangements from one election to the next, addressing the lessons learnt from experience. In a world in which election results are often compromised because of faulty technology, the importance of these innovations should not be underestimated.[7]

Research among people who serve as election officials shows that they are fully aware of the responsibility vested in them and, as a result, they anticipate their duties with a mixture of excitement and dread. As government of India officials, their careers are governed by the grade on their Annual Confidential Report. A mistake committed while on election duty can lead to a black mark in that year's report. It is no wonder that one of these officials said, "*Yeh pariksha bhi hai aur shaadi bhi!*" (It [elections] feels simultaneously like an exam and a wedding!)

In order to serve as officials, they are required to undergo training in three stages to learn their way around the electoral procedures and the enormous paperwork entailed. Much of the training also anticipates what needs to be done when things go wrong or when the unexpected happens, such as the case of a visually-impaired voter who requires help with an EVM. The day before the election, each polling team of four officials is required to be present at a gathering of all officials in a particular district, where election materials are distributed. Each package contains about 60 different items, including multiple forms, stationery, tags, seals, wax, and the all-important EVMs. Auxiliary needs of officers who are expected to spend the night at the polling booth after preparing it for the next day are also covered, with medicines and mosquito repellent provided for. All these are packed into a white *jhola* (cloth bag) that each team of polling officials is issued, although the senior presiding officer carries the small vial of indelible black ink on his person for utmost security. From here, the officials are transported under armed guard to their respective polling stations—a trip that, given India's immense physical diversity, can be sometimes extremely arduous. Election officials routinely trek through snow, ford rivers, and walk through forests to set up their polling booths. In some cases, the number of officials outnumbers the electorate, but the effort made for even a single voter is the same as for a thousand.

In the last 24 hours before election day, all remain poised for the finale. Campaigning has stopped, families are tense as last-minute material inducements by political parties have left their menfolk in an alcoholic stupor, and officials wait nervously to discharge this most crucial of all duties. Party workers try to continue the campaign unobtrusively, going from door to door distributing voter slips— small pieces of paper on which the party's symbol and the candidate's name are printed alongside the voter's name, roll number, and other details—as last-minute coercion. Meanwhile, the local school building has undergone its metamorphosis into a polling station. This involves cleaning, rearranging furniture, designating separate entry and exits to the booth, removing all campaign materials from the vicinity of the building, and making provisions of drinking water for the voters. The walls are covered with posters detailing various aspects of the voting process, including the design of the EVM, instructions in the local language on how to cast a vote, and information about the observers and the importance of free and fair elections. Further, the area outside the building must be demarcated as a special zone in which all talk of "politics" is to be avoided. A 100-meter line is drawn on the road to indicate this area, as well as a 200-meter line further down the road, to indicate the wider area within which full law and order must be maintained; not even raised voices are tolerated within that zone.

When election day dawns the next day, the weeks of preparation and hard work are finally put to the test. In India, unlike in most other countries, election day is declared a public holiday, so it already feels special for everyone. It begins early for the officials, who need to complete the formalities of the mock poll before opening the doors of the polling booth. They do this in the presence of the party agents to satisfy them that the machine is "clean," after which the EVMs are attested and sealed. The sealing process is an elaborate one. The party agent signs the first sealing strip, followed by the presiding officer. With the consent of the polling agents, a tag bearing the details of the particular EVM and polling booth is attached to the flap of the EVM, which is then shut and finally sealed with wax. The doors are opened at 7 a.m. and the wait for the voters begins. Outside the polling station, armed guards take up their posts.

The voters, too, go through their own rituals of preparation. Party workers start early, often offering prayers after a bath, before making their way toward the polling booth. Voters rearrange their chores to enable them to go and vote before it gets too hot or inconvenient. Men tend to go earlier than women, who tend to children and urgent domestic chores. For women, the trip to the polling station provides a rare outing, a legitimate reason to travel beyond the confines of their dwellings with their friends. For young brides who were married outside their villages, election day provides an excuse to visit their natal villages and see old friends and relatives. They therefore make a special effort to look presentable. Women often wear their best sari that they have saved for special occasions, such as weddings and festival days.

Rambati (46), a Gujjar woman in western Uttar Pradesh, summarized it all: "It was a hectic day for me since I had to finish all the household work in addition to bathing, wearing make-up, and making sure that I had a new sari. It took me the entire morning to wind up the household chores, including taking care of the cattle." Others had taken even greater pains to make the journey. One man in Kolkata had arranged for his mother to be present at the polling center by transporting her from a hospital in an ambulance. Examples such as these are by no means isolated events; on the contrary, they abound across the country.

At a polling booth during the 2009 elections, the atmosphere was solemn, as people formed separate and orderly queues for men and women, waiting patiently even when they were long, and keeping conversation to a minimum, at most discussing the weather or similarly innocuous subjects. The sobriety of the occasion was particularly noticeable given that social gatherings anywhere in India tend to be noisy affairs.

Many people commented after election day on the radical social mixing at the polls—the unexpected sight of people from different social strata rubbing shoulders. One low-caste Chamar woman explained how, in her experience, intercaste proximity is rare, if it happens at all. At Panchayat meetings or religious gatherings it is customary for castes to sit in groups of their own. In urban centers, too, class usually divides people. Even though untouchability is illegal in contemporary India, its social effect continues in traditional and unexpected ways. Upper-caste people, too, commented on this forced social mingling with a mixture of disbelief and grudging admiration at what a radical alteration a simple election queue could achieve, forcing even supporters from rival parties to stand cheek by jowl.

The polling booth thus provides a space for the social drama of the election to be played out. Its rules and etiquette facilitates the suppression of everyday social discrimination and the assertion of a more egalitarian vision of society. This temporary assemblage of an undifferentiated group of people could generate an awareness of the virtues of political equality. As a former untouchable Chamar woman put it, "I am realizing my vote has the same value as anybody else's, having stood in the same line as people of different castes."

Further, many felt the actual process of casting their vote was itself deeply transformative as they reemerged blinking into the bright sunshine. One woman said, "Once I stood in front of the EVM, no one, not my husband, or father or mother-in-law, could dictate which button I pressed. It was my choice and my choice alone." Another young woman, despite an early marriage and motherhood, felt that the act of voting was the real rite of initiation into adulthood. "Now that I have voted for the first time, I feel truly grown up," she said shyly. The solemnity of the queues, the polite officials who kept conversation to a minimum, and the privacy of the EVM heightened the importance of the occasion. All the various aspects—the silence, the darkness, the officials, the unhurried pace, marking the body as a sign of participation, the importance of individual faith—resonated with the experience of other sacred spaces that people were familiar with. As one man said, "The polling station is like a *garba griha* [sanctum sanctorum] where we perform this important rite." And perhaps in recognition of this sentiment, it was reported in Gujarat that some women removed their shoes before entering the polling station, as they would do as a mark of respect for any important and sacred space.

It was noteworthy how immensely relieved and happy voters looked as they emerged out of the gates of the polling station, clutching their precious voter ID cards with newly inked fingers. Each voter who emerged from the booth could testify to having been treated with fairness and dignity, regardless of their caste or social station. The excitement and relief rendered the erstwhile somber voters into loquacious informants, and it was thus a good moment to ask them directly: "Why do you vote?" Respondents used imaginative metaphors such as comparing their single vote to an atom that is small but powerful, comparing their votes to weapons that could be wielded against the powerful, and describing how their voter identity cards were the proof that they even existed. For poor voters and those who live in remote parts of the country, their act of voting was a clarion call to the nation that they still existed and were not to be forgotten. People were keen to exercise this most basic of constitutional rights, since it took minimal effort but enabled future agitations. As an illiterate Dalit activist put it, "If I don't vote, how can I ask for better roads, or schools, or health services? Voting is free, easy, and no one can stop me. So I should start by doing that."

People also saw voting as a duty that was borne out of reciprocity. A number of people felt that, given the effort the Election Commission expended in holding elections, an effort that was most visible to them for the last 24 hours or so, the least they could do in return was to turn up to vote. It would be almost churlish not to do so; it was a feeling of *noblesse oblige*.

But most of all, people remarked on how the culture of the polling station facilitated the radical experience of social levelling, otherwise tolerated mostly only in temple queues or Friday prayers, as an indication of a possible future egalitarianism in society at large. The queue's liminality facilitates direct unmediated communication between individuals free of social structure and generates a rare egalitarianism among the participants, overturning the hierarchies of the normal social order. As one voter joked, but only partly in jest: "After this mark [on our fingers], we are all one, and have become the same after voting. One vote has one value. That makes us all equal today."[8]

CONCLUSION

As we have seen, the reasons people continue to vote in large numbers and with enthusiasm in India lie mainly in the importance that they themselves place on the electoral process in itself. The weeks of campaigning that culminate in election day are a *communitas* that suspends the rules of normal social order and brings instead a rare flowering of egalitarianism. This experience in turn heightens people's awareness of their most fundamental and universal attributes as citizens of India. Political scientists and philosophers call this the "expressive" aspect of voting, the "theatre of politics" so to speak, when people are able to present themselves as good citizens who discharge their duty as voters, regardless of a specific electoral result (Tuck 2008).

In conventional discussions of politics, this expressiveness is not considered a serious enough reason for voting because in a democratic system, it is argued, elections are mainly a means to an end. The assumption here is that people ultimately vote to make their candidate win and any other reason for voting is therefore ancillary to this. Thus, the expressive or performative aspects of voting are considered valuable but not essential to the meaning of the electoral process as democracy's arithmetic. However, on the basis of the material from India presented here, this approach seems to limit the meaning of voting quite severely since this reading of elections, when combined with a cynicism that views all politicians to be ultimately the same, unsurprisingly leads to voter apathy. That is to say, the instrumental aspects of voting are futile because whomever one votes for will be corrupt and ineffectual. The expressive aspects of voting are mere window dressing, so one may as well stay home.

Instead, Indian voters, while voting for their favored candidates and political parties and even while under the pressures of coercion and patronage, believe that the electoral process is a worthwhile end in itself. This is so because the electoral process alone allows for the flowering of democratic values that are otherwise hidden in the inequities of everyday life, the increasing criminalization of politics, and the election result. Elections alone allow for the performative expression of the fundamental values of democracy—citizenship, duty and rights, equality, cooperation, the ability to imagine a common good—values that are otherwise wholly missing from the polity. Like the collective rice pudding, elections demonstrate how cooperation can result in creating something much larger than the sum of the parts.

It was precisely because of the absence of these values in daily life that people feel the urge to embrace and celebrate these values when they are available during elections. Elections therefore emerge as aesthetic and ritual moments that allow for the inversion of the rules of normal social life. In this elections emerge as classic anti-structural liminal moments that lie betwixt and between everyday states of inequality. As Victor Turner noted in his analysis of Ndembu ritual, such liminal periods are characterized by a mode of social relatedness that he calls 'communitas' which is a community of feeling that is tied neither to blood or locality and instead tends to be undifferentiated and egalitarian. As the evidence in this paper demonstrates, this is the nature of the shared feeling among voters at a polling station during their participation in their act of voting. An Indian election thereby creates a heightened awareness of what is missing in everyday hierarchical life, while simultaneously providing a glimpse of democracy's ideals of egalitarianism and cooperation. People participate in elections in the hope that the extraordinary awareness and visceral experience of egalitarianism will in turn infuse into everyday time and eventually bring genuine social change. It is for this reason that elections have become sacrosanct in India and continue to keep India's democracy alive.

NOTES

1. The argument in this essay is drawn from the findings of ethnographic research on Indian elections, conducted over a period of several years. The characteristics of campaigns or election day described in this paper are applicable to any or all elections in India. I use the findings from my personal long-term village-level study in the state of West Bengal that were then tested on a national scale during the 2009 elections, through a comparative ethnographic project conducted in villages, small towns, and metropolitan cities in the states of Bihar, West Bengal, Chattisgarh, Madhya Pradesh, Tamil Nadu, Kerala, Maharashtra, Gujarat, Rajasthan, Delhi, and two sites in East and West Uttar Pradesh. Typically, ethnographic data does not rely only on what people say when asked questions, but also on the observations of what people do, how they behave—in this case, both on election day as well as at other times, whether politically or not. In this, it differs from other field methods, including surveys and questionnaires. In this paper, the data and the quotes are drawn from research conducted during the 2009 elections and my own research in West Bengal over several elections.

2. This is not dissimilar to the symbolic meanings of other ritual markings that Indians frequently carry on their bodies, such as the henna designs on a bride's palms, threads tied around wrists during Hindu rituals, foreheads marked with sacred ash, or the discoloration on the forehead of a pious Muslim who frequently touches his head to the ground in prayer. They all convey a specific meaning and indicate a coveted membership, and are therefore not erased or removed by the participant.

3. It should therefore come as no surprise that voter turnout rates tend to be lower in the larger metropolitan cities of India than in small towns and villages. And it is to perhaps create peer pressure in other urban democratic contexts that during the 2010 midterm elections in the United States, the virtual game of "Four Square" introduced the "I have voted" badges that players could acquire and display on their web-based profile after they had voted. In Switzerland, a study by Patricia Funk revealed that turnout dropped when postal ballots were introduced, as people valued "being seen" to have voted (Dubner and Levitt 2005).

4. This loan word from English has now been thoroughly assimilated into the Indian lexicon and is used alongside other such appropriations: *party, leader, public, vote,* and so on.

5. The most startling example of this was the widespread public discussion in April 2009 (months before the United States elected its first black president) about the possibilities of a Dalit woman becoming India's prime minister.

6. Article 324 of the constitution of India vests in the commission the powers of superintendence, direction, and control of the elections to both houses of Parliament. Detailed provisions are made under the Representation of the People Act (1951) and the rules made thereunder. Under the same act, the ECI nominates officers of government as observers and they report directly to the commission.

7. See the introduction to Bertrad, Briquet, and Pels (2006) for a comparative account of the technology of voting across different countries.

8. The value of political equality is obviously felt most by those who are among the most deprived in society, and it challenges the orthodoxy of the view that "poor people make poor democrats." For a cross-country analysis that challenges this view, see Krishna (2008).

REFERENCES

Bertrad Romain, Jean-Louis Briquet, and Peter Pels, eds. *The Hidden History of the Secret Ballot.* Bloomington and Indianapolis: Indian University Press, 2006.

Dubner, Stephen, and Steven Levitt. "Why Vote?" *The New York Times,* November 6, 2005.

Jaffrelot, Christophe. *India's Silent Revolution: The Rise of the Lower Castes in North India.* London: Hurst, 2003.

Krishna, Anirudh, ed. *Poverty, Participation and Democracy.* Cambridge: Cambridge University Press, 2008.

Marriott, McKim. "The Feast of Love." *Krishna: Myths, Rites and Attitudes.* Ed. Milton Singer. Chicago: University of Chicago Press, 1971 (1966).

NES Surveys. Conducted by Lokniti and based at the Centre for the Study of Developing Societies. Available at <http://www.lokniti.org/>.

Tuck, Richard. *Free Riding.* Cambridge: Harvard University Press, 2008.

India's Liberal Democracy

Gopal Guru

Generally speaking, liberal democracy in India, which has emerged in the context of anticolonial nationalism, has remained differentially attractive to social groups. For example, the modernizing elite in India was drawn toward liberal democracy primarily because it promised them an opportunity to recover and expand the power and influence that was constricted during colonial rule. However, they did not seem to be in favor of extending the benefits of liberal democracy beyond their own interests. In fact, as historian of ideas Sumit Sarkar has noted, they were compelled to show some degree of commitment to democracy as an expansive framework (2001: 30). Similarly, Rajeev Bhargava, a leading political theorist, maintains the view that Congress nationalists had little interest in liberal democracy (2000: 28).

On the other hand, historically disadvantaged segments of the population found liberal democracy attractive because it offered them an opportunity to acquire and then expand normative spaces involving not just equality, liberty, and rights, but self-respect and dignity. Liberal democracy as an attractive ideal thus invokes different degrees of subaltern involvement in the project of producing an egalitarian India. In the anticolonial phase, liberal democracy and the idea of the nation are constituted in a symbiotic relationship. It is in this

I thank Gurpreet Mahajan for helping me to revise this essay from its earlier version. However, I remain responsible for the final version. I also want to thank Arjun Appadurai and Arien Mack for their vital input.

context that Bhargava's observation becomes relevant: "Democracy came to India as nationalism and therefore, arguments for nationalism were coterminous with arguments for democracy. The character of this democracy had to be liberal not only because of its commitment to civil liberties but also because of its vision of equality and social justice" (Bhargava 2000: 26).

The idea of democracy, which somehow managed to emerge within the nationalist imagination in India, seems to have provided the context for two different sets of language: the language of self-rule and national pride representing nationalist elites, and the language of self-esteem and self-respect that different marginalized groups deployed for the articulation of their normative aspiration (Guru 2007: 221-238). Nationalist imagination in India has also led to the emergence of two rather intersecting notions of self-esteem, one nurtured by those who were of the socially privileged elite but who felt humiliated on account of denial of self-rule within the colonial configuration of power, and a second pursued by Dalits in opposition to the local configuration of power (Brahminism and capitalism) that involve Dalit humiliation (Guru 2009: 3).

The Dalit response to Indian nationalism also differs from the mainstream notion of nationalism in another important respect. While the mainstream nationalist imagination draws its emotional power from the register of collective pride and humiliation (Guru 2009: 3), the Dalit response puts *swabhiman* (self-respect) before *abhiman* (pride) of nation (Khairmode 2002: 286). For Dalits, self-respect acquires its meaning and *social* dimension through interrogation of the local configuration of power and domination, whereas the notion of national pride as invoked by the nationalist elite acquires its significance and *political* character in the context of the confrontation within the colonial configuration of power.

The primacy of *social* over *political* needs to be understood in terms of Dalit skepticism regarding the political promise that involved nationalist resolution of the caste question. During the anticolonial struggle, a segment of the upper-caste population was violently opposed to social reforms, thus raising doubts in the minds of the Dalit (led by Bhimrao Ramji Ambedkar)[1] about the nationalists' sincerity when it came to resolving the caste question. Dalits were not sure whether the nationalist elite, which was divided on social issues, would support a "nationalist" resolution of the caste question. In fact, Dalits led by Ambedkar feared that the socially dominant sections would hijack independent India and manipulate liberal democracy in order to consolidate and expand their own power through the reproduction of the old hierarchical order that placed Dalits at the bottom (Ganveer 1980: 54).

Dalits, however, treated liberal democracy as the initial rather than the sufficient condition for the realization of their normative goals (Khairmode 2002: 286). Ambedkar expected that the Indian constitution as a moral text would create spaces that would enable the Dalit to acquire self-description as subjective agents, and liberal institutions would help them reject the negative description of servile objects that had long been imposed on them. Self-esteem, equal respect for persons, equality before law, and equal civil and political rights, which are central to the practice of liberalism, were the cornerstones in the Dalit struggle for emancipation.

However, efforts involving increasing institutional proliferation and periodic examination of legal provisions proved inadequate, and the normative and political focus on Dalit emancipation was undervalued both in the institutional response to the Dalit question and in the way it was imagined by intellectuals, as well as in the academy. As we shall see in the following sections, scholars of Indian democracy seem to have privileged the question of institutional well-being over welfare of human beings. Yet, some of these scholars treated the question of social inequality as a crucial factor in their own assessment of liberal democracy (Kaviraj 2000: 112).

I would like to argue that an assessment of liberal democracy from the point of view of the Dalit would be quite inadequate if it were done solely on the basis of the structural aspects of inequality and distributional aspects of injustice. For a more comprehensive assessment of liberal democracy, it is necessary to bring into central focus the discussion of the language of self-esteem and self-respect, which seems to have escaped the attention of scholars of Indian democracy. First, I would like to offer a brief explanation of different notions of self-esteem, which will help us in assessing the impact of liberal democracy on the Dalit pursuit for self-esteem and self-respect.

According to Robert Nozick, self-esteem is based on social comparison—that is, evaluating oneself according to one's position relative to others (see Lane 1982: 44). Avishai Margalit, on the other hand, defines self-esteem in terms of individual achievement and social ranking. However, Margalit goes one step beyond Nozick, distinguishing between self-esteem and self-respect. Thus, for Margalit, self-esteem in some sense is different from self-respect inasmuch as the latter is based on treatment of self by others, while the former depends on personal efforts duly supported by government job opportunities existing in liberal democracy (Margalit 1996: 44-45). Taking a cue from both Nozick and Margalit, let us try to address the central question: to what extent has liberal democracy, through institutional intervention at different levels, created opportunities for Dalits to enhance their self-esteem and gain self-respect? How do Dalits articulate and maximize their sense of self-esteem and self-respect?

Through transgression of social boundaries the self is foregrounded and, simultaneously, self-esteem is asserted. Self-esteem is also asserted through speech acts and body language. Liberal democracy provides the necessary background conditions for the articulation of this self-esteem, including adult franchise, political rights, access to public office, and so forth.

The social composition of institutions has implications for the concerns of self-esteem and self-respect, particularly of Dalits. Following Nozick and Margalit, it could be argued that the realization of self-esteem has three key elements. First, realization itself requires social comparison or ranking. Second, valid comparison or significant ranking requires institutions with hierarchical standing (role differentiation) and mixed social composition (caste, race, and gender) but equal talent and caliber. It is true that comparisons and ranks are morally painful and sometimes dangerous since they involve a destructive sense of envy, but they are a precondition for the definition of self-esteem. Finally, endorsement of one's achievement by individuals in different social strata plays a vital role in the definition of self-esteem.

To what extent do Dalits have these three conditions available in India? Liberal democracy must accommodate Dalit interests in different institutional structures created from time to time as a constitutional mandate. Thus, every five years, the representative institutions (including the lower house of the Indian parliament, state legislative assemblies, and local self-government) have to take Dalit members into account. The Indian parliament has to have nearly 80 Dalit members in its lower house (the Lok Sabha), more than 500 of them in legislative assemblies in different states, and several thousand Dalit members at the level of local self-government. In addition, the Indian government recruits several thousands Dalits at different levels of its bureaucratic structures in accordance with the quota system given in the Indian constitution.

Dalits in postcolonial India have made tangible achievements that have led toward enhancement of their self-esteem. For example, they have moved from their traditionally inferior designation as *Dhed* (repulsive untouchables) to being entrusted with heading different representative institutions in liberal democracy, whether as minister, commissioner, or president *sarpanch* (elected village head). Many Dalits also head bureaucratic institutions.

The Dalit hold on these institutions has led to a vicarious sense of empowerment for those who are not themselves in positions of power, but succeed in deterring an upper-caste local adversary by making reference to the Dalit who is in fact in power. This is often evident in the Dalit assertion that "If you torment me I will have you fixed by my person occupying the influential position." Thus, Dalits gain self-respect, show that that they cannot be cowed, and retaliate against persecution by drawing on the self-esteem of powerful Dalits. By making this possible, liberal democracy certainly plays a crucial role in making the articulation of self-respect and self-esteem possible. On the other hand, Dalits have been considered the most important source of sustaining liberal democracy in India (Kothari 1997: 441). One could, therefore, argue that there is a symbiotic relationship between liberal democracy and Dalit political participation: self-respect and self-esteem are both externally induced by liberal democracy and internally driven.

However, a Dalit audit of liberal democracy over the past 60 years suggests that liberal democracy has proffered a skewed response to the Dalit question, one hinging on everyday forms of humiliation, degradation, and repulsion. Among the non-Dalits, self-esteem evokes at best continuous and humiliating taunting directed at Dalits—for example, Dalits are referred to as *sarkar ke jawai* (free rider)—and at worst, it leads the upper caste to violent reactions against Dalits' own pursuit for self-esteem. There are crude as well as cunning methods that the adversaries of the Dalit deploy with the intention to deny the latter a sense of self-esteem and self-respect, with the effect of reducing the Dalit to a squalor that has been described as a "hellhole" (Dorairaj 2011: 90-93).

In fact, the reduction of the Dalit to wretchedness is achieved through maltreatment by institutions and maladjustment of Dalits into such institutions. Such a callous attitude is more shocking when it is displayed by the government, and more shattering when it is inflicted with deep contempt by civil society toward the very government institutions created for the Dalit (Dorairaj 2011: 90-93). This callousness, leading to the folding of the of Dalit into "filthy" spaces, in turn gives rise to a public perception among the elite that the Dalit are the source of environmental hazard. This morally objectionable attitude adopted by the government and civil society tends to diminish the self-worth of Dalits, to make them feel worthless. To put it differently, no one feels elevated by being part of filth. It would be absurd to treat a "hellhole" as the moral source of self-esteem. Similarly, in the culture of liberalism, where honesty is a regulative norm, it would be equally absurd to treat a criminal background as the source of self-esteem. When Dalits face an increasing degree of criminalization/lumpenization by the state, particularly in the age of neoliberalism, how can they feel morally self-esteemed? These are some of the cruder forms leading to the loss of Dalit dignity and self-esteem.

However, denial of self-esteem to the Dalit takes subtle forms as well. This happens through insinuation and insulation, which form part of the upper caste's moral universe. The upper caste, in their desire to remain ritually pure and socially superior, seek to insulate themselves from public institutions that are exclusively created for Dalits. In the upper caste's perception, Dalit presence in these institutions becomes, at the symbolic level, a source of repulsion and therefore sociologically/ritually dangerous. The reduction of modern institutions to what are perceived to be ghettos is reflected in the repulsive attitudes that non-Dalit legislators and bureaucrats adopt toward, for example, social welfare departments. It has been observed that many upper-caste bureaucrats do not want to be posted to such ministries even on promotion.[2] Those who cannot avoid transfer to such institutions use *Gangajal* (holy water) to purify them. There are several instances in which an upper-caste judge has been found purifying an office after it had been vacated by his Dalit predecessor, or stories of an upper-caste professor purifying his university house after it was vacated by a Dalit professor, or even upper-caste members who, for ritual reasons (so-called purity-pollution), do not want to sit with the Dalit *sarpanch*.

The moral universal also forces the upper castes to insulate themselves from the institutions occupied by Dalits. They may do this with some subtlety. For example, they may try to insulate themselves from institutions that have a strong Dalit content and orientation, either by staying out of them[3] or creating a new institution.[4] This deliberate design of exclusion or insulation has implication for Dalit self-esteem, in that it hardly encourages Dalits to treat their association with such institutions as a source of self-esteem. Moreover, exclusion has a much deeper implication for the lofty ideals of egalitarianism. Exclusion, which is constitutive of an element of vanity, seeks to deny egalitarian ideals their inclusive character. At another level it also leads to the conceptual compression of these ideals, in the sense that these attitudes reduce the universal content of public institutions to a parochial intent. To put it differently, the idea of democracy or social justice or dignity, which forms the basis of modern public institutions, is reduced to Dalit identity, which in the perception of exclusion becomes just a sociological construction. Thus, ideas are compressed into identity. Conversely, institutions based on an exclusive identity—especially in terms of uniform social composition—also constrain the expansive nature of democracy, forcing them into policy-packaged identity rather than idea. The moral impact of compression thus leads to the ethical impoverishment of the institutions, which are seen as an embodiment of identity rather than ideas. These institutions that are reduced to a particular identity are converted into an object of ridicule and contempt, and thus cease to enjoy public respect.

Self-respect, however, can also be defined in terms of the positive treatment of the self or the affirmative attitude that one adopts toward oneself. The act of denying oneself one's moral worth leads to the loss of self-respect. We can also say that the struggle for relative worth rather than equal worth, which is the fondest claim of liberal democracy, results in the loss of self-respect. The struggle for relative worth necessarily results from the moral capacity to possess only compromised ambitions. This type of struggle is characterized by the kind of servile body language and speech found among Dalits operating within the framework of the same liberal democracy. As the following illustrations show, Dalits seem to be struggling less for equal worth and more for relative worth.

Dalit members of Parliament—nearly 100 are members of Parliament—by and large have remained in "silent mode" for the past five decades (Gawarguru 1986). And whenever some of them do speak in Parliament, they choose to speak on issues that have only a symbolic importance for the Dalit question.[5] Dalit representatives elected at the local level speak the language of the patron rather than the language of their social constituency. Their voices appear subsumed in the dominant voice of those who are responsible for the entry of Dalits into representative institutions at the central, state, and local levels. The subordination is further evident from a rather astonishing example of a Dalit legislator from the legislative assembly in Karnataka state. This particular legislator is reported to have refused to occupy the chair in the assembly hall of the state. Instead, he chose to sit down on the floor in a remote corner of the hall.[6] This particular behavior reminds us of the social taboo that made it impossible for a Dalit to transgress social and ritual boundaries. It is in this sense that one can argue that some Dalits are morally responsible in maintaining the division between institutions based on ritual distinction and those based on functional differentiation. While such Dalits can feel a sense of self-esteem in terms of having possession of some tangible assets (a palatial home or chauffer-driven car), they feel this esteem only at the cost of lost self-respect.

Why do non-Dalits discount the Dalit claim for self-esteem? What are the resources that they use in order to undermine the Dalit claim for self-esteem? In other words, why do Dalits develop only "handicapped ambitions" to become the head of the institutions having an implicit Dalit agenda? Why can they not aspire for more competitive positions even if they possess the same political talent and ethical stamina that the non-Dalits possess?

Let us answer the last question first. It is not something pathological about the Dalit to develop handicapped ambitions. In fact, the Dalit's inability to assert has to be understood in terms of subjective and objective constraints. Dalit politicians, of course, possess the necessary intellectual resources and skills to offer powerful critique of "paternal liberalism." But they are unable to mount this critique because of a subjective desire to remain the constant recipient of political patronage. This compels Dalits to raise their ambitions only to the level permissible within the framework of "paternal liberalism." Political patrons expect their Dalit clientele to develop ambitions that coincide with their political worth and that do not rise above the social worth the Dalit uses to compensate for his/her intellectual incompetence. The political worth of Dalits is tied up with horizontal mobility that a political patron sponsors by using the quota system. To put it differently, Dalits should not aspire to contest electorally from the general constituency, and should not aspire to become the head of powerful ministries.

Dalits, according to hegemonic designs of the powerful, must remain chained to those institutions that deal with Dalit issues. The political patrons of the Dalit use liberal institutions as patronizing devices to achieve their acquiescence. In other words, the political patron has created institutions such as the social justice ministry to contain Dalit aspirations. The political patron also seeks Dalit accommodation into some institutions so as to insulate other institutions from the Dalit "menace." It is this caste logic that can explain the division of public institutions between those implicitly based on ritual distinction and those based on functional differentiation. While this would undermine the Rawlsian agenda that assigns equal importance to every public institution created for the steady and equal distribution of self-esteem, it would please scholars who, time and again, have argued that reformatory liberal democracy has created an unprecedented problem for institutional well-being (Beteille 1998: 477). If one approaches the question of institutional well-being from Beteille's perspective, then one could argue that the quota system has been responsible for infesting modern public institutions, both representative and bureaucratic, with caste. One could further argue that the quota system constrains the spirit of rationality so important for institutional well-being.

Since caste has been considered the problem around which the nation's progress centers, scholars like Beteille and their supporters would suggest the following: let us save some institutions from the caste menace. To that end, these scholars would be heartened to know that their concern for institutional well-being has been vindicated by leaders who have kept certain institutions (the military, the judiciary) free from caste-based quotas. The contributions made by soldiers and scientists in protecting the nation have been treated as being of paramount importance. But we do not see Dalit sanitary workers—who keep the cities clean and thus save the lives of millions—receiving a gallantry award from the Indian state, which distributes these awards on January 26, Republic Day.

Some scholars have suggested that the development of modern bureaucratic institutions based on the impersonal character of the officials who staff them can make liberal democracy more robust (Kaviraj 2000: 91). They also argue that the bureaucrats' commitment to rational procedures can contribute to institutional well-being (Beteille 1998). These scholars thus find the intermeshing of caste questions with rational and rule-bound institutional practice detrimental to the very structures of liberal democracy. Intermeshing caste takes place on the assumption that people belonging to a particular caste can only trust politicians or officials from the same community. This, certain scholars argue, undermines the impersonal operation of political power (Kaviraj 2000: 91).

This kind of argument tries to indirectly convince us that public institutions, which are originally empty of any casteism, become infected with the caste element. According to this understanding, caste is the source of institutional crisis—and that this source of crisis is rendered active through the very democratic process itself (elections, for example). The question that one has to answer is: do Dalit officials working in these public institutions feel free to openly practice casteism, thus showing contempt for impersonal rule? Let us try and answer this question.

The Dalit experience challenges the argument forwarded by Beteille, which suggests that public institutions in India are empty of casteism, and the presence of large numbers of lower-caste members in public institutions is the source of institutional crisis. Let me question this argument by posing a couple of counter-questions that bear on the Dalit experience. If the public institutions were empty of casteism, then why are people working in public institutions interested in knowing the caste of a Dalit, and not his intellectual or political caliber? This question assumes importance in the context of a Dalit officer's experience, which suggests that information about his caste used to travel faster (to the upper caste) than his transfer papers (Tulsiram 2010). (This experience was shared with me by Harkishan Santoshi in Delhi on January 24, 2007). In fact, the "caste of mind" of the socially dominant bureaucracy tends to trump administrative secular procedures.

The upper castes, to the utter disappoint of Max Weber, choose to exercise their social rather than secular authority, with the intention of putting on hold the Dalit official's capacity to remain rational. To put it differently, upper-caste bureaucrats put Dalits continuously on probation. The Dalit bureaucrat's struggle to remain rational is driven by the need to keep the upper caste in good humor. Dalit officials at times become ultrarationalist—to the extent that they remove the gap between the private and the public or the social and the official. Their residence thus becomes an extension of government office, where interactions based on emotional ties are strictly prohibited. The compulsion to remain rational across time and space prevents Dalit officials from becoming progressively partisan in favor of the needy. The grounds for progressive partisanship are not arbitrarily created but are provided by the ethics of progressive governance, based on the constitutional commitment to social justice. Anxiety about remaining rational in the eyes of the upper-caste colleagues has moral consequences for Dalit officials. The need to remain ultrarational reduces these Dalits to machine-like behavior and hence without any feeling and emotions for Dalits as human beings. Second, the need to remain rational not only certifies the upper-caste officials as the natural embodiment of rationality, but also leads to a loss of confidence among Dalit officials, who then accept the legislative power that the upper-caste officials exercise, that keeps Dalits on continuous probation.

Rationality in the case of the Dalit acquires a coercive nature. This coercive form of rationality leads to a double alienation of Dalit officials: from themselves and from their social constituency. How does a Dalit cope up with this coercive form of rationality?

Dalits officials prefer to join those institutions that are relatively less hostile socially to their cultural and mental well-being. Thus, Dalits are found in the Social Justice Ministry, the Scheduled Caste Commission, the Directorate of Social Welfare, and several similar institutions that exist at the central, state, and local levels. Ironically, this "soft landing" into institutions with more or less uniform social composition results in the denial of a sense of self-esteem. As mentioned earlier, a claim to self-esteem becomes valid not in a situation of sameness but difference.

From this account of bureaucratic institutions in liberal democracy, two conclusions follow. First, the coercive character of rationality jeopardizes Dalit prospects of maximizing their self-esteem. Dalits, in their efforts to escape being ultrarational, ultimately end up in institutions that reward sameness. As mentioned earlier, self-esteem resides in difference and not sameness. Second, liberal institutions do not have control over personnel, who begin to unfold themselves into parochial (caste, religion, region, and language) colors after they are recruited into these institutions through the most secular and universal process.

Legal institutions constitute themselves as part of liberal democracy through the language of rights. These institutions neutrally adjudicate and arbitrate between individual rights and political institutions. Legal intervention thus performs a double function: it provides legitimacy to liberal democracy and, at the wider level, addresses social crisis. However, the legal system is only one way to address social crisis, the other being the domain of ethics. Interestingly, these resources—legal and ethical—have an inverse relationship to each other, in that a lack of ethical resources in a society makes legal intervention necessary. Conversely, the availability of abundant ethical resources makes legal intervention redundant.

The preponderance of laws governing ethics in India suggests that Indian society lacks ethical resources. To wit, the strong and widespread presence of caste and patriarchy, marked by an unwillingness among the upper castes to promote ethical practices, have led Indian lawmakers to codify ethics into law. Law becomes the preferred form because of its effectiveness, its immediacy, and its universal character. This effectiveness is defined in terms of its punitive power: its ability to deter those who produce crisis for society.

The upper caste seems to have preferred this legal positivism over ethics for the following reasons. First, in the social perception of the dominant castes, treating the Dalit as morally equal would amount to a greater social loss than the monetary loss that the upper castes are likely to incur should they enter the legal battle. Second, the upper castes prefer codification of ethics into law because the violation of law does not involve any serious risk as far as the dominant castes are concerned. The legal domain leads the upper castes to "deal" with Dalits much more confidently and decisively even without showing any respect for law. This is because they know that the custodians of the laws who are responsible for impartial delivery of legal justice—that is, the judges—remain closer to his and their caste than to secular laws. This is clear from the astonishing ruling delivered by a lower-court judge from Rajasthan state who belonged to one of the upper castes. While delivering his judgment in the rape case of a lower-caste woman, he observed that "touching a lower caste is not in the culture of Indian society" (Chakravarti 2003: 163). It is this kind of prejudiced approach to procedural justice that leads non-Dalits to deal with Dalits by invoking religious laws that in the historical imagination of the upper caste face serious challenge from the modern laws that were being passed on by the British colonial state (Ganveer 1980: 54).

Ambedkar has created a strong case in favor of ethics rather than law. He argues that ethics as a normative resource is preferable to law since the former creates a much larger sphere of social harmony in society (Ambedkar 2005: 382). Ambedkar thus unequivocally suggests that it is the ethical moral domain rather than the legal domain that provides stable conditions for the effective resolution of the Dalit question. He also believes that the Dalit adversary should pursue the same ethical rather than legal option to help bring about the latter's liberation.

Until now we have discussed at some length the politicians and officials who form a small part of India's 160 million Dalits. Obviously, this narrow focus on a certain segment gives us only a partial understanding of the tense relationship between Dalits and liberal democracy in India. There is a large mass of Dalits whose association with both the Indian nation and its liberal democracy differs from the Dalit segments we have been concerned with so far in this paper. It is different in degree and quality. In the following pages we are going to discuss in the context of the Indian nation and liberal democracy two very large segments of the Dalit: the toiling Dalit masses and educated, unemployed Dalits. As we will clarify shortly, even these two segments offer different responses to liberal democracy and nationalism. The Dalit toiling masses in contemporary times are the recipients of state patronage that seem to be flowing more due to fear of unprecedented unrest perceived by the global rich (Indian corporations included) and less because of Dalit mass movements. Arguably, various social welfare schemes—most notably the Mid Day Meal Scheme or the Mahatma Gandhi National Rural Employment Guarantee Act—has resulted from this concern.[8] It is in this sense that the toiling masses include Dalit matters: not because of their efforts but because of the corporatist need to prevent crisis from developing. The educated, unemployed Dalit youth do not seem to be averse to the idea of participating in the life of liberal democracy and nationalism, for the simple reason that it is these two spheres (state and market) that still hold some promise for them.

There is a third segment that does not relate either to liberal democracy or the Indian nation, and neither the nation nor liberal democracy is interested in them. This is the portion of the Dalit community that has become invisible to the state and liberal democracy: construction workers, rag pickers, and scavengers. They are politically invisible because they either constitute themselves outside or are pushed out of state structures in India. They also become politically invisible because of their inability to stake any claim on—if not control over—the state. What puts these Dalits in touch with the state and legal institutions is the language of rights, which, in a liberal democracy, acquires meaning only when the state itself is challenged. The language of rights, and the rights themselves, gain validity through legal defense. Dalits do not posses positive rights related to moral interest, such as self-respect and dignity, primarily because this language does not exist in the sphere of activities (rickshaw pulling, scavenging, or rag picking) that they engage in. Although there are efforts made by certain NGOs to provide protection to their dignity, the state does not show enthusiasm to provide any effective laws that would protect the dignity of Dalits.[9]

The absence of the language of rights by implication eliminates the possibility of Dalit assertion, which is so important in gaining the attention of both the state as well as civil society. Tragically, these Dalits become visible only through fatal accidents that occur on a nearly daily basis. In fact, invisibility imposed on rag pickers and more particularly the *safai karamcharis* (sanitary workers) results in their double death—moral and corporeal. The moral death occurs in the sense that their self-worth diminishes in the hellhole that is constitutive of manual scavenging and rag picking. It is corporeal death in the sense that they are killed since they are physically at risk. These Dalits also find themselves outside the Indian nation because they, for all practical purposes, have ceased to be the citizens of India. It is only citizens who can meaningfully relate to a nation through participation in the political process, such as voting in elections, who belong. But these Dalits have for all practical reasons ceased to be citizens. Continuous displacement leading to state of uncertainty has deprived them of resources like voting cards or ration cards, without which one cannot actively participate in the political process.

Nationalism and liberal democracy, on the other hand, appear promising at least to a sizable section of educated but unemployed Dalit youth. Intervention by the "liberal state" and now even the corporate sector continue to remain the main avenues for employment opportunities for such Dalits. Identity politics is seen as the major route by which they can articulate their demands. Identity politics, in general, requires both nationalism and liberalism. For its own recognition, identity politics requires the nation, and it also requires liberal democracy for its articulation.

Identity politics and liberal democracy become enmeshed in each other in one more sense. Claims couched in the language of rights and put forward by identity politics need to be articulated through the mediation of the state and its related institutions. Dalit identity politics invokes the language of rights and social justice in the context of exclusion. Exclusion in turn hinges on identity politics, with these Dalits found associated with pacificatory structures such as social welfare departments, university grant commissions, universities, and now, corporate NGOS. The Dalit demand for reservation in the private sector forms the logical part of this identity politics.

Identity politics in contemporary times operates through lobbying, seeking personal favors, and institutional patronage. It is in this sense that Dalit youth become trapped in identity politics. Since politics based on identity uses community resources for personal advancement, it essentially eschews the need for mass movement, which is more transparent and seeks to address collective aspirations.

Identity politics is incapable of producing transformative internal critics. Yet, it somehow offers a handle to Dalit leaders who, then, can and do use the opportunity space made available within the liberal framework to satisfy their expensive tastes and also to nurture more aristocratic desires. An aristocratic desire to remain relevant in the public memory by creating monuments to the Dalit personality can become a possibility only through entrapment of the Dalit masses into identity politics on the one hand, and the manipulation of paternal liberalism on the other.

At another level of regressive Dalit identity politics, this entrapped segment of Dalits has developed self-defeating tendencies of being internally aggressive[10] and externally appealing.[11] Some Dalit subgroups who are lagging behind in terms of access to certain welfare policies have chosen to aggressively denounce those who have taken the lead. Thus identity, which is constitutive of "paternal liberalism," stands directly in opposition to the aspiration to become an enlightened consumer or some kind of socially super-mobile if not bourgeois Dalit in the neoliberal order.

Super-mobile Dalits, driven by the ideology of neoliberalism, subscribe to the idea of participation through open competition in the limited sphere of market-based equality. At the social level, this group has started treating the Dalit community as a socially necessary burden to be warded off through patronage. These mobile Dalits paradoxically share material resources with their underprivileged lot at least to some extent—but without sharing the idealism of common Dalits, who provided the community resources that make the mobility of the former possible. The Dalit response to both nationalism and liberal democracy in the age of globalization has been quite positive only to the degree that the tiny group of super-mobile Dalits have put their critical scrutiny of nationalism and liberalism on hold.[12]

Dalits from different segments have sought to critique liberal democracy for its failure to ensure substantive change with a sense of self-esteem and self-respect. They seek to critique the Indian nation for not fulfilling the promises that it had given to different marginalized groups (rag pickers, sex workers, scavengers, and tribes and denotified tribes).[13] The presence of these Dalits even in the backyard of the Indian nation serves as a backdrop to the Dalit critique. In addition, one notices much more vocal and radical Dalit critiques of nationalism and liberal democracy. In fact, the radical critique begins with none other than Ambedkar himself. Ambedkar seeks to critique liberal democracy for its failure at multiple levels. According to him, liberal institutions cannot exorcise the ghost of caste. He further argues that bureaucratic/institutional structures have managed to remain hospitable to caste affinity, while at the same time showing increasing hostility to the ideal of bureaucratic impartiality or procedural justice. Ambedkar has also sought to critique bureaucratic liberalism for its deliberate design to facilitate only individual mobility rather than collective Dalit emancipation. Third, he has argued that the liberal vocabulary of individualism tends to destroy the moral resources necessary to build up solidarity for Dalit emancipation. He also realizes that the vocabulary of liberalism does not have the stamina to motivate Dalits to struggle for collective good. On the contrary, liberalism, in his opinion, tends to promote an insular tendency within the Dalit community. At the same time, its complementary attitude toward social hierarchy makes the fusion of social groups difficult (Bahishkrit 1990: 228).

The Dalit critique, which in its post-Ambedkar phase continued to remain radical (at least until the arrival of globalization in 1990), has been more apparent in Dalit literary writings than in social science literature. Dalit critical assertions appeared as part of the moral need for an internal critique of Dalit politics, which had already lost its credibility and capacity to expose the limits of liberal democracy vis-à-vis Dalit emancipation. Dalit politics of the 1970s, led by the Republican Party of India, lacked the moral power to critique liberal democracy, since they were its beneficiaries. The upper caste's political preponderance—especially in the electoral field—and the subjective need to achieve personal goals at the cost of Dalit collective interest: these factors explain the moral deficiency in Dalit politics. For example, Namdeo Dhasal, in one of his poems, attempts a devastating critique of parliamentary democracy in India. In his literary imagination, caste has a limiting impact on the efficacy of liberal institutions like Parliament (Dhasal 1981: 17).

The most radically articulated critique of the Indian nation is to be found in the writings of Dalit short-story writers and poets. For example, Baburao Bagul, one of the leading Dalit short-story writers, while critiquing Indian nationalism, says that "those who have committed the mistake by taking birth in India, should rectify it either by waging war for *dignity* within the nation or by deserting it forever" (Bagul 1981: 10; emphasis added). Similarly, Dhasal, one of the leading Dalit poets from Maharashtra, uses an analogy to make the Dalit critique of nation expressive. He finds, for the Dalit, a similarity between the Indian nation and the castor seed plant and argues that the Indian nation, like the castor seed plant, is vacuous from within (1981: 51). Using the literary imagination of Dhasal, one can further argue that although some believe India will achieve great heights in terms of gross domestic product, it lacks depth as it fails to achieve quality of life (dignified existence for all) for the average Indian. The Dalit experience with nation thus suggests that the Indian nation stands on a paradox. While liberal democracy can help some Dalits achieve national celebrity, it also pushes millions of Dalits into its own "backyard."

Liberal democracy has helped the Dalit to move from truth to truth, in the sense that some have become important "public" persons, transcending their stigmatized identity as, for example, scavenger or Dhed. But this journey from truth to truth is incomplete; while they have grown in their own eyes, they do not grow in the eyes of the upper caste. Their predicament is similar to that of American blacks, who, as Toni Morrison has said, do not grow in the eyes of American whites. To put it differently, while they can enhance their self-esteem (as defined by Margalit and Nozick) through personal achievement, they fail to gain self-respect since they are still maltreated by India's caste-ridden society.

Indian liberalism has helped Dalits acquire self-esteem, if not self-respect. Liberal democracy exists in the shadow of eternal truth of caste. The Dalit critique seeks to interrogate both the Indian nation and its liberal democratic structure for its failure to enable the Dalit to move from being the wretched of the hellhole to sentient beings.

NOTES

1. Dr. Babasaheb Ambedkar was born in a caste that was considered untouchable. He went on to become the leading social thinker of modern India and a leader of the untouchable masses.
2. This is my personal conversation with the person under reference and took place on August 20, 2002 at the Planning Commission, Delhi.
3. Savdekar, an upper-caste person from Aurangabad, publicly expressed his displeasure about a Dalit's appointment as the vice-chancellor of Marathwada University, Aurangabad, in 1973 by exclaiming "*Marathwadycha Maharwada zala*" (Marathwada University has been infected by the lower caste).
4. This refers to the Maharashtra state government's decision to rename Marathwada University after Dr. Ambedkar. The upper caste who were opposing this renaming finally withdrew their complaint after they were assured by the state government that they would get a new university,

which they did, at Nanded, a district place in the Marathwada region in Maharashtra state.

5. Dalit members of Parliament have created a parliamentary forum to take up the Dalit question at the Parliament level, but this forum does not have much presence.

6. This happened in the monsoon session of Karnataka Assembly, 2005.

7. At this point of analysis it is necessary to point out the flaw in the so-called authority that the upper caste exercise against Dalit officials. What is fundamentally flawed about the upper caste in the Indian bureaucracy is the fact that, while putting Dalit officials under the scope, they do not realize that they are also under the surveillance of the larger structures of domination. But members of the upper caste choose to gloss over this because it does not adversely affect their social dominance that finds its defining condition in the social subjugation of Dalits.

8. The Mid Day Meal Scheme is a program the Indian government established in 1995 with the goal of "enhancing enrollment, retention and attendance and simultaneously improving nutritional levels among children" (<http: //india.gov.in/sectors/education/mid_day_meal.php>). The Mahatma Gandhi National Rural Employment Guarantee Act (NREGA) "aims at enhancing the livelihood and security of people in rural areas by guaranteeing hundred days of wage-employment in a financial year to a rural household whose adult members volunteer to do unskilled manual work" ("The Mahatma Gandhi National Rural Employment Guarantee Act" <http: //www.nrega.nic.in/netnrega/home.aspx>).

9. Manva Garima is a network of NGOs working for the removal of manual scavenging. It operates from Ahmedabad in Gujarat and Devas in Madhya Pradesh.

10. This internal aggressiveness is evident in the tension between Dalit castes like Mala and Madiga in Andhara Pradesh, Mahars and Mangs in Maharashtar, Adi-Karnataka and Adi-Dravida in Karnataka, Walmiki and Chamar in Uttar Pradesh.

11. Dalit NGOs made this appeal to corporations for the inclusion of Dalit in private industries.

12. There are several Dalits who have been suggesting this option. Prominent among them are Dalits from the diaspora.

13. Denotified tribes are groups that under British colonial administration had been classified as criminal. This classification was repealed in 1952 and the groups were "denotified."

REFERENCES

Ambedkar, B. R. *Writings and Speeches of Babasaheb Ambedkar*. Vol.20. Mumbai: Government of Maharashtra, Publication Committee, 2005.

Bagul, Baburao. *Dalit Sahitya Aajche Kranti Vidnayan (Marathi)*. Nagpur: Buddhist Publication, 1981.

Bahishkrit Bharat. Government of Maharashtra, Education Department. Mumbai, 1990.

Beteille, Andre. *Distributive Justice and Institutional Well-Being. Democracy, Difference and Social Justice*. Ed. Gurpreet Mahajan. Delhi: Oxford University Press, 1998.

Bhargava, Rajeev. *Democratic Vision of a New Republic. Transforming India, Social and Political Dynamics of democracy*, Eds. Francine Frankel and Rajeev Bhargava. Delhi: Oxford University Press, 2000.

Chakravati, Uma. *Gendering of Caste through Feminst Lens*. Calcutta: Stree, 2003.

Dhasal, Namdeo. *Tuhi Iyatta Konchi (Marathi)*. Mumbai: Ambedkar Prabodhini, 1981.

Dorairaj, S. "Hellhole Hostel." *Frontline* 28:2 (January 15-28, 2011): 90-93.

Ganveer, Ratanakar. *The Speeches of Dr. Babasaheb Ambedkar*. Bhusawal: Ratnamitra Publication, 1980.

Gawarguru, G. N. "Party Politics in Reserved Constituency: A Case Study of Pandharpur Parliamentary Constituency in Maharashtra." PhD diss. Jawaharlal Nehru University, New Delhi, 1986.

Guru, Gopal. "Twentieth Century Discourse on Social Justice: A View from Quarantine India." *Development of Modern Indian Thought and Social Sciences*. Ed. Sabyasachi Bhattacharya. Delhi: Oxford University Press, 2007: 221-238.

———. "Introduction." *Humiliation: Claims and Context*. Ed. Gopal Guru. Delhi: Oxford University Press, 2009: 3.

Kaviraj, Sudipta. "Indian Democracy and Social Equality." *Transforming India: Social and Political Dynamics of Democracy*. Delhi: Oxford University Press, 2000.

Khairmode, C. B. *Bhimrao Ramji Ambedkar.* Vol.5. Pune: Sugawa Publication, 2002.

Kothari, Rajani. "Rise of the Dalit and the Renewed Debate on Caste." *State and Politics in India.* Ed. Atul Kohli. Delhi: Oxford University Press, 1997.

Lane, Robert E. "Government and Self-Esteem." *Political Theory* 10:1 (February 1982): 5-31.

Margalit, Avishai. *The Decent Society.* Cambridge: Harvard University Press, 1996.

Sarkar, Sumit. "Indian Democracy: The Historical Inheritance." *The Success of India's Democracy.* Ed. Atul Kohli. Cambridge: Cambridge University Press, 2001.

Tulsiram, Murdiya. *Autobiography* (in Hindi). Delhi: Wani Publication, 2010.

Accusations of Illiteracy and the Medicine of the Organ

Lawrence Cohen

EYES OVER CHENNAI

D r. Agarwal's eye hospital watches the denizens of Chennai, quite literally: the family-run hospital was rebuilt in 1976 in the shape of a great human eye and its iconic structure peers out at the busy traffic along Cathedral Road. This futuristic conjunction of function and form bespeaks fungible success: since going public on the Mumbai Stock Exchange in the early 1990s, Dr. Agarwal's has become a valued investment property.[1] The hospital has become a center for postgraduate clinical training and surgical innovation, and through the first decade of the 2000s, its management built numerous small clinics across the region that advertised themselves as providing low-cost surgical procedures, most notably for cataracts.

This essay draws on a paper presented at the 2011 meetings of the American Anthropological Association in celebration of the life and work of Carol Breckenridge. In addition to acknowledging Breckenridge's spirit and example, I would also like to thank discussants Arjun Appadurai, Joao Biehl, and Shalini Randeria. This essay also draws on a different paper presented at the Department of Sociology, University of Delhi, at which the comments of Ranendra Das, Veena Das, Tulsi Patel, Ashley Tellis, and especially Deepak Mehta informed this argument. For discussions on medicine in the making of colonial Madras, I am grateful to Eugene Irschick and Shiv Visvanathan.

The ocularity of the Cathedral Road main campus is insistent. When the hospital was remodeled in 2008, the eye got a new, shinier look, in keeping with the "international" aesthetics remaking clinical architecture across India to exemplify the "five-star" quality attractive to medical tourists. Not only was the form of the organ recapitulated on both the exterior of the main building and its lobbies and waiting rooms, but the hospital roof was reshaped as well to look like an eye from above, an explicit wink to the satellite vision of Google Earth.

Dr. J. Agarwal, third in the family line of ophthalmologists, first had the extraordinary vision of a hospital built in the shape of an organ in what hospital publicity materials termed a dream ("History" 2004). But the dream itself is a wink to a persistent mode of iconic advertisement nationwide, often but not necessarily presuming illiteracy, in which a clinic is rendered recognizable to the public in terms of an iconic lexicon of body parts. Hoardings and other signage for specialty clinics in small towns and cities routinely feature visual depictions of the organ or organ system under treatment. Eyes and teeth dominate, but I have visited clinics in numerous towns with signs featuring drawings or, increasingly, photographs of hearts, kidneys, limbs, and the digestive tract. These signs in many cases represent conventional practices of the commercial artists who produce them,[2] but when I interviewed the directors of these clinics (usually a single doctor or the head of a family of physicians), I was often told that the iconic sign makes the clinic accessible to "illiterates."[3]

THE RIGHT CAMP

This essay considers what I will term the *accusation of illiteracy* as a feature of both the history and neoliberal reformation of the clinic in postcolonial India. It suggests a possible relationship between understandings of illiteracy and the image of the organ as a way to think through both questions of the ethics and politics of organ transplantation, my research over the past decade, and broader questions about how death may be imagined.

The icon of the organ in the advertisement of the clinic is not limited to urban storefronts or freestanding hospitals. It appears, if not more frequently, in the promotion of a distinctive clinical form that circulates through much of the world and yet that has received minimal attention within the anthropology of medicine. I refer to the charitable or government "health camp." Critical attention to refugee camps as sites of emergency and humanitarian governance, as in the provision of food, medicine, and shelter to refugee populations in the wake of war, disaster, or plague, has of course emerged across several fields. This literature foregrounds a problem for humanitarian groups like Médecins sans Frontières as the urgent present of humanitarian time threatens to turn into the long-term provision of services (Redfield 2005).[4] This vexing relationship—between the government of the exceptional situation and the government of the normal situation—has characterized much political theory and social analysis (Schmitt 1976 [1927]; Agamben 1998; Zizek 1999; Petryna 2002) and has reframed debate on the government of marginal populations in contemporary India (Chatterjee 2004; Das 2004). But the ubiquitous species of camps to which I refer are not usually organized around the immediate, punctuated time of present emergency but rather the periodic and regular time of the civil gift.[5] Blood pressure camps, diabetes camps, healthy baby camps, and cataract camps presume a mass population that chronically lacks both access to and information about appropriate health resources and that depends upon the gift of these resources through a form—the camp—able to treat the mass in its entirety.

Health camps are usually rationalized into discrete problems, symptoms, or organ systems, and their promotion often utilizes the icon of the relevant body part. Contemporary camps in India tend to be characterized by two features: one, a very public, well-advertised gift relation of care in which religious, fraternal, diasporic, or other NGOs enact a transactional form of civil society through the provision of the camp-clinic;[6] and two, techniques of reason and of the body that we can anachronistically call Fordist or Taylorist, enabling camp personnel to treat large numbers of patients quickly.

The body demanded and produced in this gift-establishing civil society through the camp is thus a mass body, its massiveness addressed in both the terrain-spanning mobility of the camp circuit and the assembly line redistributing clinical functions. The figure of an assembly line is anachronistic not because we live in post-Fordist times but rather as the clinical camp with its treatment of the mass body emerged in colonial rural India well before the Fordist reformation of local industry. The treatment of cataract in the 1870s and 1880s, particularly in regions where weather, farming techniques, and the political and economic conditions reorganizing agrarian labor may have contributed to visual loss and blindness in later life, led to intensive experimentation in the 1890s by the British and Indian personnel of the colonial military Indian Medical Service. The controversial procedures that emerged were debated globally, most famously the "crude" technique of the "Smith Indian Operation." The Smith Indian Operation was a high-risk intracapsular procedure, particularly for those clinicians whose hands had not yet been schooled into the repetitive work of the camp.

The inventor of this eponymous procedure, Colonel Henry Smith, cultivated controversy, most notoriously in his practice of smoking a cigar while operating. But as he was able to accomplish tens of thousands of operations with his new method, his skills were high and failure and iatrogenesis relatively low. Smith's justification for his operation drew upon the impressive evidence of his experience, and behind it that of unnamed Indian colleagues who assisted or carried out many of the procedures. His defense of new *mass techniques* of surgery, enabling the care of the population body, parallels the justification by Sir Henry Maine for the new pedagogy of "cramming" that was threatening to allow Indians to outstrip British candidates in examinations (Cohen 1998: 139-140). That is, both Smith and Maine suggest that the emergent global condition of empire required a series of new techniques to compress time more effectively and govern multitudes (Ravin 2005). The efficacy of the vulgar operation depended on the cultivation of a clinical disposition in which many people had to be treated quickly and effectively in order for the mass body to see.

Rachel Prentice (2007) has intriguingly conceptualized the cultivation of just such an embodied clinical disposition in surgical training as "ethical."[7] Indeed, many clinicians a century after Smith, working in the sterilization camps (whose form, capacities, and justification echoed the history of cataract) of the family-planning state, would claim against accusations of violent iatrogenesis the *ethical* nature of their touching the mass body.

If cataract surgery inaugurates the deployment of mass technique in the camp-based assembly-line surgeries of the late nineteenth century, tubal ligations and vasectomies become closely identified with the figure of the camp in the twentieth. Emma Tarlo has offered one of the most compelling accounts of the biopolitics of mass sterilization during the 1975-1977 Indian Emergency, when elections were suspended and Prime Minister Indira Gandhi effectively ruled by decree. Tarlo's focus is on the circulation of documents that marginal households were required to show in order to gain access to state-controlled housing, employment, and subsidized food—documents demonstrating that a member of the household had been sterilized (2003). This version of the presence of the camp in relation to everyday life stands in contradistinction to narratives of grosser coercion, such as in Rohinton Mistry's 1995 novel, *A Fine Balance*. In the novel, Ishvar and Om, two low-caste marginal men, are in a public market when they and others are grabbed by police and taken to a camp. The effect of camp surgery on their bodies is brutal. Ishvar's legs become infected and eventually he must have a *second* operation: the legs must be amputated. An upper-caste landlord the two men have offended presses the medical team to conduct a second operation on Om as well. The doctors comply, and Om is castrated. When Ishvar accuses the doctors of having castrated Om, another doctor returns the accusation: "We are fed up with you ignorant people! How many times to explain?" For the doctor, "it was just another instance of [the ignorant] confusing sterilization with castration." But the accusation is false: Ishvar and Om struggle to be adequate to a world in which operations double up.

THE UBIQUITY OF THE OTHER OPERATION: CONFUSION OF ORGANS

Mistry's account in its reliance on the poetics of extremity may fail to account for what Tarlo sees: an emergent economy of documents, as the extraordinary compulsion for the family-planning operation comes to inhabit the everyday distribution of life chances. Some households are able to purchase or lay claim to the sterilization certificates, and thus the operations, of others: scars are no longer the legible documentation of the clinical event.[8]

But the scene of accusation and counter-accusation Mistry imagines became unexpectedly familiar to me in my own work on the transplant operation, in Chennai and elsewhere. Word got around in the neighborhood of Mylapore where I was staying and in Ayanavaram, where I was interviewing organ sellers and other donors, recipients, and brokers, that either I was a foreign doctor looking to buy a kidney or was some manner of social worker looking either to help or to penalize persons who had improperly circulated their organs. In the context of such rumors, I found myself repeatedly asked, by men: would having the kidney operation make one a eunuch?

I mentioned this concern to one of the resident doctors at a government hospital dialysis ward where I was also spending time. As I recall he laughed, and said, these illiterates confuse their operations.[9] I returned to talk with him and his colleagues a few days later, after another man in my neighborhood whom I had come to know asked me if it were true that I was a kidney doctor. When I said no, expecting another suddenly frequent offer of a kidney for sale, he persisted in asking for advice and gestured toward the outline of a large testicular hydrocoele stretching the fabric of his pants leg. I met his gaze, and before I could suggest a clinic he told me he had asked me since it was obviously a kidney problem. This man had come to Chennai from a village to the north and had found a job as a cook. When I asked him why it was so obviously a kidney problem, he pointed to the swollen testicle as if I had not seen it: it is my kidney, he said. Yes, another of the resident doctors told me, we often find patients confusing their kidneys with their genitals, it is common. The first doctor added, it is like I told you before, these illiterates confuse their organs.

I cannot fully trust my rendition of this scene: it may draw too readily upon the circulation of easy indignation one gets from reading the novel, one reason perhaps for the book's subsequent fame. And yet the ubiquity of this figure of a doubling of operations and its rendering as a confusion of organs has persistently dogged my research. This short essay reflects a struggle to define what kind of persistence may be at stake in this situation.

METONYMIC FAILURE

How might we engage such claims of an illiterate relation to the body? Within modern pedagogic regimes in many parts of the world, the order of language and the order of the parts of the body have long been rendered as metonymic or syntagmatic chains through the form of the chart or pedagogic exercise. Footpath vendors throughout urban India offer hope in the form of inexpensive children's picture books that promote learning the alphabet or the body as a colorful series of parts. The form of learning—metonymic, in the terminology of structural linguistics (see Jakobson 1956) in its framing of the body or of language as a sequence—carries a dense history. Among its sources is the rationalization of colonial rule. Within the examination structure Henry Maine identified as particular to the demands of empire in India, competency was most efficiently assessed through *performances of metonymy*—so-called rote learning attentive to reproducing the order of knowledge in its entirety.

Accusations of illiteracy, to the extent that they presume a failure of metonymic performance, read the particular metaphoric operations of situated language as metonymic confusion. The Indian illiterate, so closely identified through what Thomas Blom Hansen has termed the double discourse of Indian colonialism with the passionate subject of "the masses" or mob constitutively outside of reason (1999), is thus particularly legible in terms of the metonymic failure of his or her mass body. The illiterate, assessed in the terms of such failure, is thus particularly vulnerable to a confusion of parts and thus to trouble with surgery, as the clinic par excellence of the body in parts.

To the extent the illiterate mass can be imagined as failing to perform the metonymic totality of its parts, as in my conversations with the medical staff at the government hospital in Chennai, what kind of medicine is then imaginable as an intervention? This essay began with a hospital built as a giant body part, gesturing to a clinical world steeped in the iconicity of parts as a response to the presumptive failure of the illiterate mass to recognize the body's parts adequately.

Many economic and cultural forces promote the emergence of a privatized clinical landscape organized around a specialist medicine of parts. My intent is not to reduce the iteration of the iconic organ only to the historical incitements for a mass pedagogy. Nor is it to explain the dream of Dr. Agarwal to build a hospital shaped like a giant eye as but the pedagogic remediation of the mass. When Dr. Agarwal's Eye Hospital went public and built many smaller clinics targeting the poor—arguably challenging its not-for-profit rival Aravind, the famed humanitarian eye clinic—the new buildings for this less elite clientele lacked iconicity of any such grandeur. The giant eye on Cathedral Road stares at far more than the presumptively illiterate urban poor unlikely to walk through its pupil-shaped doorway. It celebrates a family legacy, through the cultivation of a shared clinical disposition, one of service. It affirms and acknowledges participants in the urbane civil society surrounding it, who in the shadow of the eye could recognize themselves as donors to the vision of the poor.[10]

Thus I am hesitant to reduce this extraordinary structure to the use of one family's surplus capital to memorialize its ethical cultivation, over generations, of a generalized surgical disposition.[11] The public organ here signifies more: it is an architectural performance within a bourgeois landscape of the duty and achievement of private medicine in relation to the mass body. Private clinics, particularly in the mid-1970s when the ocular architectural vision of the Agarwals was achieved, occupied an ambivalent moral position within then state-dominated medical modernity, their commitment to the mass body implicitly in question. And yet the family capital of medical dynasties had long been an important component of the mercantile forces that, scholars like Aparna Balachandran have argued, were central to the shaping of urban space and civic order in colonial Madras (2008). The giant organ is a claim for a civil relation of care that links the elite clinic to the mass camp through the surgical cultivation of expertise: through the ethical. What I am suggesting is that the giant eye on Cathedral Road *in its iconicity* extends the relation between medical capital and civic virtue, offering the clinic as civic gift and winking to the metonymic governance of the mass body.

THE PUBLIC ORGAN

If the organ finds its way into the monumentalization of civic aspiration in Chennai, it also comes to mark other forms and affects of belonging. Lisa Mitchell has chronicled the shift of language ideologies in South India over the late nineteenth and twentieth centuries, enabling an emergent conception of the purified and ordered regional language to become the ground of subject formation, productive of intensities of affect (2009). If the regional alphabet and the body can be read as homologous grids of literate citizenship, Mitchell's argument about self-sacrifice (as an affective response to the perceived insult to the regional language) can be extended to the metonymic chain of bodily organs.

I have earlier written about an imagined sacrifice I heard of more than once in an Ayanavaram housing project in Chennai, in the wake of the widespread publicity since the late 1980s of periodic kidney-selling scandals, referring to the late Tamil Nadu chief minister M. G. Ramachandran (or MGR), who died, notably, of kidney failure. In Mitchell's analysis, the passionate experience of language extends to self-sacrificing violence incited by the untimely death of the leader of the new linguistic states. If I had known what a kidney was, went one form of the imagined sacrifice relayed to me, I would have given a kidney to MGR. Or in another instance, more extravagantly offered and yet demanding a reckoning, I was told that "I would have given him *both* of mine" (Cohen 1999). The moment of such an unexpected gift was sometimes framed, given the structure and incitement of my interviews, just after an acknowledgement of bodily illiteracy: that "I did not then know about the kidney." If a marginal subject of the order of language and the body was denied the virtue of the gift because of her non-cognizance of the parts of this order, the publicly elaborated narrative of kidney-selling nonetheless substantializes her imagined gift.

These women had, according to widespread media and scholarly accounts, *sold* a kidney: that is why we were meeting. But their accounts of the circulation of the organ framed it as a particular kind of *gift* relation necessitating a prior money exchange. What they called the "kidney operation" was a sacrificial gift by which the money from the organ's sale reanimated the possibility of everyday care for children, parents, spouses, and themselves. The recipient of the "real" organ was usually not central to this exchange. In fact, the act of imagining a sacrificial gift through the monetization of the kidney extended far beyond participants in the organ market.[12]

The situation of selling an organ is rendered inordinately shameful for those having the operation, in part by the transnational scale of the audit apparatus examining and troubling the malfeasance of the transplant clinic (and including numerous anthropologists like myself). The ubiquity of accounts linking the seller's recognition of the organ to a life-saving gift to the leader ("I would have given him both of mine") served to recode the kidney and its scar not as a track of shame but— shorn of confusion—as the fleshly ground of an actual order of care.

I have argued that decades of family planning incentives have rendered sterilization an ever-present figure, which functions differentially across differences of gender and religion, to mark the future of any body forcibly inserted into the mass body (Cohen 2004b). Family planning has long promised the future through surgery: it has long been entangled with planned development and its expectations of modernity. The promissory structure of the development state has in many places eroded: its dreamworld of mass utopia, to borrow from Susan Buck-Morss, lies in fragments (2000). But surgery's relation to that promise—the possibility of carving out a future by submitting one's mass body to the clinical disposition of the camp, and the fear, especially for men, that such an act is castrating—appears reanimated in the promise of the kidney operation, in conversations I again and again encountered: "Maybe I'll sell my kidney...." This reanimation brings different parts and different surgeries together—the surgery of the development state and the surgery of its aftermath, the "family planning operation" and the "kidney operation"—but its confusion is not an effect of illiteracy but of the challenging conditions of hope and of virtue.

If, again and again, men in Chennai either asked about the emasculating effects of kidney surgery or explained their failure to achieve the same degree of sacrificial commitment as women in these neighborhoods, they described a particular relation *in time* to debt and economic marginality. Both women and men described thinking about the possible dangers and apparent benefits of the "kidney operation."

Most women with whom I spoke had earlier had the "family planning operation." It was a familiar feature of a life course and a condition for relative autonomy in financial and kin relations. The *time* before surgery these women spoke of was a time to talk with other women who had had this second surgery. For men, this sense of available time was framed in terms of a far more anxious spiral, allowing for a worrisome sense of the emasculating risk of such operations to return to thought. To put it differently, it was as if the recurrent publicity of the kidney operation opened up the feel of the Emergency and its gendered legacy of camp vasectomies, and allowed these to descend into the everyday. Most of these men were too young to have experienced that earlier moment of coercive family planning. The doubling of the operation at stake for men here is not a traumatic return.

For both women and men, these *surgical* conditions of imaging care and the limit to care in the age of intensive transplant publicity call to mind and into conversation other operations and other parts. I am terming *metaphoric* the challenges of attending to these other parts, as earlier and in some cases ongoing moments of state family planning policy make unexpected demands on a body and its future. What is at stake is not a proper ordering or combination of parts, but rather the conditions of thinking and living through forms of surgical governance in which operations double and parts address one another in compelling, if at times differentially gendered ways.

THE DEATH OF THE LEADER

MGR's death, and the deep affects it called into public suffering, was organized around a then emergent category of kidney failure. I term kidney failure (and more generally organ failure) emergent not because this conception of death due to the cessation of organ function was at the time particularly novel. Rather, I want to suggest that this rendering of dying due to organ failure becomes an available language for death to the extent that one is in the position of imagining one's life extension through the replacement of failing organs by transplantation.[13]

We might term this condition of being able to imagine one's own death or that of another in terms of organ failure a question of one's *supplementarity*. To be supplementable, in this sense, is to live in a condition of simultaneous lack—one is a metonymic collection of failing parts—and surplus—one has the ability to make claims upon the parts of others. The woman who offered MGR *both* of her kidneys suggested that the body of the leader may come to evoke a particularly intense kind of supplementarity in the age of the transplant. I met a man in a park in Bangalore who had started a nongovernmental organization to help low-income recipients of a kidney afford the costly medication preventing organ rejection. His own motivation for this civic virtue was his having purchased several kidneys in succession to keep himself alive. "I'm the man with four kidneys," he told me.

Over the first decade of the twenty-first century, the deaths of political figures have been increasingly framed in terms of organ failure. What may have been striking in the moment of MGR's death is now ubiquitous. But there has been a shift in the available language of political death.

One term that has circulated widely in clinical-political reportage has been *multi-organ failure*. Thus, the death of longtime chief minister of West Bengal, Jyoti Basu, was reported through close attention to his progressive multi-organ failure. In Basu's case, his presumptively collectivist commitment as a Communist leader was underscored by the widely noted fact that he had pledged not just one but most of his organs to help unknown others. Here the supplementarity of the leader could enact and mirror the supplementarity of the people.[14]

In other cases, the new figure may do different work. It has entered the language of interparty relations, as when the Hindu nationalist Bharatiya Janata Party, or BJP, attacked the energy policy of the governing coalition as a severe case of "multi-organ failure" ("Check Out" 2006).

Perhaps the most publicly watched political death ascribed to multi-organ failure was that of Pramod Mahajan, a rising star in the BJP gunned down by his own brother. Mahajan hung onto life for several days, and extensive reports detailed the damage of the bullets to each of the several involved organs. Detailed body charts appeared in newspapers, the metonymic assemblage of parts reminiscent of footpath pedagogy. When some years later the late Pramod's brother and murderer Pravin was allowed out of prison on furlough to visit his wife and children, he suddenly succumbed to an illness and died. This death was also and somewhat uncannily named in the media as multi-organ failure. If the metonymic display of parts in the first brother's death conveyed a desperate sequence of pathological events as one after another organ appeared to fail, in the latter death it seemed in its multiplicity to cover up a more specific cause of death: rumors abounded.

Death by its nature usually involves the "failure" of multiple organs. The question of the term's growing ubiquity, particularly in standing in for the death of the leader, conveys a shift in reality: what once went without saying becomes a meaningful account of the end of life for public figures.[15] I have suggested that this shift is in the broadest sense tied to the possibilities of life extension through the transplant organ for those able to mobilize access to clinical diagnosis, treatment, and supplementation by the parts of others. That the dying leader becomes a site where the language of organs intensifies—from the gift of "both of mine" to the ubiquity of multi-organ failure—reflects these distributed conditions of supplementarity. The availability of the diagnosis of organ failure, let alone the availability of the transplant organ and the medication needed to accept it, is globally distributed to a relative minority. Organ failure, in this distributional context, is a kind of privilege, or as I have been putting it, a supplement, a condition of lack that at the same time suggests the possibility of excess, of being able to claim the organs of others. In the figure of the supplementable leader, the outsized, excessive nature of this claim meets its match, as it were, in a form of contemporary sovereignty marked as itself excessive.

If the rise of "multi-organ failure" as a figure both of sovereign excess and its biological limits continues to have traction, it may mark a development in how the political relation of leader to citizen can be thought. The MGR of tomorrow will need far more than your kidneys. The pedagogy of multi-organ failure reaches beyond that population for whom death has already become the medicine of replacing organs. It reaches toward the mass body, extending that body's imaginable sacrifice. Against the new figure of death—the body of the leader that can be rendered as a metonymic collection of organs, each necessary to the life of the state, awaiting supplementation—there is the other body, the body that in its operability, its "confused" metaphoric condition in which one organ comes to stand for another, becomes available as biological surplus.

On the other hand, in the face of the intensive publicity of transplant sales, audits, and scandals, talk of the "kidney operation" becomes a widely available way for a marginal subject to imagine or to fear a different kind of future, not through organ failure but through an operation that *promises* to turn one's organ into money and thus into a host of possible gift relations to kin and to others. The erstwhile promise of the development state, bound up in government medicine and the underside of its mass utopia in the technocratic demand for family planning, finds itself uncertainly inhabiting the sacrificial potential of surgical monetization. Far in excess of the actual giving over of the kidney to surgery, it is the imagined sacrificial gift of the organ, in the fullness or sometimes the horror of its potentiality, that has become a mass phenomenon.

NOTES

1. The provenance and authority of such a claim, moving virally across Internet-based financial website reports (see, for example, Value Pick 2010 and Gireesh 2011) may be questionable. Many other claimants to top profitability have been asserted during the decade of the 2000s. At the least, Dr. Agarwal's has been effective in mobilizing information for investors through new media. In fact, its distinctive eye-shaped building often appears on the Internet in conjunction with its financial data. The conjunction draws upon technologies of display in the hotel and hospitality industry (Cohen 2004a: 89), linking innovations in architectural form (in particular, the rise of the category of the "boutique hotel") to Indian medicine's increasing feel for the global. Whether or not Dr. Agarwal's is or remains the second-most profitable Indian hospital chain, its pattern of intensive capital investment—with the exponential growth of new Dr. Agarwal's clinics across South India over the decade of the 2000s—mirrors that of the leading private hospital group, Apollo.

2. Interviews with clinicians and with commercial artists were conducted in Varanasi in 2004 and 2011. Artists drew upon academic training or apprenticeship in their conventions of representing clinics as body parts. The mode of authorship of these signs bears some resemblance to Prasad's discussion of the "subsumption" of artisanal labor in the film industry (1998), though I am not making a conceptual claim for subsumption in these cases.

3. That I was recognizably white and foreign determined in some measure the emergence of the figure of illiteracy in these interviews, often quite explicitly. Thus, in response to my enquiry, during the course of a longer conversation or formal interview with a clinic director, about the visual icon on the clinic's hoarding, I was often told some version of the following: you see, here *you* must understand that many patients are not literate, unlike the West, and so *we* must organize our practice around their needs. But the figure of illiteracy, as I will suggest below, far exceeds its immediate reference in such moments to my own partial embodiment of the West.

4. In a related species of the time scale produced by humanitarian governance, Arjun Appadurai writes of the "project time" by which government and nongovernment organizations attempt to intervene in the life of the urban slum, here in Mumbai: Appadurai famously terms the refusal of this time by an assemblage of slum-based organizations a "politics of patience" (2001). As I note below, the time of the health camp, though it may draw upon the short-term horizon of project time, is usually famed as a circular and iterative form of gift, something that performs the relationship constituting civil society as a *perennial* gift of care from the middle class to the very poor.

5. The term "punctuated time" is from Guyer (2007).

6. The daily listings for the city and town found in local newspapers provide one measure of this *public* gift of the camp. Through the 1980s into the present, the period over which I have followed these listings in Hindi and English newspapers in north India, they have been dominated by announcements for the varied health camps offered that day and including a mention of the donor organization.

7. Prentice's earlier 2007 formulation has more recently turned to the work of Mahmood (2005) in developing this conception of ethical *habitus*.

8. In this reading of Tarlo I am drawing on the work of Das (2004).

9. These were his words as I inscribed them into a notebook some minutes after the conversation. Here and below, unless words have been captured by a tape recording device, I do not use quotation marks.

10. Quite literally: I attended a meeting nearby of a Lion's Club whose charitable activities centered on both the provision of cataract camps and the support of other eye treatments. The Lions are internationally committed to eye care—the organ all but brands their particular fraternalism—but numerous other religious, fraternal, and service groups in Indian cities also provide camps for specific organs, including eyes.

11. Nor do I want to draw primarily on the cultural logic of the icon, for example, to the possibility of the Agarwals' recognition, as they moved south early in the twentieth century from Delhi's Chandni Chowk down to Madras, of a presumptive order of particularly Tamil iconicity (Daniel 1987).

12. For example, among young men I interviewed in the north Indian city of Varanasi, talk of the "kidney operation" came up in relation to imagining their limited economic horizons. The gift relations that sustained families and communities were falling apart: gifts were unaffordable as their fathers' generation had failed to "settle" their families adequately. The example most often used by these men was analogous to a popular 1985 Hindi film, *Saaheb*. In both the film and the discussions by these men years after, a father cannot give away his daughter as he lacks the means to afford the dowry. The son must step in, selling his kidney and using the money to monetize and reanimate the gift of a daughter. This is a double sacrifice as the "kidney operation" somehow emasculates the young man. Note that these men were not then actually considering the operation, but as with the women in Chennai, the kidney as a gift was not set against monetization—the way it is in the elite discourse on ethics in medicine—but in a necessary relation to it.

13. To be in such a position, of imagining one's life extension through the medicine of the organ, depends upon access to the surgical clinic. In the United States, such access for older persons has depended on shifts in Medicare policy that drive overall insurance coverage in late life and remake conceptions of death itself (Kaufman 2010).

14. An earlier anthropology of India, to which I retain some ties, might have rushed to see in Jyoti Basu's declared gift of his organs a classical form, the gift of the sovereign that establishes him as the disseminator at the center of a commonwealth. What is interesting in this vein about the emergent figure of multi-organ failure is that it produces sovereignty, if that is what we can ascribe to political leaders, not as a gift but a counter gift, of the citizen-subject who gratefully offers the politician "both of mine."

15. Multi-organ, or multiple organ failure, is in fact a clinical category that emerges with transformation in the organization of death for those with access to end-of-life intensive care. Intensive care unit (ICU) survival is a problem of the homeostatic management of multiple biological systems, "system" in this sense a legacy of the cybernetic reconceptualization of physiology of the early to mid-twentieth century. Over the second half of the twentieth century and into the current one, conceptions of system failure have proliferated, as ICU technology enables the management of homeostatic crises that would have previously resulted in failure and death. Thus "shock", as it becomes manageable, gives way to a new form of unmanageable system failure, often conceptualized as acute respiratory distress. With the improved management in turn of acute respiratory distress, conditions of failure in the space of the ICU become legible in the 1970s as multiple organ failure (MOF). Over succeeding decades MOF (and later MODS [multiple organ dysfunction syndrome]) became increasingly ubiquitous as a cause of mortality in the critically ill patient. To die of multi-organ failure is to have access to the technology of the contemporary ICU.

However, despite the global reach of the concept in intensive care medicine, death in North America, unlike death in India, is seldom publicized as MOF or MODS. The ICD-10-CM (International Classification of Diseases) does not accept multiple organ failure as a primary classification, and, therefore, the structure of billing and insurance and more generally of clinical accountability does not allow MOF or MODS to emerge as reported causes of death in many countries. Its ubiquity in the Indian public sphere is a striking phenomenon.

REFERENCES

Agamben, Giorgio. *Homo Sacer: Sovereign Power and Bare Life.* Trans. Daniel Heller-Roazen. Stanford: Stanford University Press, 1998.

Appadurai, Arjun. "Deep Democracy: Urban Governmentality and the Horizon of Politics." *Environment and Urbanization* 13 (October 2001): 23-43.

Balachandran, Aparna. "Of Corporations and Caste Heads: Urban Rule in Company Madras." *Journal of Colonialism and Colonial History* 9 (Fall 2008).

Buck-Morss, Susan. *Dreamworld and Catastrophe: The Passing of Mass Utopia in East and West.* Cambridge: MIT Press, 2000.

Chatterjee, Partha. *The Politics of the Governed: Reflections on Popular Politics in Most of the World.* New York: Columbia University Press, 2004.

"Check Out UPA's 'Multiple Organ Failure.'" *Express India,* July 8, 2006. <http://www.expressindia.com/news/fullstory.php?newsid= 70742>.

Cohen, Lawrence. *No Aging in India: Alzheimer's, the Bad Family, and Other Modern Things.* Berkeley: University of California Press, 1998.

———. "Operability, Bioavailability, and Exception." *Global Assemblages: Technology, Politics, and Ethics as Anthropological Problems.* Eds. Aihwa Ong and Stephen J. Collier. Malden: Blackwell, 2004a.

———. "Operability: Surgery at the Margins of the State." *Anthropology in the Margins of the State.* Eds. Veena Das and Deborah Poole. Santa Fe, N.M.: SAR Press, 2004b.

———. "Where It Hurts: Indian Material for an Ethics of Organ Transplantation." *Daedalus* 128 (Fall 1999): 135-165.

Daniel, E. Valentine. *Fluid Signs: Being a Person the Tamil Way.* Berkeley: University of California Press, 1987.

Das, Veena. "The Signature of the State: The Paradox of Illegibility." *Anthropology in the Margins of the State.* Eds. Veena Das and Deborah Poole. Santa Fe, N.M.: SAR Press, 2004.

Gireesh, P. K. "Dr. Agarwal's Eye Hospital to Invest Rs.45-cr in AP, to Open 3 Facilities in Hyderabad Soon." *Pharmabiz.Com.* January 27, 2011 <http://www.pharmabiz.com/PrintArticle.aspx?aid=60881& sid=1>.

Guyer, Jane I. "Prophecy and the Near Future: Thoughts on Macroeconomic, Evangelical, and Punctuated Time." *American Ethnologist* 34 (August 2007): 409-421.

Hansen, Thomas Blom. *The Saffron Wave: Democracy and Hindu Nationalism in Modern India*. Princeton: Princeton University Press, 1999.

"The History behind Creation of Dr. Agarwal's Eye Hospital." *Agarwalhospitals. Org*. 2004 <http://www.agarwalhospitals.org/html/ history.asp>.

Jakobson, Roman. *Fundamentals of Language*. Gravenhage: Mouton and Co., 1956.

Kaufman, Sharon R. "Making Longevity in an Aging Society: Linking Ethical Sensibility and Medicare Spending." *Medical Anthropology* 28 (October 2009): 317-325.

Mahmood, Saba. *Politics of Piety: The Islamic Revival and the Feminist Subject*. Princeton: Princeton University Press, 2004.

Mistry, Rohinton. *A Fine Balance*. New York: Vintage, 1995.

Mitchell, Lisa. *Language, Emotion, and Politics in South India: The Making of a Mother Tongue*. Bloomington: Indiana University Press, 2009.

Petryna, Adriana. *Life Exposed: Biological Citizens after Chernobyl*. Princeton: Princeton University Press, 2002.

Prasad, M. Madhava. *Ideology of the Hindi Film: A Historical Construction*. New Delhi: Oxford University Press, 1998.

Prentice, Rachel. "Drilling Surgeons: The Social Lessons of Embodied Surgical Learning." *Science, Technology, and Human Values* 32 (September 2007): 534-553.

Ravin, James G. "Henry 'Jullundur' Smith's 'Extraction of Cataract in the Capsule': A Landmark Article." *Archives of Ophthalmology* 123 (2005): 544-545.

Redfield, Peter. "Doctors, Borders, and Life in Crisis." *Cultural Anthropology* 20 (August 2005): 328-361.

Schmitt, Carl. *The Concept of the Political*. Trans. G. Schwab. New Brunswick: Rutgers University Press, 1976 [1927].

Tarlo, Emma. *Unsettling Memories: Narratives of the Emergency in Delhi*. New Delhi: Permanent Black, 2003.

Value Pick from Indian Stock Markets. July 28, 2010 <http:// value-picks. blogspot.com/2010/07/dr-agarwals-eye-hospital-ltd-buy.html>.

Zizek, Slavoj. "Carl Schmitt in the Age of Post-Politics." *The Challenge of Carl Schmitt*. Ed. Chantal Mouffe. London: Verso, 1999.

Terrorism, Conspiracy, and Surveillance in Bombay's Urban Cinema

Ranjani Mazumdar

ear, as many suggest, is a response to perceptions of danger that
penetrates social memory, thrives on ambiguities, and generates states
of paranoia. The fear associated with the memory of explosions, bomb
blasts, and other such cataclysmic events is partly linked to our inability to
comprehend, systematize, and judge these sites of conflict. The number of
times we hear about an event and its magnitude shapes our relationship
to paranoia, and technologies of information have played a pivotal role
in making media "events" rule our "present." Television news spectaculars
transform traumatic events in the world into narratives of suspense and
surprise (Lutticken 2006). This is now fundamental to the way the media
functions and it is here that "conspiracy" as a form of narrative with dramatic
explanatory power becomes a convenient intervention, opening historical
wounds to a parade of detail, documents, plans, security discourses, and
technology (Jarett 1999; Christensen 2002; Keeley 1999; Nadel 2002). This
media theater of crisis management depends to a large extent on emotional
geographies of fear, located in the archives of our memory. In the recent
past, conspiracy has entered the terrain of Bombay cinema to dissect and
produce the illusion that the "truth" can be known once the gaps are filled.

I would like to thank Ravi Sundaram, Shikha Jhingan, Shaswati Mazumdar, Shohini
Ghosh, Sabeena Gadihoke, Ira Bhaskar, Kalpana Ram, Ravi Vasudevan, Kuhu Tanvir,
Arjun Appadurai, and Arien Mack for their comments and suggestions.

This essay looks at three films from Bombay that take the issue of terrorism to mediate the landscape of conspiracy, surveillance, and the city. The films are Anurag Kashyap's *Black Friday* (2005), Raj Kumar Gupta's *Aamir* (2008), and Neeraj Pandey's *A Wednesday* (2009). All three films belong to a body of cinema that has emerged in relation to what is now commonly referred to as the Multiplex era.[1] The filmmakers belong to a community of cinephiles and are therefore extremely conscious of and dedicated to their craft (Mazumdar 2010). These twenty-first-century films refer to various terrorist attacks of the last two decades and work with an investigative cartography, staging the city through narratives cluttered with evidentiary details, an aggressive marking and arranging of information, and a constant presence of the visual media as the ultimate arbiter of knowledge. Unlike popular melodramas, the films discussed here open out cataclysmic events through reenactments and precision-style unraveling; in this process a "mobile script" is carved out to mediate the relationship between paranoia and citizenship (Sturken 1997).[2] If the social practice of paranoia is rooted in the belief that the truth is not fully available, then in these films, conspiracy is the form through which the spectator is provided the illusion of comfort and control over contemporary events, the city of Bombay, and history. Conspiracy selectively opens out an archive of memory to frame a city's present, ironing out rival visions of truth for a unified and singular projection.

In his work on the presence of conspiracy narratives in American culture, Gordon B. Arnold suggests that for the ordinary person, conspiracy does not signify a literal or criminal act, but more a generalized perception that people are targets of deception and manipulation (2008: 4). As a cultural narrative and as a mass phenomenon, conspiracy acquires widespread circulation when everyday life is disrupted by a traumatic event. In such a situation, conspiracy emerges as a seductive force since it helps explain complex situations in a simple cause-and-effect narrative. The conspiracy narrative is not a frozen structure in time but a constantly shifting horizon of meaning, that has changed since the early days of the Cold War to the present global context of uncertainty and fear (Arnold: 4). The history of investigative journalism in India, which started in the 1980s, may have provided a template for the consolidation of the conspiracy form. The sensational structure of investigative journalism lends itself to narrative unraveling and disclosure techniques. In the films discussed here, the language of conspiracy is deployed as the organizing template through which urban paranoia, civil disturbance, and political intrigue linked to terrorism find a voice. Central to the unraveling of conspiracy is the appropriation of obsessive surveillance techniques in the cinematic language of looking, mapping, and processing information. The surveillance form caters to a desire for transparency and provides illusory control over traumatic events (Levin, Frohne, and Weibel 2002). But where and how did the city of Bombay get mired in the discourse of conspiracy and surveillance? How does this template showcase the city? Where did all this start? For this, we need to look back at the recent past.

THE ARCHIVE OF MEMORY

The destruction of the Babri Masjid in December 1992 marked a major moment in the subcontinent's history, representing a break with a particular self-image of modern India. The demolition itself as a widely photographed event emerged as a major sign in the construction of a memory archive of conflict. The sixteenth-century mosque located at Ayodhya was the site and subject of a long-drawn dispute with Hindu militants. They claimed it was the birthplace of Ram, over which the mosque had been built. Fueled by the Hindu nationalists, the dispute took a politically ugly turn and on December 6, 1992, a mob of almost 150,000 Hindu militants brought the mosque down (Jaffrelot 2007; Menon and Nigam 2007: 36-60). The demolition was followed by riots in different parts of the country, but the grizzliest effects were felt in Bombay, where almost 2,000 Muslims were killed. In January 1993, a series of bomb blasts at several marked locations in Bombay followed the riots. For many residents, the riots and the blasts have become the temporal mark to divide the city's history into the before and after of 1992–1993.

Anthropologists, historians, journalists, and filmmakers have tried to make sense of the cityscape following the blasts. Thomas Blom Hansen's engagement with the "Muslim Mohalla" in his account of Bombay and the Shiv Sena provides a history of violence within the informal networks of the city. Blom Hansen sees both the 1993 blasts and the decline of Bombay's famous textile mills as critical to the consolidation of a Muslim identity in the city. His vivid description of life in Central Bombay remains one of the most powerful accounts of the city's internal disenchantment and despair (Hansen: 2001). In a somewhat similar vein, Radhika Subramaniam carries out a phenomenology of Bombay's crowd to build a vast archive of terror and suspicion, located in the daily rhythms of the city. The context for Subramaniam's exploration of this "culture of suspicion" is Bombay after 1993 (Subramaniam 1999). Arjun Appadurai suggests a process of "ethnicization" that started with the consolidation of the Shiv Sena in the 1970s and reached its apogee in the post 1992–1993 moment, when Hindu militants pushed for a rewriting of "urban space as sacred, national, and Hindu space" (Appadurai 2000: 630). The desire for a space without Muslim bodies emerged as a specific response to the problem of scarce housing space, and the language of cleansing was conveniently adopted to deal with Muslim presence (644). More recently, Gyan Prakash, in his account of Bombay's "mythic imagination," acknowledges that the riots and the bomb blasts caused considerable damage to the city's cosmopolitan ethos (Prakash 2010). Bombay cannot but address the transformation of the city after the events of 1992–1993. It is as if the city has been marked forever.

The demolition of the mosque itself as an event of medieval intensity resulted in an almost unmanageable archive of photographs, documentary footage, and television news—all of which continue to circulate via print to video, television to the Internet, and persist as a spectacular memory of the recent past. The presence of saffron flags atop a solid mass of architecture, the unruly crowd gathered all around, images of destruction after explosions and riots in various parts of the country, men holding swords, pictures of political leaders: these images are now firmly ensconced, stoking speculation, anger, hatred, bewilderment, and even complete apathy. This complicated weave of images has congealed into a "technology of memory," playing an important role in the power dynamics of memory production (Sturken 1997: 10). In her fascinating work on the production and constant transformation of memory linked to the war in Vietnam, Marita Sturken writes that recognizing the "changeable script" of memory today is crucial to understanding its cultural function (1997: 17). For Sturken, camera images have a special power to hold and contain memory and in this the still photograph is particularly potent.[3] However, it is not just the camera image's ability to contain memory that makes it significant but also its role as a producer of memory. As I have already noted, the vast archive of photographic and video images on the demolition of the Babri Masjid and the violence that followed circulates across diverse media formats. It was produced immediately after the events in almost every magazine and newspaper cover. Islamic and Hindu fundamentalist groups have also used the demolition in propaganda videos and pamphlets to voice opinions against each other. Dislodged from its original moment of production, the visual force of the demolition now circulates freely and is reproduced whenever the subject is discussed. Given that the site has been embroiled in a court battle for a long time, photographs of the mosque that once stood in Ayodhya are frequently placed in some news item every now and then. Only recently the controversial court verdict by the Allahabad High Court (September 30, 2010) brought the images back into circulation, including those of destruction. The three-member bench ruled that the land should be divided three ways between the three groups involved in the dispute (Roy 2010). Today, the photographic account of the demolition and its aftermath remains a powerful sign of destruction that can stoke a range of passionate responses.

Memory archives write the present in complicated ways. Feelings of loss and bewilderment, anger and humiliation can get channeled into sites to evoke a density of narratives that get attached to the memory archive. No archive is unified and singular in its affective force field. Riots, terrorist attacks, and bomb blasts become attached to the memory archive when they are described or discussed in newspapers, magazines, television, and on the Internet. Bombay has witnessed a series of terrorist attacks since the demolition. The first reaction came in the form of 10 blasts in March 1993, which killed 300 and injured more than 700. In July 2006, seven bombs rocked a suburban train in the city, killing 174 people and injuring more than 300. In November

2008, the city witnessed more than 10 coordinated shooting and bomb attacks, including the three-day terrorist takeover of the Taj Hotel in South Bombay. This event was televised globally and a documentary based on the surveillance footage accessed later, now circulates on the Internet. When a city's contemporary history gets marked by such cataclysmic events, the details of which still remain obscure, the events are replayed constantly through an extended memory archive within which all the events appear connected. The paranoid narrative is therefore constituted through a series of such attachments and is one of the ways in which the idea of the "mobile script" can be thought of (Sturken 1997).

The first direct reference to the demolition and its effects on Bombay was seen in Mani Ratnam's *Bombay* (1995). Soon, other films such as Mahesh Bhatt's *Zakhm* (1998) and Khalid Mohammed's *Fiza* (2000) followed. These films have relied on the emotional contour of redemption and Hindi cinema's moral universe to narrate what they saw as a crisis of humanity. In this last decade, the events in Bombay have been deployed to create another kind of paranoid urban cinema. Drawing on both the memory archive for its conspiracy narrative as well as the technological world that has emerged in the thickets of urban life after globalization, this new form of urban cinema deploys the aesthetics of surveillance to evoke an affective world of anxiety. As we will see, various forms of communication technologies are drawn into a new loop of sensations that generate fear, helplessness, and paranoia. In these films the city is not presented as knowable, but as an abyss of decrepitude.

BOMBAY'S TAKEOVER IN BLACK FRIDAY

Anurag Kashyap's film *Black Friday*, based on the Bombay bomb blasts of 1993, was perhaps the first to deploy the structure of a conspiracy film. Largely committed to reproducing the structure of the book authored by S. Hassan Zaidi, *Black Friday* uses real names and places. This became the primary reason for a long delay in its release due to legal worries that the film could influence the 13-year-old trial into the synchronized bomb attacks. That trial ended in September 2006 and the film was released soon after to critical acclaim, receiving favorable reviews both in India and abroad. Matt Zoler Seitz of the *New York Times* described the film as "raw and epic," a mix of "shocking, agitprop-inflected imagery (disfigured bombing victims, police torture of suspects); cool-headed police procedural details; and documentary devices (including numbered, white-on-black chapter titles) and a nonlinear structure that spends the entire second half explaining the origins of the bombers' alienation" (Seitz 2007). Arnab Bannerjee's review in the *Hindustan Times* referred to the film as "passionate throughout, not once making judgmental claims or being irresponsible" (Bannerjee 2007).

Black Friday provides us with extensive shooting of Bombay and tries to recreate the events before and after the 1993 serial blasts. At one level the film is a revenge narrative that shows Tiger Memon and Dawood Ibrahim as the kingpins behind the planned attacks. At another level we have Badshah Khan (Aditya Srivastav), one of the prime accused in the conspiracy, who is manipulated emotionally to join Tiger Memon's gang to participate in the blasts after his working life was destroyed by the riots. There are several other characters in the film, but it is Badshah Khan as the foot soldier who offers the crucial testimony in the film, to open out a terrifying world of terrorism. The investigation of the conspiracy is led by Rakesh Maria (Kay Kay Menon), the principal investigator on behalf of the police. The film is divided into five chapters, each pushing a particular dimension of the conspiracy.

Black Friday also uses terrorism as the template to penetrate the layers of the city and its gangster world. A reviewer of the film in *The Times of India* took special note of how the "camera penetrates through the dark and grimy interiors of a city which is quite literally a tinderbox, waiting to implode anytime. The plot of the 1993 bomb blasts is painstakingly recreated and the long list of characters in the transnational drama, are given body and form" (*The Times of India* 2007) This X-ray-like penetrative quality became the high point of the film, enabled by the presence of characters who take us through various sites with their testimonies. Right from the beginning, *Black Friday's* perceptual economy depends on a form that draws in testimony and witness accounts to galvanize a truth discourse in accordance with the point of view of the police. This discourse relies to a large extent on Khan's account, which in the film becomes increasingly problematic.

Black Friday unfolds like an investigative narrative. The confessions extracted by the police out of suspected terrorists form a visual and aural track through which the conspiracy is accessed. The film begins with such a confession leading up to the blast at the Stock Exchange, and then inhabits the point of view of the police to push the investigation. The police interrogation sequences are shot using a red filter, while the rest of the narrative appears in standard color. This movement and juxtaposition between the interrogation scenes and the larger universe of action that unfolds through the extracted confessions privileges the police point of view. It is in the course of the investigation that we stumble upon Badshah Khan, through whom the entire conspiracy is laid out for the spectator. At one level this is a conventional police procedural form where witness accounts are generated to tightly structure information and details. At another level the movement from scenes of interrogation at the police headquarters to dramatic detailing across the city deploys the aesthetics of surveillance. As the narrative unfolds, we gain access to a powerful terrorist network moving with a camera that literally operates like an X-ray machine, scripting a desire for social and spatial control. In the course of this journey, Islamic signage is liberally deployed: we encounter people reading the namaz, there is conversation about Ramzan, the sound of Qawwali occasionally plays on the soundtrack, and mosques dot the city. The X-ray vision as I use it here is a way of identifying the camera as penetrating through multiple layers of the city. The clutter of the object world does not prevent the X-ray vision from moving aggressively through the thickets of the city.

Badshah Khan willingly becomes a witness for the state after he recognizes and admits to Rakesh Maria that he became a terrorist because of Allah, but soon realized that Allah was not with them. Khan's confessional voice is played over other images and mesmerizes the spectator to embark on a journey with him, to see the chronology of involvement from his point of view. We travel to Islamabad and Dubai; we access discussions on meat and vegetarianism. Khan's voice operates as his memory, to take the spectator to where Khan has already been.

Within the structure of the film, Badshah Khan is witness, interviewee, and narrator all rolled into one. Without this play of testimony, *Black Friday*'s desire to reveal the truth about the conspiracy could not have been achieved. Khan's speech as an act of bearing witness appears in the narrative to lend credence through the power of confession. To confess is to admit to a crime, creating an order of truth telling that has been deployed so inventively in nonfiction cinema. Khan sits in front of Rakesh Maria as his crystal-clear voice takes us on a flashback journey to different sites and spaces. While Khan's testimony is meant for the police officers, his voice is essentially meant to mesmerize the spectators. Kashyap encourages us to engage with the narrative, to look at the scale of the plan that moves beyond borders. Khan's narration of the plan works through a back-and-forth structure where the voice comes and goes. While at one level the voice merges with the world that is being recounted, it is also reinstated as the testimony of a state witness. There is a doubling of truth value as the voice and the visual narration of the past provide two tracks of visual and aural evidence.

Khan's testimony has a travel structure as he recounts his visits to places and narrates times, events, and memories. The narration is dotted with details of training camps, the airlines they traveled by, the hotel where everyone met, issues related to visas, and so on. The narrative is mesmerizing as it collates a soundtrack of Muslim names, Islamic fervor, and Pakistani involvement. We hear what the police wants us to hear and we move through the film inhabiting the point of view of the police. Despite Khan's mesmerizing voice, the method of recall gives the police the authoritative evidence that they are searching for. Factual documentation serves as evidence, but evidence of *what* becomes a fundamental question. Badshah Khan's voice narrates the world of individual responsibility, social context, everyday hardships, and common sense, confronting a charged historical moment along with the mundane. The testimony acquires an emotionally powerful expression, presenting Khan as a figure who stands in for the country's misled and troubled Muslim youth. With this testimony, Anurag Kashyap was clearly hoping to complicate the world of the conspiracy, but the use of the testimony in the service of the police ultimately creates serious tension in the film.

If Badshah Khan's testimony generates a cross-border sweep, the testimony of Asgar Muqadam (Tiger Memon's manager) offers a different account. Muqadam has clearly been tortured by the police. He sits there only in his underpants narrating the actual planting of the bombs. We hear Muqadam's voice as he walks us through the major sites of the city where the bombs have been placed. We see Badshah Khan along with a man named Farukh Pawle, in a car with a bomb, desperately looking for a convenient place to leave the car. We see the stock exchange, the Air India building. We hear the conversation between Farukh and Badshah Khan as they express their anger about the Shiv Sena and their desire to destroy the passport office. The dense crowd of Zaveri Bazaar is laid out as a man named Mushtaq walks through the busy market to park a two-wheeler with the bomb. Muqadam's confession showcases the city through the terrorist plan and the process is laid out quite literally as we move through different sites. Neighborhoods are named, strategies described, and the planners are placed at the heart of the city. Bombay's takeover by terrorists remains overwhelming in these sequences and the ability to paralyze the city with the blasts appears frightening. In a very balanced review, Smita Mitra recognized the implications of the film's structure. For Mitra "the torture sequences taken from Maria's point of view implicate the spectator as we enter the problematic terrain of strategies and mechanisms of evidence and confessions that most police investigations routinely deploy. If the police investigation is the 'protagonist' of the film then clearly Maria is the figure through whom that negotiation is enacted for us" (2007).

The urban map of *Black Friday* is no doubt spectacular. Kashyap used hidden cameras to mount the cityscape, which could not have been done without a careful plan. In an interview on the making of the film, Kashyap recounts,

> We did research to re-create things. I saw the real locations, I saw the actual footage of the films from [the government's] Film Division, I read all the newspapers. I read a book called *Voices* written by Sebastian, a human rights lawyer, looked at lots of press photographs.... It was a difficult film. The most difficult thing was to create 1993 when there were no cell phones, no satellite television

and the latest car was Maruti 1000. We had to shoot on the streets of
Mumbai and avoid all the modern cars.... We had to avoid people
with mobile phones. While shooting in that atmosphere, we had 25
cars of our own. It is worse than making a period film because there
you know you can't shoot here so you go to a place that suits your
script. But I needed the city, so I had to shoot here, at the same time
I had to trim the city. I somehow managed it. I shot mostly from a
top angle and focused on my characters. There was a lot of guerrilla
type shooting where nobody in the city came to know—we shot with
hidden cameras (Kashyap 2010).

Kashyap's narrative confirms the X-ray vision that I see as central to
the strategy of the film. The use of non-stars and hidden camerawork
was also influenced by the strategies adopted in sting operations.[4]
Kashyap was determined to map the city as a character and in several
conversations emphasized how Bombay had never been captured on
film like it had been in *Black Friday*. The ability to move through a
dense landscape of architectural and human mass, television and radio
technology, lavatories and garbage, to unearth the men behind the
conspiracy, marked *Black Friday's* X-ray vision. Perhaps the best example
of this remains the six-minute chase staged in the film when Imtiaz
Gawate is arrested. A cop team arrives in Central Bombay after a prisoner
names Gawate during the interrogation. They start questioning various
people to pick up clues on the whereabouts of Gawate. This search soon
results in an extended chase through squalor, wires, alleyways, water
pipes, underground tunnels, train tracks, and more. The soundscape and
the kinetic carving out of diverse perspectives to map the chaos and
density of Central Bombay is indeed quite spectacular. A tired Gawate is
finally picked up, slapped, and taken away for what is perhaps the most
brutal form of police torture. The chase exists in the film as a marker of
this desire for a penetrative vision, a scanning of spatial density to pick
up the body that will be brutalized for more testimony and confession.
No matter how dense the space is, the cops manage to penetrate the
layers and the camera strives to capture this process of unraveling.

The sensorium of *Black Friday* is accentuated by its powerful
soundtrack. While the musical score is deployed to enhance the

seductive universe of the conspiracy, the soundtrack also contains audio produced by television and radio to mark the time of the events. Each testimony offers an account of the conspiracy and as we move through the film, the voice is dislodged from the body of the speaker, independently producing information on global financial transactions, RDX (colloquially referred to as *kala sabun,* which means black soap), smuggling, the underworld, Islam, Pakistani camps, and more. The combined effect of strong visuals and a mesmerizing soundtrack adds to the roaming surveillance style of the film. Kashyap felt the film's power lay in its assemblage of all the men responsible for heinous crimes against the state and the web they got caught up in. Kashyap felt no one was singled out by the film, everyone was interrogated— the conspirators, the victims, and the powerful network of the police (*Hindustan Times* 2007). This supreme confidence in being able to put the whole story together "objectively" remains the fundamental problem with *Black Friday.* Despite Kashyap's belief that the film indicted everyone, Rakesh Maria remains the figure who processes all the information produced by the investigation. The fascination for the details of the conspiracy and the step-by-step account of the plan, accessed via testimonies produced after torture, reaffirms faith in this conduct of the police. All uncertainties and difficult questions are ironed out, and detection is accorded a special place. The X-ray vision with its powerful intensity makes the prisoners turn their life into a form of public spectacle and by default become accomplices in the surveillance tactics of the police, the filmmaker, and the spectators.

THE ARCHAEOLOGY OF THE STEREOTYPE IN AAMIR

If *Black Friday* directly engages with the conspiracy behind the 1993 blast, *Aamir* is located in the present, in a world that we can now refer to as post-1993. Directed by Raj Kumar Gupta, *Aamir* is the story of a Non-Resident Indian (NRI) doctor from London named Aamir Ali (Rajeev Khandelwal), who arrives in Bombay to meet his family. At the airport he experiences discrimination at the hands of a customs officer, who gets his bags checked three times. If his name was Amar, not Aamir, would the officer do the same? asks Aamir. This opening stages the rising conflict in the city and the "culture of suspicion" that operates in everyday life. The airport sequence plays out the Hindu–Muslim divide and we assume the film is now going to engage with these issues. However, as soon as Aamir exits from the airport, he is drawn into a nightmarish experience in which he is the sole "good" Muslim up against a hidden and powerful Islamic network in the city. Aamir's family has been kidnapped and for their release, he must perform a role for the terrorists and plant a bomb in a crowded bus. Like in *Black Friday,* we enter the interior world of the conspiracy, which is masterminded for the spectators by the Muslims of the city. However, unlike *Black Friday,* Aamir's world is an entirely Islamic world with no representatives of the state mediating the conspiracy.

The moment Aamir steps out of the airport, a cell phone is handed over to him by two unknown men on a bike. Thereafter he is constantly tracked by an ominous voice on the phone. While Aamir can only hear the voice, we as spectators can see the anonymous caller on screen, framed in expressionist style shadows, the face revealed only partially. This is the Kingpin of the terrorist network, whose powerful control of the city is made explicitly clear throughout the film. In a dramatic moment staged at a restaurant where Aamir has been asked to wait, we hear the cell phone ring. The sound of the ring electrifies the atmosphere and there is palpable tension on Aamir's face as he picks up the phone. The Kingpin on the other side issues some instructions and a reluctant Aamir comes out with the phone to buy dry fruits at a local store. When Aamir tries to stuff the dry fruits in his pocket, the Kingpin asks why he is not eating what he has bought. A bewildered Aamir looks around wildly to see several people talking on cell phones. The protagonist is trapped by the cell phone, his every movement watched and communicated via all Muslims who have the phone in their possession. We follow a bewildered Aamir through a decrepit urban landscape as he tries to make sense of all the instructions given to him by the voice on the phone. The network expands when Aamir is asked to call Karachi. Next, he encounters a prostitute who speaks with a Bengali accent, clearly marking Bangladeshi Muslims and their presence in Bombay within the network. Video images of Aamir's kidnapped family are revealed to him on the screen of the cell phone. The film plays with the ring of the phone throughout, creating a soundscape of cellular technology—the ominous threatening voice of the principle Kingpin and the ambience of traffic. The city is overwhelmingly under surveillance, not by the state but by the Muslim terrorists. They possess the All-Seeing Eye, the omniscient gaze, and a network of committed members who are working toward a revenge on the system. The figure of the terrorist is given a voice that is even more threatening as it pervades the film via phone conversations.

In establishing this network the filmmaker accesses spaces of Bombay through two stereotypes of Muslims in South Asia—that of food and filth—both deployed to convey the emotive charge of "disgust." In his philosophical treatise on disgust, Winfred Menninghaus writes that "the fundamental schema of disgust is the experience of a nearness that is not wanted. An intrusive presence, a smell or taste is spontaneously assessed as contamination and forcibly distanced" (2003: 1). Gupta plays out this logic of "disgusting nearness" by forcing Aamir and, by the same logic, the spectator, to confront the city's squalor identified in the film with the Muslim community. The form of observation is decidedly tactile, with Aamir forced to walk through sites where he can smell, hear, and touch that which is perceived as "disgusting." As we watch in horror and fascination, a parade of stereotypes unfolds on screen. Almost every serious response has expressed discomfort at the use of the social and cultural landscape in the film. Shohini Ghosh saw a double purpose in the depiction of urban squalor: to educate Aamir on the plight and living conditions of Muslims and to show how this congested space operated as a "hostile panopticon" monitored by "seen and unseen eyes" (2009). Aarti Wani and Kuhu Tanvir have also referred to the hostile presence of the Muslim crowd and the grotesque usage of eating habits to articulate cultural difference (Wani 2009; Tanvir 2010). There are some moments that remain more troubling than others.

In one sequence the protagonist is led to a toilet across a *chawl* area and we see him enter the filthiest possible makeshift bathroom, where the stench makes him sick. Aamir finds a little note tucked in the wall of the toilet. When he takes it out we can see his face contorted as nausea overwhelms him. Aamir finally runs out, and in a long shot we see him vomiting in the middle of waste and garbage. Raj Kumar Gupta's desire to touch the senses was part of his shooting strategy. Rajeev Khandelwal recalls how during the shooting of the toilet sequence, "the entire crew was wearing medical masks because the stench was so strong" (Rajendran 2009). Not only does this showcase a typical NRI nightmare, the sequence also makes filth a visible sign for the representation of Muslim spaces. The same strategy is adopted in the hotel where Aamir is made to wait in a room. The hotel is architecturally Islamic, has decaying walls, windowless rooms, and sinister looking men. Aamir is taken to a room where the television seems incongruous. A tray full of food is brought into the room and the sight of meat combined with the claustrophobia of the room adds to his sense of despair.

Like filth, the play with food is equally revolting. The unnamed Kingpin is constantly presented with piles of food. The camera deliberately plays with close-ups of meat while the sound of chewing is highlighted on the audio track. The film appears to revel in this grotesque ensemble, completely oblivious to the stereotypes it is mobilizing. These sequences are repeated often and the discourse of food itself is strategically located to establish the iconography of a community (Tanvir 2010). The most troubling sequence, however, showcases Aamir's walk across a butcher's alley holding a red suitcase with the bomb. A song plays on the soundtrack, intercut with close-ups of raw meat being chopped. The cold faces of men with their cloth caps are placed behind the carcasses. The walk is stylized and the association of butchers and butchery with a community is made quite directly. This sequence in particular draws on the aesthetic power of disgust, which relies on the simultaneous ability to repel, captivate, and enthrall the spectator. The affective charge of disgust has played a critical role in the workings of the social world we inhabit. Disgust usually has a physical and fleshy quality and is generated through experiences of touch, sight, smell, taste, and sound. As some have argued, both disgust and contempt play a role in reinforcing social hierarchy. Modern democratic structures rely far less on tolerance and respect, and much more on the widespread circulation of contempt. Disgust operates through the schisms of daily life, and functions with a supreme confidence in the belief that the lower order smells and pollutes. When this takes an extreme form, the threat to democracy becomes a potent force (Miller 1997). *Aamir's* director, Raj Kumar Gupta, expressed no qualms in playing with such feelings of disgust. Gupta wanted to show Aamir's isolation from the larger community and the use of primitivist iconography to distinguish between the educated Muslim and the others seemed important to him (Raj Kumar Gupta 2009). This marking of locations inhabited by the Muslims in *Aamir* produces space as diseased and terrifying through a carefully crafted geography of filth, decay, and garbage. Space is structured to cry out for action and cleansing, and Aamir's predicament in the midst of this horrifying landscape of enveloping space only adds to such an appeal.

Aamir's filmic strategy is a dense accumulation of crisis images to feed a spectator implicated in a paranoid visual economy. The methods adopted for such a strategy were quite inventive. Alphonse Roy, a wildlife photographer, was hired to shoot for the film. Roy drew on his own skills and used telephoto lenses from a distance where the crowd could not see the camera. Given that Khandelwal was not so well known, he was asked to mingle with the crowd. This would not have been possible with a big star, so having an unknown face helped set the design for the urban landscape. Roy used two cameras: one for the close-ups and one for the long shots. This allowed him to carve out Bombay's urban blight as well as showcase the despair writ large on Aamir's face, creating the desired field of affect (Roy 2009). It was this combination of the un-selfconscious crowd (not knowing that a camera was looking at them) with a demoralized Aamir caught in a network of surveillance, that generated a terrifying experience of fear. As Zygmut Bauman says,

> Fear and evil are Siamese twins; you can't meet one, without meeting the other. Or perhaps they are but two names of one experience— one of the names referring to what you see or what you hear, the other to what you feel; one pointing "out there" to the world, the other to the "in here" to yourself. What we fear is evil; what is evil is fear (2006: 54).

Perhaps the biggest fear today is the fear of insecurity, which results in the endless pursuit of protection and the search for security. The inability to provide that full security and freedom from all fears feeds the language of insecurity and the demand for more surveillance technologies. The mapping of space in *Aamir* is paradoxical—the surveillance mechanism appears to be in place, but it is in the hands of the Muslim terrorists. They can see and track, navigate and plan, terrorize and be ubiquitously present. This is where the technology of vision meets the evil of terrorism, defining and marking space as we move through Bombay's by-lanes. In *Aamir,* the terrorist conspiracy invades Bombay, producing the ubiquitous paranoia for greater control of spaces marked as "other".

THE CORRIDORS OF POWER IN A WEDNESDAY

Like *Aamir, A Wednesday* (Dir.: Neeraj Pandey) deals with one day in the life of Bombay. The sequence of events gathers intensity in a narrative that showcases the point of view of both a police officer and a "common man" who takes to vigilante action. *A Wednesday* also boasts of performances by two veteran character actors, Naseeruddin Shah and Anupam Kher, both products of the National School of Drama and both known for their acting skills. Drawing these two stalwarts into the film, the director situates them as opponents who at heart believe in the same thing. An ordinary man sick of his life of fear decides to take the law into his own hands. Imagining himself as a vigilante, this unnamed "common man" (Shah) challenges the cops to a game in which the ultimate targets are the jailed terrorists who, according to him, continue to operate from their prison. The cops do not seem to have an adequate plan to fight terrorism and so the "common man" decides to act. He settles down with his cell phones, SIM cards, and a laptop on the roof of a half-constructed building to proceed with a plan.

Prakash Rathod (Kher) is the commissioner of police, who gets a call from the "common man" demanding the release of four militants in exchange for information on bombs that have been planted in various parts of Bombay. At first, Rathod thinks the caller is a prankster, but soon changes his mind when the bomb planted right opposite his police headquarters is found. Soon, a cop team swings into action (along with a computer hacker) to help track the location of the anonymous caller. The suspense builds and finally Rathod agrees to hand over the militants. It soon transpires that the common man himself wants the militants dead and masterminds blasts to have them killed. The cops bypass the law in an extraconstitutional move to hand over the militants. At the end of the film, the common man talks about the plight of the ordinary citizen. Unlike *Aamir* and *Black Friday*, *A Wednesday* does not take us through the alleys of the city. Instead, the view of the city is deliberately refracted through surveillance technologies, television, and police headquarters. *Black Friday* is an investigative return to an event, *Aamir* the step-by-step chronicling of a hapless victim's journey across Bombay's dense neighborhoods. The street-level view so central to these films is largely absent in *A Wednesday,* which draws on the stylistic features of the Hollywood conspiracy film much more to chart out the simultaneous unfolding of spaces linked to power.

A Wednesday was received quite well by critics and almost all noted the film's technical finesse and good acting. But there were several who felt a sense of disquiet about the film's moral vision. Khalid Mohammed in his otherwise favorable review for the *Hindustan Times* said, "like it or not, there is in-between-the-lines Muslim thrashing here besides the ongoing obsession of associating terrorism with Islam" (2008). Namrata Joshi's review in *Outlook* said, "It is gripping, terse and well crafted, has a twist that throws you off kilter. But this twist which makes it so distinctive a thriller leaves you deeply disturbed" (2008). Even Nikhat Kazmi, who gave the film four and a half out of five stars, wrote in 2008 that, "One might quibble with the fascist end of the film where the rule of law is given a go by." Disturbed by the vigilantism of the film, Shubhra Gupta ended her 2008 review for the *Indian Express* with the question, "Do we blow up people who blow us up? Does an eye for an eye take us anywhere?" So what is the main problem with the film? Why does it evoke turmoil? The answer lies in the way a dense interplay of information is processed through a panoptical surveillance citadel crafted by a lone figure who is made to stand in for a man of the crowd.

A panoramic view of the city can be seen from the rooftop where the common man sits with all his gadgets. This view is dramatically shot to make him appear like a messiah figure out to rescue the city.

The events unfold in compressed time, filled with action, suspense, and excitement. This common man communicates through the Internet and his cell phone and is in touch with a television reporter, the chief of police, and the police officer escorting the militants. Several spaces and people are drawn into the loop of action: the chief minister, the truck carrying the terrorists, the TV station, the police station, the highly technologized "war room" at the police station. There is a communication network established between these spaces through the relay of phone conversations as we move at a pace across different sites. The "corridors of power" are depicted literally, generating a vision of the city that is refracted through the world of the police, the media, informants, and state functionaries. The constant movement in the film from the common man on the terrace adds to its dramatic pace. The unknown vigilante controls the view of the whole city and successfully masterminds an operation drawing in the government and media. New technologies of information such as SIM cards, the Internet, and the computer provide the vigilante figure access to the corridors of power.

Surveillance, writes McKenzie Wark (2002: 396), is "only one element of an integrated form of power, vectoral power. Its other elements are the capacity to receive and transmit information, the capacity to archive and analyze information, and the capacity to move resources to and from given destinations in a timely and accurate fashion." There are two kinds of vector technologies: one that moves physical objects and one that moves information. The movement from one point to another under specific conditions is crucial to vector technology, which ultimately translates into the ability to order the things one perceives (398). Vector power depends on the quantitative and qualitative transformation of perceived spaces of the world into a resource that is then deployed to order the movement of resources in that world. What emerges in the process is a new world and a plan that can be drawn on a map (399). In *A Wednesday,* we see this attempt to create a new vision of Bombay through a careful relay of bodies and information. As the common man maps a circuit across different spaces through the movement of people in positions of power, the police, the TV crew, and the terrorists, vectoral power combines with the panoptical vision of the city from the rooftop. This attempt at a transcendental position occupied by the common man structures the morality of the film. He is neither Hindu nor Muslim; the common man's worldview is supposedly the vision behind the film.

A Wednesday manages to highlight the communication network of a high-speed society. The *Hindustan Times* review said the film contained "speed, energy and technical dazzle" (Mohammed 2008). The technologies responsible for the flow of information operate like a roving surveillance machine and the pathologies linked to the experiences of a high-speed society are foregrounded in the imagination of the film. The common man's iconic presence operates at several levels. He moves from being an ordinary man of the crowd to a figure in control of the city. The credit sequence at the beginning is superimposed on a montage of typical Bombay shots—a combination of heritage buildings, traffic, overpasses, bridges, the train platform, and the walking crowd. The common man is set up as a figure of the crowd. He walks, takes the train, and has the demeanor of an ordinary middle-class man. This force field changes once he inhabits the rooftop. Now the common man is able to inhabit two orders of experience—both required in any surveillance mechanism. First, he can feel the pulse of the people, knows their anxieties, and their daily experiences. Second, he can play the messiah who is supremely confident about his ability to clean up the city. The nature of this reaction to government impotence and the explanation for extraconstitutional means is situated via a dramatic speech in reply to Rathod's questions during a significant conversation between the two. The speech contains the following lines:

> What do you do if a cockroach enters your house? You do not treat them as pets, you kill them.... I am someone who is afraid to get into a bus or a train these days.... I am someone whose wife thinks he is going to war.... I am someone who suspects the person carrying a rosary. I am also the one who is afraid to grow his beard and wear a cap.... I am just a stupid man of the crowd wanting to clean his house...this has nothing to do with my religion.... I just want to remind you that people are very angry. We are resilient by force, not by choice...the fault is ours, we get used to things quite easily.... Instead of fighting, we begin to get used to it.... But we have our compulsions, we have

to maintain a family. That is why we appoint a government to run the nation. All of you, the government, the police force, intelligence. But you are doing nothing.... Why are you not nipping them in the bud? It takes you ten years to prove a person guilty?... All this has to stop. This whole system is flawed. If you don't clean up this mess then we will have to do something about it. I know this will create an imbalance in our civilized society. The blast was not just a terrorist attack but a question posed by them—We will go on killing you, what can you do? They asked us this question on Friday, repeated it on Tuesday, I am just replying on Wednesday.

It is in this speech that we are provided some clues to the common man's religious identity, even as nothing is literally specified. The speech mediates the emotional terrain of the ordinary citizen's anxieties and becomes critical to the strategy of the film. A reviewer referred to this as a "meticulously worded common man's discourse," which sought to address "every single question that might arise in the audience's mind out of ambiguity, if any" (Malani 2008). This abstract positioning of the "audience" and the "people" both in the film and in some of the reviews elides the structuring of power and paranoia to position the spectator.

A Wednesday presents surveillance as an empowering force to make visible the red tape and delays involved in making the city free of terror. Through the common man's strategic location, action, and dramatic speech we are provided access to a distant world of material resources and bodies, as well as information in constant movement. The movement of the imprisoned terrorists, the television crew, and the police force combines with the flow of information that circulates between the common man, the police, the TV reporter, and the terrorists. The film appears to be in constant motion, the messiah figure placed at a high-altitude position as he monitors and tracks the result of his actions with the help of TV newsfeeds provided by the reporter. Through this figuration of vectoral power, urban paranoia is given a voice, acted upon and played out as an extraconstitutional force and surveillance emerges as a populist "weapon of the weak."

THE TECHNOLOGICAL UNCANNY

The role of technology and new media in the channeling of fear is palpable in all three films. The rhetorical strategy of *Black Friday* is aided by the conscious use of the television as an information machine. Television news is placed within the narrative world as both image and sound, operating as a knowledge-structuring device. Spectators are shown watching TV for news on the riots and the blasts. Its recurring presence in the film operates as a heuristic device drawing our attention to a highly charged soundscape where evidence, causality, and motivation are understood through certain techniques. The constant sound of the news also functions as a unifying device, acting as an imaginary bond. If the Internet and cell phone form the main thread for the staging of action in *A Wednesday*, then in *Aamir* the network that generates the narrative loop is the cell phone. These objects of audiovisual knowledge production generate tension in the narratives, operating as sites of possibility and negative energy. They operate as uncanny mediums without which the films cannot tell their story. At one level they are necessary objects that mark the time, the structure, and the unfolding of events. At another level they produce fear, paranoia, and the uncertainties of life.

A Wednesday uses a PowerPoint presentation to encapsulate within three minutes the scale of the terrorist network. An officer does a presentation for Prakash Rathod with projected photographs of the four terrorists at the heart of the negotiations with the common man. The profiling of the four is authoritatively rattled off at a rapid pace by the officer. The four men are convicts who have not yet been through a trial. The officer's presentation, however, expresses no hesitancy. Rather, all speculation and ambiguities are resolved by a narrative that marks each one of the four within a truth regime generated by the police. The production of details adds to the truth-telling form, the rapid movement of slides displays the hyper-real choreography of guns, freeze frames, crowd scenes, faces, ships, the sea—a random collation of eclectic images. Speculation based on information gathered through surveillance strategies is transformed into a narrative of the factually known. No trial is required here as information is laid out for the police chief and the spectator. It is this moment that makes Rathod take the decision to hand over the four terrorists to the "common man." The officer's speech, with words like jihad, guns, the names of the terrorists, Pakistan, Lashkar, and Al Qaeda, combines with the swishing sound of the PowerPoint to form a sonic effect and an affective tonality of sensations. Fear is given a form, a body, and a force through audiovisual technology and contributes to the creation of an immersive atmosphere of dread.[5] This modulation of affect in compressed time via a complex circuit of emotions that moves across technology, the body, still photographs, and sound design creates a vibrational force that ends up influencing all subsequent decisions. The rapid pace of the film is in fact largely created through a careful management of sonic frequency. Neither the audience, nor the police, nor the media is given much time to reflect. The ability to make quick decisions is made possible with the help of new technologies. The surveillance power of the film ultimately makes the case for an expanded, and yet flexible, notion of the law in the hands of the police (Mukherjee 2009).

All three films produce visual and sensory knowledge as they map the city of Bombay. In this urban cartography, the signs of globalization emerge not from the display of lifestyle images and consumption but through the overwhelming presence of communication technologies. While all three films pose a counter-globalizing cartography, they mediate terror through realist strategies of representation, drawing on the repertoire of the stylistic devices deployed by news programs, reality TV, surveillance cameras, and police procedures. The resultant archive is one in which the urban landscape emerges as a site taken over by Muslims who are desperately in need of social control. Terror in all the films becomes a communication strategy, a social fact that alters our sense of place. Terror transforms regions into landscapes of fear. Viewers are drawn into a cartographic mapping of sites coded by violence, sites that perform their backwardness, their decay, and their crumbling ruin. We are then positioned to speculate about the history of the city. Bombay is presented as a space that demands action on itself, a strategy of cleansing that must first understand the truth about its decay. This is a city deeply affected by the archive of memory associated with the demolition of the Babri Masjid. The spiral of events that followed the demolition opened the city's subterranean geography for discussion, speculation, and intervention. Bombay's recent past of cataclysmic events now haunts these spaces.

The 9/11 attack on the twin towers in New York forms a memory archive that has made us into what Marita Sturken refers to as the tourists of history (Sturken 2007: 7). Through kitsch and consumerist products, the twin towers circulate, feeding contemporary paranoia and fear. The archive of memory linked to the demolition of the Babri Masjid and the bomb blasts that followed find two different articulations in Bombay cinema. The first is the melodramatic form dealing with the emotional texture of conflict, division, and loss. The second is the kind of cinema I have discussed here, where cinematic technology colludes to produce the desire for surveillance and spatial control, drawing spectators into a new way of navigating Bombay. The obsessive translation of a complex situation into a cartography of space, conspiracy, and fear becomes highly problematic as the overwhelming desire to control the city and its Muslims comes to the fore in all three films.

NOTES

1. The Multiplex era is now used as a term to periodize exhibition history. While the multiplex has had a history in other parts of the world since the 1970s, in India, the first multiplex opened in Delhi in 1997. The transformation of single-screen theatres to multi-screen ones has created a situation where different kinds of films are often screened in the same complex. The rise of a new group of filmmakers attempting to break out of a typical "Bollywood" form is located in this period since they can now find a venue at the multiplex. The new form coexists with the typical Bollywood film at the multiplex. The new architectural form of the multiplex has transformed the circuits of production and circulation of cinema.

2. Hindi cinema has historically dealt with Hindu–Muslim conflict through narratives of community and redemption. There was always a line that would not be crossed by filmmakers. It is this boundary that is bypassed in this new genre of films dealing with paranoia.

3. In her analysis of the Hollywood films dealing with Vietnam, Marita Sturken suggests that the experience of the war and its aftermath produced a constantly shifting and mobile script. This mobile form can be accessed across several textual forms that include photographs, objects, films, and art.

4. In March 2001, under what it called Operation West End, *Tehelka*, an independent weekly newsmagazine, conducted a sting operation to expose officials of the Indian government. *Tehelka* reporters used spycams and masqueraded as arms dealers offering bribes to several government officials. They shot their transactions with army officers and friends of the ruling party, finally forcing several people to resign after the expose. For an account of the *Tehelka* sting operation see Mazarella (2006). Also see Tejpal, *The Tehelka Expose.*

5. Sound contributes immensely in the creation of atmospheric ecologies. While we tend to foreground the optical form of cinema, the aural dimension remains equally important, particularly in creating affective regimes of dread, fear, and terror. The films discussed here significantly deploy the soundtrack to generate the sensorium of dread.

REFERENCES

Appadurai, Arjun. "Spectral Housing and Urban Cleansing: Notes on Millenial Mumbai." *Public Culture* 12 (2000): 630.

Arnold, Gordon B. *Conspiracy Theory in Film, Television and Politics.* Greenwood, Conn.: Praeger Publishers, 2008.

Bannerjee, Arnab. *Hindustan Times*, February 12, 2007.

Bauman, Zygmut. *Liquid Fear.* Cambridge: Polity Press, 2006.

Blom Hansen, Thomas. *The Wages of Violence: Naming and Identity in Postcolonial India.* Princeton: Princeton University Press, 2001.

Christensen, Jerome. "The Time Warner Conspiracy: *JFK, Batman,* and the Manager Theory of Hollywood Film." *Critical Inquiry* 28 (Spring 2002): 591-617.

Ghosh, Shohini. "Style and Prejudice: A Reading of Aamir." *Communalism Combat* 15 (September 2009).

Goodman, Steve. *Sonic Warfare: Sound, Affect and the Ecology of Fear.* Cambridge: MIT Press, 2010.

Gupta, Raj Kumar. Interview by author. Delhi, October 28, 2009.

Gupta, Shubhra. "A Wednesday." *Indian Express*. September 6, 2008.

Jaffrelot, Christophe. *Hindu Nationalism and Indian Politics*. New York: Columbia University Press, 2007.

Jarett, Greg. "Conspiracy Theories of Consciousness." *Philosophical Studies: An International Journal for Philosophy in the Analytic Tradition* 96 (October 1999): 45-58.

Joshi, Namrata. "A Review of *A Wednesday*." *Outlook* (September 2008): 86.

Kashyap, Anurag. Interview. Delhi. August 24, 2005.

Kazmi, Nikhat. "A Review of *A Wednesday*." *The Times of India*, September 5, 2008.

Keeley, Brian L. "Of Conspiracy Theories." *The Journal of Philosophy* 96 (March 1999): 109-126.

Levin, Thomas Y., Ursula Frohne, and Peter Weibel, eds. *CTRL Space: Rhetorics of Surveillance from Bentham to Big Brother*. Cambridge: MIT Press, 2002.

Lutticken, Sven. "Suspense and Surprise." *New Left Review* 40 (July/August 2006): 95-109.

Malani, Gaurav. "A Wednesday: Movie Review." *Economic Times,* September 5, 2008.

Mazarella, William. "Internet X-Ray: E Governance, Transparency and the Politics of Intermediation in India." *Public Culture* 8 (Spring 2006): 473-505.

Mazumdar, Ranjani. "Friction, Collision and the Grotesque: The Dystopic Fragments of Bombay Cinema." *Noir Urbanisms: Dystopic Images of the Modern City*. Ed. Gyan Prakash. Princeton: Princeton University Press, 2010.

Menninghaus, Winfried. *Disgust: The Theory and Sensation of a Strong Emotion*. Albany: State University of New York Press, 2003.

Menon, Nivedita and Aditya Nigam. *Power and Contestation: India Since 1989*. New York: Zed Books, 2007.

Miller, William Ian. *The Anatomy of Disgust*. Cambridge. Cambridge: Harvard University Press, 1997.

Mitra, Smita. "*Black Friday*: A Review." *Economic and Political Weekly* 42:16 (April 21, 2007): 1408-1409.

Mohammed, Khalid. "A Wednesday." *Hindustan Times*, September 5, 2008.

Mukherjee, Rahul. "A Reply to Terrorism on *A Wednesday*: A Citizen Vigilante's Prescriptions for Governing Terrorism." *Sarai Reader 08: Fear* (2009): 242-249.

Nadel, Alan. "Paranoia Terrorism and the Fictional Condition of Knowledge." *Contemporary Literature* 43 (Summer 2002): 406-421.

Prakash, Gyan. *Mumbai Fables.* New York: HarperCollins, 2010.

Rajendran, Priya. "I Want to Create a Brand for Myself: Rajeev Khandelwal." *Hindustan Times,* October 31, 2009.

Roy, Alphonse. Interview. Delhi, October 28, 2009.

Roy, Kumkum. "Issues of Faith" *Economic and Political Weekly* 45 (December 2010).

Seitz, Matt Zoller. "Madness in Mumbai." *New York Times,* February 8, 2007.

Singh, Prashant. "Anurag Kashyap: Rebel with a Cause." *India Today,* March 21, 2009.

Sturken, Marita. "Reenactment, Fantasy and the Paranoia of History: Oliver Stone's Docudramas." *History and Theory* 36 (December 1997a): 64-79.

——. *Tangled Memories: The Vietnam War, the Aids Epidemic, and the Politics of Remembering.* Berkeley: University of California Press, 1997b.

——. *Tourists of History: Memory, Kitsch, and Consumerism from Oklahoma City to Ground Zero.* Durham, N.C.: Duke University Press, 2007.

Subramaniam, Radhika. "Culture of Suspicion: Riots and Rumor in Bombay: 1992-93." *Transforming Anthroplogy* 8 (January 1999): 97-110.

Tanvir, Kuhu. "Myth, Legend, Conspiracy: Urban Terror in Aamir and Delhi-6." *Fear: Sarai Reader* 8 (2010): 248-253.

Tejpal, Tarun. "The Tehelka Expose: Reclaiming Investigative Journalism in India" <http://www.taruntejpal.com/TheTehelkaExpose.HTM>.

The Times of India, February 10, 2007.

Wani, Aarti. "Aamir at the Multiplex." *Film International* 6 (2008).

Wark, Mckenzie. "To the Vector the Spoils." *CTRL Space: Rhetorics of Surveillance from Bentham to Big Brother.* Eds. Thomas Y. Levin, Ursula Frohne, and Peter Weibel. Cambridge: MIT Press: 2002, 396-401.

"We Shot *Black Friday* with Hidden Cameras: An Interview with Anurag Kashyap." Rediff India Abroad, February 7, 2007 <http://www.rediff.com/movies/2007/feb/07anurag.htm/>.

"An' You will Fight, Till the Death of It....": Past and Present in the Challenge of Kashmir

Suvir Kaul

THE SITUATION TODAY

On my last three visits to my family home in Srinagar, Kashmir, I have been working with a local scholar to collect and translate recent poetry in Kashmiri into English. Our project is particular: we ask how poets have responded to the bloody disruption of civic and political order in Kashmir in the last two decades. In the winter of 1989, a full-blown insurrection led by heavily-armed and well-trained militants broke out against the Indian government. These militants styled themselves the new cutting edge of a decades-long drive for Kashmiri independence. Some of them acted in order to amalgamate Kashmir with Pakistan, which is what they believed should have happened during the partition of Pakistan and India in 1947. The insurrection precipitated a chain of events that has destroyed peace and normality in the Kashmir valley.

I thank Aijaz Hussain, Tariq Thachil, Ania Loomba, and Sanjay Kak for helping shape this article, and Arjun Appadurai for his editorial suggestions.

Within a year or two of the conflict breaking out, the majority
of the Kashmiri Hindu population fled the valley, and few of them
have returned permanently since. It is safe to say that no one in this
small minority (less than 5 percent of the population) sympathized
with the desire for independence. Some of them were targeted by the
militants and their civilian sympathizers, and the resultant fear caused
the large mass of them to leave. Their flight allowed most Indians
to believe that they were dealing not with a political movement for
independence but with Islamic secessionism, and the government
response was, not surprisingly, heavy-handed and draconian. Further,
state administrators insisted that the militants were fighting a proxy war
on behalf of Pakistan, and refused to acknowledge that this uprising
might have indigenous roots. Many militants were Pakistani and Afghan
veterans of battles against the Soviets in Afghanistan, and there is no
question that the most organized of the militant groups were funded
and trained in Pakistan (Jamal 2009). However, most militants were
young Kashmiri men who crossed the border to join one or the other
of the many groups that formed, splintered, and reformed in the 1990s
and they—as well as civilians caught in the cross-fire—bore the brunt
of the casualties in their battles against Indian forces.

The massive presence of Indian armed forces along the borders—
"lines of control," really, since no nation agrees about their legitimacy—
with Pakistan and China, in addition to the tens of thousands of
militarized police, such as the Border Security Force and the Central
Reserve Police Force, meant that Kashmir turned into an armed camp.
Civil liberties were all but suspended, and in crucial arenas, civilian
authorities were superseded by their military counterparts. Indian armed
forces and agencies routinely behaved like an occupation army that
defines itself as distinct from, and ranged against, the local population.
(As we will see, this opposition is, for historical reasons, understood as
that between Hindu occupiers and a subject Muslim population). For
every militant apprehended or killed, scores of other Kashmiris were
picked up, tortured, or imprisoned on suspicion of being affiliated with
some form of pro-freedom activism. Worse, there were large numbers
of those who simply disappeared, and whose unidentified bodies
now lie in unmarked graves, some of which have been investigated

by human rights groups in the last few years (International People's Tribunal 2009). Also, as is the case with most such militant movements across the globe, conflicts between different groups and factions led to large-scale internecine killings. The government played a role here too, encouraging "surrendered" militants to turn their arms against each other, and enrolling them into loosely regulated, much-feared ancillaries of the uniformed police force (Human Rights Watch 1996; the recent trove of diplomatic cables released by Wikileaks provides unusual corroboration—see the *Guardian* report on December 16, 2010). The numbers of the dead mounted: estimates range from 70,000 to 100,000 killed in the last 20 years. The numbers of those maimed physically and psychologically by this conflict are correspondingly larger.

I offer this bare-bones summary here to make a simple point: there exists no Kashmiri family that has not suffered from the war raging around them. There are material reminders of their suffering everywhere: thousands of gravestones now sprout in fresh graveyards all over Srinagar and other towns in Kashmir, and their inscriptions bear witness to martyrs who have sacrificed themselves in the cause of independence. Hospitals and dispensaries report astonishing numbers of people afflicted with mental illnesses (Wax 2008). In times of conflict, including during the new "intifada" of summer 2010,[1] which featured large protests often fronted by young men keeping up a barrage of stones against the police, these hospitals are barely able to cope with the influx of the dying and the damaged. Local newspapers, magazines, and the electronic media are full of reports of human misery. Various "fact-finding missions" originating in India, and some international human rights organizations, have long documented the military and civil abuses that accompany "crackdowns" (this is the word used locally) on civilian populations. Details of these abuses are not hidden, even if the crisis itself, in spite of media attention in recent months, has not become a definitive political problem for contemporary India or indeed for the international community. A generation and more have come of age in Kashmir knowing only the brutality and the everyday suspicions of a civic order riddled with informers for the state or for anti-state groups, and for many of them it remains incomprehensible why a nation lauded as the world's largest democracy has remained immune to their suffering.

As a literary critic who is particularly interested in the way poetry, that fragile and yet most perdurable of artistic forms, engages with its historical moment, I sought to put together an archive of poems that might offer us another entry point into this theater of conflict. Poets are artisans who are bound by past practices (formal and generic conventions, arresting images or turns of phrase, powerful insights into existential or historical conditions) even as they generate innovations in theme and language that allow them to engage with the present in order to imagine different futures. Poems, that is, can be read as bearing witness to, or more precisely, *performing*, the fracturing or forging of cultural assumptions. In Kashmir, poems have provided a remarkable number of everyday colloquialisms and aphorisms, and have thus long played an important role in the historical formation of *Kashmiriyat*, the idea of a collectivity different from others outside the language-community. For instance, phrases and lines from the poems of the fourteenth-century mystics Lal Ded and Sheikh Nooruddin (Nund Rishi) are treated as maxims, and spoken often enough to constitute the common sense of the land.

While *Kashmiriyat*, as an idea and as a description of shared lives and cultural assumptions across religious communities, has been belittled as a utopian, retrospective back formation that attempts to paper over age-old sectarian and social divides, there is no question that the melding of Buddhist, Hindu, and Muslim ideals provided Kashmiris with a vast reservoir of spiritual ideas at odds with more doctrinaire and prescriptive forms of religious belief. Many of these ideas are central to the Sufi tradition, with its concomitant devotion to local shrines, that differentiates both Muslim and Hindu forms of worship in Kashmir from practices elsewhere (not seamlessly or without contestation, of course, but certainly definitively). Thus, the disappearance of crucial elements of this way of life—the loss of trust between Hindus and Muslims that led to the mass exile of the former; the breakdown of the civic compact under the pressure of militants and the state—is bound to result in poetry that mourns, resists, denounces this state of affairs. At least, that is what I assumed when I began this project in the summer of 2008.

As I discovered very quickly, the scholarly pursuit of poetry is no more immune to the ravages of civic strife than is life itself: in two weeks in Srinagar, I was able to meet and work with my collaborator for all of two days (this has been the pattern in two subsequent visits). Strikes and curfews, public protests and police responses, ensured that no one left home unless it was absolutely necessary. I spent days indoors or on our balcony instead of in conversation with writers or aficionados of poetry, and the sounds that carried occasionally were the slogans and shouts of massed crowds, as well as the sharper retort of tear-gas guns and rifles. Occasionally, wisps of tear gas would float past our home, located as it is on the edge of a volatile neighborhood that has long been a stronghold of the Jammu and Kashmir Liberation Front (one of several political groups allied under the banner of the Hurriyat Conference, which now leads the movement for political self-determination). The musicality, formal cadences, and intelligence of poetry seemed very far away, replaced by the muscular and polarized noise of a violence-torn public sphere. It was fitting then that one of the first arresting poems I read, brought to me in manuscript by a friend, resembled neither of the forms that are the staple of Kashmiri poetry: the *ghazal* and the *nazm*. This is (in our translation) what I read:

> I am bundling the winds
> I am making the night the day, day the night
> I die slowly, steadily, and continue to live on
> I see the desert and pull on the desert
> From my eyes, oh, a river flows
>
> I wouldn't care if they killed me
> Dead, beaten, they keep me alive
> I will come out of here, emerge with renewed resolve
> What will they do to me, these rods and hammers?
> I have, like a tear, left
> Does a tear ever return
> All that I have seen, don't ask me, oh
> Those adored ones, whose flesh was burned by them
> How many did not find graveyards or burial
> How many were burnt on snow-mountains

How do I forget all this
What will their money and adornments do for me

I have sworn oaths on the forests
I have made to gardens this promise
I will keep watering the Spring

Let them make a dog of me in prison
Once I am outside I will become a lion again
Inside, for them, I am just a lump of flesh

We will call this poet Muzaffar "Kashmiri." I learned that he had been in prison for many years without trial, and that he was a *tehreeki*, a member of the movement, who had taken to guns and bombs in pursuit of the dream of *azadi* (freedom). He was educated, but not as a poet—he began to write in prison, and his untitled poem is written in a conversational (rather than literary) idiom. Its immediacy is the product of everyday speech, of a felt urgency, and its certainties are arrived at despairingly, in the face of imprisonment and torture. The poem's contrasts are derived from the representations of nature that are the staple of Kashmiri poetry: the valley is a garden, spring breezes bring life and color, forest canopies dress the high mountains; the desert is the life-denying polar opposite of all that constitutes Kashmiri lives lived in harmony with nature. But in this poem the incarcerated poet knows only paradox—he loses the distinction between day and night, makes the desert his own, draws it around himself like a covering, lives on even when his torturers make death attractive. What follows is the hope brought alive in the act of the poem, the articulation of a further resolve, the refusal to let "rods and hammers" break his will, and all this condensed into a delicate image of no return, the tear that drops, and never climbs back.

Hope behind bars: this is the irony that anchors renewed determination in the fragility, evanescence, and finality of a shed tear. It is important though that the shed tear is not for himself, but part of a collective mourning for all those comrades, the "adored ones," whose flesh was burnt "by them" and who now lie, without proper obsequies, somewhere in the snowy mountains. Their memory, and their sacrifice, is the more certain ground of commitment that allows him to resist the promises and bribes offered by his captors (again, the unnamed "them"). In the next lines, Kashmir itself, or rather, tropes conventional to its poetic self-representation, provide the continuity of memory and commitment necessary for sustained faith in a political ideal:

> I have sworn oaths on the forests
> I have made to gardens this promise
> I will keep watering the Spring

The idealism of these lines veers into cliché, but the closing lines arrest that movement in an idiom, and a reality, stark and brutal:

> Let them make a dog of me in prison
> Once I am outside I will become a lion again
> Inside, for them, I am just a lump of flesh

Both this incarcerated body, beaten into a "lump of flesh," and the unextinguished hope of release and redemption into renewed political activism ("I will become a lion again"), offer a powerful challenge to the political agents and theorists of Indian nationalism in the twenty-first century. Condensed into these last three lines is the egregious and dehumanizing practice of state power, in which the unwilling "citizen," especially one who takes to arms, is captured, tortured, and, in this process, reduced to the brutalized materiality of a lump of flesh. Not everyone in Kashmir is a violent *tehreeki*, far from it, but there will be few Kashmiris who will not sympathize with the scenario and the sentiment explored by this poem. To that extent, it is representative of the collective experience of a people subject to long-drawn-out and often indiscriminate state violence.

COLONIAL CONTEXTS

The scenario of incarceration and torture in Muzaffar "Kashmiri's" poem is familiar from a variety of contexts. It is noteworthy here because it plays out crucial contradictions of the modern democratic, putatively *postcolonial* state. The success of European colonialism meant that subject populations the world over were forced to experience imperialism in its own self-image, as the *modern* form of governance. Not unlike earlier feudal regimes, the imperial state held territories and ruled people via the strategic use (and the constant threat) of violence. It extracted surplus enough to enrich the imperial metropolis and fund the expansion of the colonial apparatus of rule, all the while arguing that such governance was necessary for the extension of the highest form of human development ("civilization") to those not yet within its specific Eurocentric and capitalist historical trajectory. However, the founding rationale for postcolonial and democratic nation-states is the consent of the different subnational communities in whose name anticolonial movements demanded and gained independence. Further, postcolonial democracies are meant to enable more equitable and indeed sustainable forms of development, especially those that will encourage the restructuring of historical socioeconomic and cultural hierarchies, intensified or precipitated by colonial rule.

In practice, as we know, most once-colonized nations (including those which are electoral democracies) continue to reinforce many of the socioeconomic arrangements and administrative and policing functions bequeathed to them by the colonial state. This economic and institutional history lies outside of the scope of this essay, though I have argued elsewhere that such continuities are crucial to the dynamics of contemporary India (see Kaul 2011). This history partly explains the increasingly centripetal and rigid form of nationalism that came to dominate the political cultures of newly independent nations, and it is certainly crucial to understanding the relationship of the Indian state with Kashmir. Postcolonial nations did not, of course, invent this form of militarized patriotism; over the course of the nineteenth century, imperial nations put its ritual, administrative, and civic forms on display in their colonies and celebrated it as the ethical core of modern citizenship.

The formation of colonial "nations" (if territories brought under foreign rule could be called that) also emphasized this sort of centralized military power. As colonial rulers cobbled together territories through conquest and alliance, they reshaped the forms of political collectivity that had defined these territories. Smaller territorial entities ruled by kings, their feudatories, or even large landowners, with poorly defined, porous, and shifting borders between them, were yoked together under a common authority. In many cases, it was the practical limits of colonial authority that demarcated what were to become the borders of new nations. Thus, when anticolonial movements demanded the right to self-determination and political governance, they spoke for a "nation" that was often the product of a comparatively recent colonial history and which contained disparate communities historically unequal in their relations with each other, but now tenuously united in their opposition to colonial rule. In British India, for instance, several communities at the extremities of the new nations of India and Pakistan found themselves, for various reasons, incorporated into these new nations.

At its greatest extent, the British empire in South Asia ranged from its northwestern reaches in what is now Afghanistan to its southern tip in Ceylon (today's Sri Lanka) to its eastern territories in Burma (now Myanmar). Large sections of these lands were not ruled directly by the British. There existed many kingdoms nominally under the control of local maharajas and nawabs, even though all of them were bound in treaty relations with, and existed as vassals of, the British monarch, and several had British Residents supervising their political, military, and civic administration.

Such was the case with the state of Jammu and Kashmir. The modern contours of the kingdom were put into place by the Sikh Maharaja Ranjit Singh of Lahore, whose forces took large territories in Jammu and the valley of Kashmir in 1819, spoils of their successful campaigns against the Afghan Durrani rulers. Three years later, he confirmed one of his highly successful Dogra generals, Gulab Singh Jamwal, as raja of Jammu.[2] By 1840, Gulab Singh's armies extended the kingdom into Ladakh and Baltistan. In 1846, after the British East India Company, victors of the First Anglo-Sikh war, gained control of Punjab, they signed treaties confirming Gulab Singh as the maharaja of Jammu and Kashmir, a state they saw as a buffer between them and the Afghans, Russians, and Chinese. For the British, Jammu and Kashmir was central to their forward-areas policies in the northwest of India, whose mountain ranges, valleys, and high altitude passes they thought critical to their defense against Russian expansion, or even Chinese control of trade routes in Tibet and Ladakh. Thus, between

1888 and 1892, the state's territories were extended into Gilgit, Hunza, and Nagar by troops commanded by British officers acting ostensibly on behalf of Kashmir's ruler, Ranbir Singh (Gulab Singh's son).

This brief outline of the extension of Dogra rule and British authority suggests more clarity of command and control than was the case in these oft-contested territories and their fought-over and poorly demarcated boundaries (for an overview, written largely from the points of view available in British imperial archives, see Huttenback 2004). As a matter of imperial policy, the British had allowed princely states throughout India their formal apparatus of independent governance and revenue collection, while making sure that they maintained British trading, military, and diplomatic priorities. This process often involved considerable give and take between the British and the local ruler, whether it involved the raising of troops, the waging of war, or the setting up of revenue, judicial, and educational institutions within the state. Jammu and Kashmir was no different, with the proviso that its strategic location meant that, in the second half of the nineteenth century, the British were primarily concerned with the fixing and strengthening of the state's northwestern borders. If they intervened in the internal affairs of the state, they did so largely because they believed misrule, especially excessive taxation, would produce social instability that would weaken the state's authority in its border areas (Rai 2004: 142-44).

The most consequential feature of the state of Jammu and Kashmir was the fact that its Dogra Hindu maharajas ruled over a majority Muslim population. This was not in itself unique among princely states in India, where there are many instances of "minority" rulers developing policies that did not differentiate egregiously between their subjects in favor of their co-religionists. However, as Mridu Rai has demonstrated persuasively, the Dogra rulers' policies so derived from (and bolstered) their identity as Rajput Hindus and so resolutely catered to their Hindu affiliations, within the state and outside it, that the Dogra state became, in effect, a Hindu state (Rai 2004: 7). The vast majority of Muslim peasants and indeed, city-based artisans, saw none of the benefits of centralized administration; they continued to live at subsistence levels while being forced to yield both unpaid labor (*begar*) virtually on demand, as well as crippling taxes on their produce. This was not the case with Kashmiri Hindus (known as pandits); no more than 5 percent of the population, they wielded disproportionate power as revenue-gatherers, accountants, civic administrators, and landholders. Pandits had developed levels of literacy that made them indispensable to the lower rungs of the administration (particularly given historically abysmal levels of formal learning amongst Muslims), and this fact, combined with the Dogra emphasis on Hindu affiliates, meant that many pandits functioned visibly as extensions of the maharaja's power. It is another matter that the Dogras excluded pandit elites from the higher administration in favor of Dogras or bureaucrats recruited from Punjab and elsewhere; particularly for the large mass of Muslim peasants, pandits were the Kashmiri-speaking face of state power (Zutshi 2004: 52).

Both Mridu Rai's *Hindu Rulers, Muslim Subjects* and Chitralekha Zutshi's *Languages of Belonging*—books essential to understanding the contemporary crisis in Kashmir—make clear to us the sociology and political force of these social and communitarian divides, as well as their lingering effects into the present. Zutshi develops a careful argument about the growth of political consciousness among Muslims in the last two decades of the nineteenth century and the first two of the twentieth: such political mobilization, even when centered on Islamic community, was, not surprisingly, an internally contested process, as leaders of different groupings derived their priorities from particular regional, sectarian, and socioeconomic affiliations. However, the communitarian "ritual and legal framework" within which all such mobilization was permitted was defined by the Dogra state, and occasionally by British administrators (Rai 2004: 118-121). Zutshi also points out that an important concern of newly politicized Muslim elite, particularly those educated outside Kashmir, was the educational backwardness of the community. Their focus on education had a particular end in view—the creation of teachers or bureaucrats in the state administration—which had systematically excluded Muslims. Inevitably, the rise of educated Muslims seeking employment in these services led to tensions between them and the pandits, who had long presumed on such positions. It was also the case that since Urdu was the official language of the state, no one argued for instruction in Kashmiri, which meant that illiteracy remained an enormous problem, especially in agricultural areas, perpetuating divides between the urban Muslim elite and the rural poor in whose name they claimed to speak (Zutshi 2004: 169-209).

In the 1930s and 1940s, political movements in the state veered between communitarian, regionalist, or pan-nationalist emphases. At different moments, political leaders spoke of a Kashmiri collectivity, ostensibly contained within the boundaries of the princely state, so distinct from political identities elsewhere that it called for its own process of self-determination. At other times, they saw themselves as participants in larger nationalist movements, led by the Indian National Congress or the Muslim League, for independence from British rule. As an example, Zutshi tracks shifts in the positions taken by Sheikh Abdullah's All Jammu and Kashmir National Conference, arguably the most important and mass-based political party in Kashmir, which changed its profile considerably over the course of two decades. During this period, political demands made of the Dogra state for Muslim representation in administration developed (in tandem with anticolonial political mobilization in India) into a movement against Dogra rule and for representative government. By the mid-1940s there was a great deal of debate in Kashmir about the pros and cons of allying local movements against the Dogra state to anticolonial movements in British India, and certainly there were full-blown critiques of the National Conference's policies available, both from those who argued that Kashmiris should pursue their own political ends and from those who argued that Kashmir's future lay with the Pakistan that Muhammad Ali Jinnah's All-India Muslim League was bringing into being (Zutshi 2004: 227-322).

The give and take of politics within and without the state was also shaped by British policies vis-à-vis the princely states (formally enunciated in the Indian Independence Act of 1947), which allowed the possibility that a state like Jammu and Kashmir would not amalgamate with either India or Pakistan once those nations came into being. Such constitutional open-endedness has caused Alastair Lamb, a historian of the Raj, to write that in "one sense the Kashmir problem can be seen as a consequence of the British failure to find a satisfactory method for the integration of the Princely States into the independent India and Pakistan that succeeded the British Raj" (1966: 3). By 1947, even though the strength of people's movements for representative government was clear, as were the ties between Jawaharlal Nehru's Indian National Congress and Sheikh Abdullah's Jammu and Kashmir National Conference, the then maharaja, Hari Singh, hoped to retain his position as the ruler of an independent nation even after the British withdrew as the paramount power in India.[3] Jinnah had in turn visited Kashmir in 1944 and had greatly strengthened ties with the (now revived) Kashmiri Muslim Conference, which allowed this organization to represent an alternative future for Kashmir as part of Pakistan. It was also the case that even as Sheikh Abdullah and Nehru considered themselves allies, there had been no substantial discussion (at least not any that was public knowledge) about Kashmir's future after August 15, 1947. British rule was to end, but there were no certainties about the maharaja's rule in Kashmir, against which the National Conference and other Kashmiri political parties continued to campaign, even though many of their leaders were in jail.

As both Rai and Zutshi make clear, political activity in Jammu and Kashmir had long been driven by connections established between people within the state and their compatriots elsewhere in British India, even though some Kashmiri nationalists argued that they needed to address problems of governance within the state rather than getting caught up in the larger anti-colonial movement. This was even then an untenable idea, as borders, no matter how heavily policed, cannot prevent the transmission of political ideas and policies, and in particular cannot guard against the urgency of momentous current events as they hurtled along at this moment of supercharged social turmoil. The idea of Partition, as we know well, brought along with it the possibility of unprecedented dislocation of populations, as millions of Muslims prepared to move to Pakistan and an equal number of Hindus and Sikhs to India. In fact, these massive relocations were far more frantic and haphazard when they took place, and that frenzy was directly caused by communal attacks, massacres, and riots in different parts of India in the run-up to Independence, as well as just after. A great deal of recent scholarly work has clarified for us the mix of motivated violence (that is, violence arranged by individuals or groups designed to gain land, property, or goods by driving out particular communities) and fearful uncertainty that precipitated these massive population shifts; most immediately, such violence seemed to demonstrate, even legitimize by dramatizing spectacularly, the unbridgeable divides between Hindus and Muslims insisted upon by ideologues of communal difference (Brass 2003; Pandey 2001).

PARTITION LEGACIES

The forced movement of populations as well as the religious polarization confirmed by Partition violence are of great consequence to the history of the last half-century in Jammu and Kashmir. In fact, it is impossible to separate all that happened in 1947 in Jammu province, particularly in Poonch, from the larger mayhem in Punjab, to which of course Jammu was very well connected. Victoria Schofield is the most recent of commentators on the Kashmir conflict to remind us that, in March 1947, an anti-maharaja "no-tax" campaign (tantamount to a revolt) had begun in Poonch. There were particular reasons for this: Muslims from Poonch and Mirpur had supplied most of the state citizens who fought in the British Indian army in World War II (and some had fought against the British in the Indian National Army); when they were demobilized, the maharaja refused to enlist them in his army, and they returned to an oppressive taxation regime enforced by Dogra troops. Further, as communal disturbances broke out in Punjab, and spilled over into Jammu, the maharaja ordered the disarming of Muslims, particularly of those who possessed weapons from their military service, and some of these guns were used to arm Sikhs and Hindus. Already disaffected from the maharaja, Poonchis became the fighting arm of the pro-Pakistan sentiment in the state, and were then mobilized accordingly by Pakistanis (Khan 1970). Schofield, like Alastair Lamb, believes that in order to fight, Poonchis contacted tribal affiliates in the northwestern areas to raise men and armaments, and this link became one of the reasons why, in October 1947, tribesmen from these areas chose to cross the border into Kashmir in support of their beleaguered co-religionists (Schofield 2010: 41-47; Lamb 1966: 37-38).

In addition, after the riots in Rawalpindi and elsewhere in March 1947, large numbers of Hindu and Sikh refugees from western Punjab were forced into the Jammu area, and their presence, and the stories of the horrors they had faced, exacerbated communal divides in the city. By October, as elsewhere in Punjab, sporadic acts of retributive violence had multiplied. In Jammu, a combination of orchestrated violence (eyewitnesses say members of the police and Dogra forces attacked Muslim localities and refugee convoys) and generalized fear caused a huge demographic shift in Jammu city and the *tehsils* to its west (Saraf 2004: 161-97; Snedden 2001; Symonds 2001: 68). Estimates suggest that half a million Muslims were displaced, and 200,000 were either killed or died of epidemics or exposure as refugees (Stephens 1953: 138, 112; Hasan 2005; Chattha 2009).[4] Members of these displaced groups went on to play important roles in the politics of the territory that Pakistan calls Azad ("Free") Kashmir (a narrow strip of territory to the west of the populous areas of Jammu and Kashmir, which are under Indian control) or, in Indian terms, Pakistan-occupied Kashmir. Memories of their dispossession and dislocation are often invoked by Pakistani and insurgent groups seeking freedom for Kashmir today.

In effect, the city of Jammu became largely Hindu, and, in a pattern of resettlement that marked Partition events, refugees from Pakistan were resettled into properties that once belonged to Muslims (for a study of parallel resettlement practices in Delhi and Karachi, see Zamindar 2007). In a 2009 interview, Ved Bhasin, the long-time editor of the *Kashmir Times*, described these riots as a deliberate attempt to change the demographics of the plains areas of the state and thus to influence its future (Khan 2009). As Yasmin Khan, another recent commentator on Partition puts it, "the mass killing in Jammu and Kashmir in 1947-48, which is usually forgotten or incorporated into the history of Kashmiri wars, shared far more characteristics with other Partition slaughters" (such as those population-clearing exercises orchestrated in the princely states of Bharatpur and Alwar) (Khan 2007: 135; for Bharatpur and Alwar, see Copland 1998 and Mayaram 1997).

For ten weeks after India and Pakistan came into being, the maharaja of Kashmir maintained a tenuous hold on power and the hope that he would rule an independent state. It was clear that if he had to choose, even a majority Muslim population and contiguous borders would not convince him to accede to Pakistan (he was too much the Hindu partisan). As it turned out, the issue was forced by the incursion into Kashmir of an estimated 5,000 armed tribesmen from northwestern Pakistan (with some support from Pakistani army and retired soldiers, as well as fighters from Poonch and Mirpur). By October 24, 1947, they had taken several towns en route to Srinagar, which caused Maharaja Hari Singh to ask for Indian military help, and then, two days later, to sign an Instrument of Accession that legitimized the landing of Indian troops in Srinagar airport on October 27. (The sequence, and hence the legal validity, of these events is disputed; for the debate, see Schofield 2010: 52-60 and Jha 1998). For the next 14 months, the Indian army battled regular units of the Pakistani army and local militia and irregulars in a number of theaters in Jammu, Kashmir, and Ladakh.

On January 1, 1949, a ceasefire under the auspices of the United Nations was declared between Pakistan and India, and the forward positions of each army became, over time (and via other battles in 1965 and 1971), the lines of control between the two nations and thus the boundary between India and Pakistan in this state. But even more consequentially, such prolonged military activities meant that what might have once been a constitutional question of accession became part of the long-drawn-out (and ongoing) drama of the partition of British India, and thus one sequence in the unseemly pageant of violent nation-formation across the subcontinent. As Vazira Zamindar argues, the history of early postcolonial state formation in India and Pakistan revolved around managing and shaping the "colossal displacements of Partition." In her words, the "highly surveillanced western Indo-Pak border, one of the most difficult for citizens of the region to cross to this day, was not a consequence of the Kashmir conflict, as security studies gurus may suggest, but rather was formed through a series of attempts to resolve the fundamental uncertainty of the political Partition itself" (Zamindar 2007: 3).

This history is of great and continuing importance in understanding the Kashmir conflict in India and in Pakistan, as the divides between Hindus and Muslims that were confirmed in the Partition, and its attendant violence, continue to frame all perceptions of the genesis—and any ideas about the potential solution—of the problem. As it is, the former princely state has been divided ever since 1948, with Pakistan controlling Baltistan and Gilgit, the vast swathe of mountains and valleys in the northwest as well as Azad. India also controls Ladakh, while China holds the Aksai Chin plateau in the northeast. For Indian nationalists, the secular credentials of the Indian state are visible in Kashmir's membership of the union, given that it is a Muslim-majority state, and thus a rebuttal of the "two-nation" theory that birthed Pakistan as the putative homeland of the subcontinent's Muslims. For Pakistani nationalists, Kashmir, precisely because it was and is a Muslim majority state, and because it shares contiguous borders and land routes with Pakistan, was stolen from them by the Dogra Hindu maharaja aided by India's armed forces. For them, this is a land and a people held only by the force of the massive Indian military deployment at the borders and within the state.

The Indian claim was complicated by the fact that the Instrument of Accession itself contained clauses suggesting that the maharaja was not signing away his sovereignty (Clause 8) or agreeing to function within "any future constitution of India" (Clause 2). Thus, in various fora, both in India and at the United Nations, Jawaharlal Nehru and officials of the Indian government reiterated their belief that this accession had to be ratified by the population at large. It is a moot point whether India was ever going to stage the plebiscite it promised. In any case, the prolonged warfare at the borders of the state, and the need to resettle Partition refugees as well as those created by the fighting, meant that the plebiscite was indefinitely set aside. Internally, too, Sheikh Abdullah's popularity meant that the National Conference and its pro-India stance prevailed, and he strengthened his hold by arresting or exiling consequential politicians of a pro-Pakistan bent. He did not, however, give up his bargaining chip with India, which was the idea of an independent Kashmir. As a result of the military and then the political give-and-take of the years after 1947 (when the Indian constitution was drafted), it included an Article 370, which recognized and guaranteed the special circumstances of Kashmir's accession, and thus its difference from the other states in the union. All political and administrative processes in the state, including elections to a constituent assembly, were to derive their form and function from this arrangement, which was, as subsequent events were to show, flawed in conception and unsustainable in practice.

Most Indian politicians, even those who respected Kashmir's "special status," presumed it was only a question of time before the state would become so economically and socially integrated with India that the provisions of Article 370 would be rendered obsolete in practice. Other national political parties, like the Jan Sangh and their allies in the state, the Praja Parishad, mobilized to try and abrogate Article 370, and made the incorporation of Kashmir into India an important feature of their political agenda. In any case, even in the early 1950s, as part of their attempts to contest the internal hegemony of Kashmiri politicians based in Srinagar, an India-identified set of Hindu political leaders from Jammu and Buddhist leaders in Ladakh argued for formal integration within the larger nation. Their efforts did not end in success, but they were reminders that Jammu and Kashmir was by no means a state unitary in its populations or its political aspirations, which remains the case today.

Over the next three decades, politics in Jammu and Kashmir continued to be a powder keg of repression (in 1953, Sheikh Abdullah was arrested by the central government and detained, on and off, for two decades after; other politicians suffered similar fates). Election after election was rigged to keep out pro-Pakistani candidates. Relations between the state and central government were often strained, as the latter often intervened in local politics and administration. However, while large sections of the rural, and particularly the mountainous, areas of Jammu, Kashmir, and Ladakh remained poor, central investments in development and infrastructure did create visible reminders of the benefits of affiliation with India. Ironically, much of this infrastructure, especially in the border areas, derived directly from India's military priorities, since war against Pakistan in 1965 and 1971 meant a huge build-up of soldiers and armaments in some of the highest and most inhospitable locations in the world. The Indian government could claim to budget enormous funds for Jammu and Kashmir, but a very high percentage of these funds went into the consolidation of military power at the line of control.

The mid-1960s also saw the emergence of the armed militants of the Jammu and Kashmir National Liberation Front and the beginnings of skirmishes between such groups and security forces, which continued into the next decade. Even when, or perhaps particularly when, Sheikh Abdullah and Prime Minister Indira Gandhi signed an accord in 1974 that was widely considered to represent an understanding that no plebiscite would ever be called for and that Jammu and Kashmir was to be considered a constituent state in the Indian Union, these armed militants began to capture the imagination of Kashmiris and to represent an unlikely force for change.

Another turning point came in the rigged elections of 1987, when candidates of the Muslim United Front, who spoke in the name of freedom and Islam, were arrested or sidelined in order to let a National Conference–Congress alliance come to power. Several of these candidates, now convinced that Indian democracy did not extend to Kashmiris, left to join armed militant groups operating out of Pakistan. Not long after, violent attacks and bombings became a regular feature in Kashmir; Pakistani support for militant camps in Azad Kashmir meant that larger groups of young Kashmiris (from both sides of the border) as well as veterans of the anti-Soviet war in Afghanistan could swell the ranks of anti-India militants. If the idea of Kashmiris armed and willing enough to take on far superior military forces came as an unwelcome surprise for Indians and for the Indian political establishment, the popular support the militants enjoyed so many years after the accession of the state in 1947 was quite stunning. Few Indians or mainstream politicians had paid attention to the uneasy history of the accession as well as the continuing history of undemocratic functioning in the state. Not surprisingly, there was little by way of imaginative political or administrative response to these new circumstances. The state simply fought back: from 1990 onward, the Indian army and paramilitary forces clamped down and, squeezed between the militants and the military, Kashmiri lives descended into the misery and brutality I touched upon in the opening section of this essay.

LOOKING AHEAD

My discussion so far has called attention to three elements that structure the Kashmir problem: the gross and widespread violations of human rights that have defined Kashmiri lives for two decades now; the history of Kashmiri Muslim alienation from a de facto Hindu state; and the long tentacles of the partition of India, whose malignant grasp allows for no conception of political collectivity not defined by the fortified borders of India and Pakistan. I will now return to the challenge of Kashmir today, especially because July, August, and September 2010 saw a remarkable shift in the forms of protest in Kashmir (Kak 2011). Since the seven to eight years has seen the decimation of the insurgents by Indian forces (estimates suggest fewer than 500 militants are operating now), it seems clear to all that armed insurgency will not lead to any resolution of the Kashmir conflict. However, even as the militancy has been contained, the anger and disaffection of Kashmiris is far from dissipated. Even with an elected state government in place, massive strikes and protests recur. (In the summer of 2008, Kashmiri Muslims mobilized in particularly large numbers to resist the reapportioning of land along a Hindu pilgrimage route to the Amarnath shrine; these protests often turned into mass demonstrations for *azadi,* freedom.) As I noted earlier, in the summer of 2010, after a 17-year-old, Tufail Ahmed Mattoo, was killed by a tear-gas canister fired by the police, Kashmir saw continuous street battles between stone-throwing protesters and the police and paramilitary, who threw stones back, used tear gas, and shot to kill and maim (for a diary of six days in Srinagar during that time, see Kaul 2010). 110 Kashmiris died, newspapers lost count of the wounded, and between strikes and curfews, life ground to a halt. The map of protests radiated across Kashmir, bringing civilians into bloody conflict not only with the police and paramilitary, but also with army detachments (Bukhari 2010).

For many military and civil administrators, this remained a problem of law and order, to be sorted out through displays of force. However, the intensity of the protests, and indeed of the state response, was such that many Indian civil society groups, journalists, and important politicians focused their attention on the ongoing conflict in Kashmir.

As more and more young men were killed, the tone of discussion in the Indian public sphere did change, and even centrist intellectuals began to call for the repeal of the Armed Forces Special Powers Act (AFSPA), which allows virtual impunity to officers and soldiers, and the Public Safety Act (PSA), which allows police to detain individuals up to two years without charge or trial. No progress along these lines was made; senior army officers made statements insisting they could not function without the legal cover provided by the AFSPA, and the PSA continues to be routinely used to imprison people. (Margaret Sekaggya, the United Nations Special Rapporteur on the Situation of Human Rights Defenders, has, after a recent visit to Kashmir, demanded the repeal of these laws; see "Begin Healing Process" 2011).

There is considerable evidence now that various organs of the Indian state function at odds with each other when it comes to Kashmir: elected officials are distrusted by their military and police counterparts, the central paramilitaries are often at odds with the state police, and even the central home and defense ministries do not agree about weighty matters like troop deployment in civilian areas. And of course Kashmir remains the playground of national electoral politics: recently activists of the Bharatiya Janta Party, the major Hindu nationalist party now in parliamentary opposition, decided to journey from different parts of India to Srinagar to unfurl the Indian flag there on January 26, India's Republic Day (for a pointed editorial on such provocations, see Varadarajan 2011). In response, political parties in Srinagar called a strike (in any case this annual celebration meets with stony silence in the city), and the state government blocked the activists from entering the Kashmir valley. The situation remains as polarized as ever.

The future—certainly the possibility of a political resolution of the problem of Kashmir—looks bleak. India grows increasingly powerful economically and militarily, and its aspirations for regional superpower status (with the hope of a seat on the United Nations Security Council) means that its strategic planners will deny any possibility of self-determination for Kashmiris. Pakistan, bloodied internally by militants and religious insurgents, needs more than ever to demonstrate its commitment to a muscular nationalism the equal of India's, and will continue to treat Azad Kashmir as a captive launching pad for actions against Indian Kashmir. Kashmiris themselves are a deeply divided people, and not just because most Kashmiri Hindus no longer live among their Muslim neighbors in the valley. Kashmiri Muslims too are divided by denominational (primarily Sunni–Shia) differences and political loyalties (the National Conference and the People's Democratic Party are the most prominent mainstream parties, with the separatist groups affiliated as the All Parties Hurriyat Conference). Even among the separatists, wide divides exist between the "moderates," who believe that demilitarization, the prosecution of crimes committed by soldiers and paramilitaries, and a return to the autonomies granted to Jammu and Kashmir by Article 370 will allow for a functional rapprochement with India. The more "hard-line" members of the Hurriyat insist that independence, or the creation of an Islamic state amalgamated with Pakistan, is the solution. Political positions aside, there are other divides that are even more disturbing: those caused by two decades of covert operations and lives lived under the continual threat of violence. There is little trust left in government or civil society organizations, for so many of them have turned out to be tainted, vehicles for the extension of state surveillance or patronage. Some journalists estimate that up to 150,000 informers are on the secret payrolls of different agencies of the state. Such state-sponsored corruption, if we can call it that, has the effect (or has been designed to have the effect) of creating a pervasive public culture of suspicion, distrust, and fear.

Kashmiri lives today are burdened in ways that few outsiders can imagine. An extraordinary percentage of the population has personally experienced the casual violence of agents of an intrusive security state. For most civilians, Indian authority (and indeed that of the police agencies of Jammu and Kashmir state) is understood as uncaring, even murderous, and this is true also of those who believe that India's economy and institutional vitality offers great benefits to Kashmiris. The events of the past year have not helped: in spite of strictures on the media, images of young men battling the police—and suffering the consequences—circulated on cell phones and the Internet (as a casual search on YouTube reveals). Middle-aged women, too, took to the streets in protest, part of the tens of thousands of Kashmiris who defied curfews, and images of these protests brought home to Indians the full extent of their alienation, as well as their determination to articulate their political grievances.

For the last 20 years Kashmiris have been on a wild and dangerous roller-coaster ride, high hopes giving way to depths of despair. Mourning and anger go hand in hand now, each fueling political rage against their treatment by India. Two decades of trauma and loss have caused many to question how long they can afford to resist state power, but equally, this period has seen the coming into adulthood of a generation of young people who have known no other lives, and are thereby confirmed in their political opposition. Where this sorry political history will lead is far from clear.

I will close by quoting in its entirety a song that became an anthem of resistance and mourning in 2010. This is the Srinagar-based rapper M. C. Kash's "I Protest (Remembrance)."[5] This rap too invokes a longer history of crisis: the unfulfilled promise of a plebiscite and the ongoing public skepticism about the fairness of "democratically held elections." Most pressingly, Kash repeatedly calls attention to atrocities and repression, but also, tellingly, to the national media Kashmiris so mistrust, the "Sponsored Media Who Hide This Homicide." The last sequence of the song has the rapper intoning the names of those who were shot by the time he wrote it, and this (incomplete) list is chilling, a memorial to the young mowed down by police actions. M. C. Kash's combination of protest and remembrance, indictment and memorialization, anger and sorrow, is a powerful testimonial to the Kashmiri suffering that shapes its politics today, as is the pledge with which he closes: "An' you will fight, Till the death of it...."

They say when you run from darkness all you seek is light.
But when the blood spills over you'll stand and fight!!
Threads of deceit woven around a word of plebiscite, By
Treacherous puppet politicians who have no soul inside.
My paradise is burnin' with troops left loose with ammo,
Who murder and rape then hide behind a political shadow.
Like a casino human life is thrown like a dice.
I'll summarize atrocities till the resurrection of Christ!!!
Can you hear the screams now see the revolution!! Their

Bullets our stones, don't talk restitution.
'Cause the only solution is the resolution of freedom, Even
Khusrow will go back an' doubt his untimely wisdom!!
These killings ain't random its an organized genocide.
Sponsored media who hide this homicide.
No more injustice we wont go down when we bleed, Alive in
The struggle even the graves will speak!

Chorus:

I Protest, against the things you done! I Protest, For a mother
Who lost her son!
I Protest, I'll throw stones and neva run! I Protest, Until my
Freedom has come!
I Protest, for my brother who's dead! I Protest, Against the
Bullet in his head!
I Protest, I'll throw stones and neva run! I Protest, Until my
Freedom has come!
Democratically held elections now that's completely absurd,
I'll tell you some stuff that you obviously neva heard!!
A ten year old kid voted with all his fingers. A whole village
Gangraped, a cry still lingers....
These are the tales from the dark side of a murderous
Regime, an endless occupation of our land an' our dreams.
Democratic politics will cut our throats before we speak,
How they talk about peace when there's blood in our
Streets?
(huh?)
When freedom of speech is subjected to strangulation!!
Flames of revolution engulfs the population.
They rise through suppression and march to be free, Face
Covered in a rag labeled a revolutionary.
Through this fight for survival I want the world to see, A
Murderous oppression written down in police brutality.
Stones in my hand its time you pay the price, For plunderin'
An' rapin' a beautiful paradise!!

Chorus:

> I Protest, against the things you done! I Protest, for a mother
> Who lost her son!
> I Protest, I'll throw stones and neva run! I Protest, until my
> Freedom has come!
> I Protest, for my brother sho's dead! I Protest, against the
> Bullet in his head!
> I Protest, I'll throw stones and neva run! I Protest, until my
> Freedom has come!

> Let's remember all those who were martyred this year.
> Inayat Khan, Wamiq Farooq, Zahid Farooq, Zubair Ahmed Bhat,
> Tufail Ahmed Matoo, Rafiq Ahmed Bangroo, Javaid Ahmed Malla,
> Shakeel Ganai, Firdous Khan, Bilal Ahmed Wani, Tajamul Bashir,
> Tauqeer Rather, Ishtiyaq Ahmed, Imtiyaz Ahmed Itoo, Shujaat-
> ul-Islaam, Muzaffar Ahmed, Fayaz Ahmed Wani, Yasmeen Jan,
> Abrar Ahmed Khan, Faizan Rafeeq, Fayaz Ahmed Khanday, Farooq
> Ahmed, Tariq Ahmed Dar, Mohammed Ahsan, Showkat Ahmed,
> Mohammed Rafiq, Nazir Ahmed, Javed Ahmed Teli, Mudassir Lone,
> Nayeem Shah, Rayees Wani, Afrooza Teli, Basharat Reshi, Irshad
> Bhat, Ashiq Hussain, Rameez Ahmed, Hafiz Yaqoob, Tariq Dar,
> Khursheed Ahmed, Bashir Ahmed Reshi, Arshid Ahmad, Sameer
> Rah, Mehraj ud din Lone, Anis Ganai, Suhail Ahmed Dar, Jehangir
> Baht, Riyaz Ahmed, Mohammad Yaqoob Bhat, Iqbal Khan, Shabir
> Malik, Ghulam Nabi Badyari, Rameez Reshi, Fida Nabi Lone,
> Farrukh Bukhari, Mudassir Zargar, Ali Mohammad Khanday, Asif
> Mir, Sameer Lone, Umar Ahmed Dar, Irshad Ahmed, Mohammad
> Abbas, Milad Ahmed Dar, Nazir Wani, Mudasir Nazir, Bilal Ahmed
> Sheikh, Umar Qayoom, Irshad Ahmad.
> An' you will fight, Till the death of it....

Lyrics © 2010 M. C. Kash (Roushan Illahi). Printed with permission.

NOTES

1. The term "intifada" is one that the Kashmiri *sangbaaz* (stone pelters) have made their own. The problem of Kashmir does not map exactly to the Israeli occupation of Palestine, but young Kashmiris see the style of

revolt—young men with stones, often masked in *keffiyehs*, facing up to soldiers with arms—as inspirational. This is not only an issue of style, of course, but of parallel historical genealogies, since both the Israel–Palestine conflict and the India–Kashmir–Pakistan imbroglio were the direct result of British colonial officers partitioning territories without any understanding of or concern for local populations (Cleary 2002).

2. The Dogra are Rajputs who migrated from Rajasthan and adjoining areas to the plains and hill tracts around Jammu. Dogras, particularly in India, are largely Hindu (most Muslim Dogras or Rajputs live in Pakistan or Azad Kashmir). They speak Dogri, a language that has more in common with Punjabi than with Kashmiri. The British considered them one of the "martial races" of India and recruited them heavily into the British Indian army.

3. Junagarh and Hyderabad, two princely states with Muslim rulers and a majority Hindu population, provide a counterpoint to Kashmir (both these states were territorially contained within India; only Kashmir shared borders with both India and Pakistan). The ruler of Junagarh sought to accede to Pakistan; an Indian blockade caused him to flee, and the state's amalgamation with India was ratified in a plebiscite conducted in February 1948. The nizam of Hyderabad wavered between independence and accession to Pakistan, but was removed from power by the Indian army in a "police action" in September 1948.

4. These numbers, as is the case with all those connected with Partition deaths and dislocations, are impressionistic. For a careful examination (and estimation) of this problem of numbers, see Corrucini and Kaul. In their analysis of Punjab, they write,

> Several methods of estimating total Partition mortality (both in present day Pakistan and India) point to a maximum of perhaps about 400,000 ± 100,000 deaths. Of these, about a third were violent deaths in the first days of attacks, and most of the remainder were cholera along the migration track or various illnesses of poor public sanitation in the early camps (1990: 37).

5. The full force of this rap becomes clear when it is heard: <http://www.reverbnation.com/mckash#!/mckashkashmir>.The song, overlaid with images from the summer's protests, is also available on YouTube: <http://www.youtube.com/watch?v=DFDrRaLcUvQ>.

REFERENCES

"Begin Healing Process in J&K, Says U.N. Special Rapporteur." *The Hindu*, January 22, 2011 <http://www.thehindu.com/news/national/article1109388.ece>.

Brass, Paul R. "The Partition of India and Retributive Genocide in the Punjab, 1946–47: Means, Methods, and Purposes." *Journal of Genocide Research* 5:3 (September 2003): 71–101.

Bukhari, Parvaiz. "Kashmir 2010, the Year of Killing Youth." *The Nation*, September 22, 2010. <http://www.thenation.com/article/154964/kashmir-2010-year-killing-youth>.

Chattha, Ilyas. "Terrible Fate: 'Ethnic Cleansing' of Jammu Muslims in 1947." *Journal of Pakistan Vision* 10:1 (2009): 117-40 <http://pu.edu.pk:82/punjab/home/journal/12/Previous-Issue.html>.

Cleary, Joe. *Literature, Partition, and the Nation State: Culture and Conflict in Ireland, Israel, and Palestine.* Cambridge: Cambridge University Press, 2002.

Copland, Ian. "The Further Shores of Partition: Ethnic Cleansing in Rajasthan, 1947." *Past and Present* 160 (1998): 203-39.

Corruccini, Robert S., and Samvit S. Kaul. *Halla: Demographic Consequences of the Partition of the Punjab, 1947.* Lanham, Md.: University Press of America, 1990.

Hasan, Khalid. "Jammu 1947: Gone but Not Forgotten" <http://www.khalidhasan.net/2005/05/27/jammu-1947-gone-but-not-forgotten/>.

Human Rights Watch. "India's Secret Army in Kashmir: New Patterns of Abuse Emerge in the Conflict" (May 1, 1996) <http://www.unhcr.org/refworld/docid/3ae6a8558.html>.

Huttenback, Robert A. *Kashmir and the British Raj, 1847-1947.* Karachi: Oxford University Press, 2004.

International People's Tribunal on Human Rights and Justice in Kashmir. *Buried Evidence: Unknown, Unmarked, and Mass Graves in Indian-Administered Kashmir* (2009) <www.kashmirprocess.org/reports/graves/toc.html>.

Jha, Prem Shankar. *Kashmir 1947: Rival Versions of History.* New Delhi: Oxford University Press, 1998.

Kak, Sanjay, ed. *Until My Freedom Has Come: The New Intifada in Kashmir.* New Delhi: Penguin, 2011.

Kaul, Suvir. "Days in Srinagar." *Outlookindia.com* <http://www.outlookindia.com/article.aspx?266544>.

Kaul, Suvir. "Indian Empire (and the case of Kashmir)." *Economic and Political Weekly* 46:13 (March 26, 2011): 66-75.

Khan, Akbar. *Raiders in Kashmir.* Islamabad: National Book Foundation, 1970.

Khan, Yasmin. *The Great Partition: The Making of India and Pakistan.* New Haven: Yale University Press, 2007.

Jamal, Arif. *Shadow War: The Untold Story of Jihad in Kashmir.* New York: Melville House, 2009.

Lamb, Alastair. *Crisis in Kashmir: 1947 to 1966.* London: Routledge and Kegan Paul, 1966.

Mayaram, Shail. *Resisting Regimes: Myth, Memory and the Shaping of a Muslim Identity.* New York: Oxford University Press, 1997.

Pandey, Gyanendra. *Remembering Partition: Violence, Nationalism, and History in India.* Cambridge: Cambridge University Press, 2001.

Rai, Mridu. *Hindu Rulers, Muslim Subjects: Islam, Rights, and the History of Kashmir.* Princeton: Princeton University Press, 2004.

"Riots Changed J & K Politics." Ved Bhasin interviewed by Shahnawaz Khan. *Kashmir Life,* October 3, 2009. <http://www.kashmirlife.net/index.php?option=com_content&view=article&id=914%3Ariots-changed-jak-politics&Itemid=163>.

Saraf, Muhammad Yusuf. "The Jammu Massacres." *Memory Lane to Jammu.* Eds. Rehmatullah Rad and Khalid Hasan. Lahore: Sang-e-Meel Publications, 2004: 161-97.

Schofield, Victoria. *Kashmir in Conflict: India, Pakistan and the Unending War.* London: I. B. Tauris, 2010.

Snedden, Christopher. "What Happened to Muslims in Jammu? Local Identity, the 'Massacre of 1947' and the Roots of the 'Kashmir Problem.'" *South Asia* 24:2 (2001): 111-134.

Stephens, Ian. *Horned Moon: An Account of a Journey through Pakistan, Kashmir, and Afghanistan.* London: Chatto and Windus, 1953.

Symonds, Richard. *In the Margins of Independence: A Relief Worker in India and Pakistan (1942-1949).* Karachi: Oxford University Press, 2001.

"U.S. Embassy Cables: U.S. Argues Against Visa for Kashmiri 'Paramilitary.'" *Guardian* <http://www.guardian.co.uk/world/us-embassy-cables-documents/110718>.

Varadarajan, Siddharth. "The Fabric of Belonging." *The Hindu*, January 23, 2011 <http://www.thehindu.com/opinion/op-ed/article1119039.ece>.

Wax, Emily. "In Kashmir, Conflict's Psychological Legacy: Mental Health Cases Swell in Two Decades." *Washington Post*, September 1, 2008.

Zamindar, Vazira Fazila-Yacoobali. *The Long Partition and the Making of Modern South Asia: Refugees, Boundaries, Histories*. New York: Columbia University Press, 2007.

Zutshi, Chitralekha. *Languages of Belonging: Islam, Regional Identity, and the Making of Kashmir*. New York: Oxford University Press, 2004.

After Midnight's Children: Some Notes on the New Indian Novel in English

Rajeswari Sunder Rajan

> Walking to the sea I carry
> A village, a city, the country
> For the moment
> On my back.
>
> —Gieve Patel, "Nargol"

The preoccupation with the nation that marks much postcolonial writing, especially the Anglophone novel in India, following the appearance of Salman Rushdie's *Midnight's Children* (1981), has been widely remarked. In this essay, I am interested in tracing how this preoccupation with the nation-thematic has persisted into—or changed in the course of—the first decade of the new century in the fiction (and prose nonfiction) that has appeared since the 1980s, in response to both sociopolitical developments (local and global) as well as changing literary trends.

Midnight's Children and its successor novels over the next quarter-century ostentatiously bore the burden of nation. "Burden" is the content of a work, its defining preoccupation. It carries as well the meaning of responsibility or obligation.[1] The intimate connection that is forged by the consciousness of "burden" between author and subject, and between individual and destiny generates, as we might expect, a range of attitudes, ideologies, postures, questions, and claims. It speaks variously of elitism, power, authority, *noblesse oblige*, possessiveness, and the custodianship of tradition assumed by self-conscious modernizers. As a ruling class, the writers internalize a subtle sense of entitlement that is often accompanied, as in Gieve Patel's poem above, by the weight of an exacerbated consciousness of responsibility. All are inescapably aware of their centrality to the nation, as intellectual leaders, prophets of modernity, and pedagogues of the people. The nation-novel is written from a recognizably ruling-class perspective, with all that the description implies in its effects as ideology, politics, style, and affect.

The generation of midnight's children among the bourgeois intelligentsia that inherited the Nehruvian mantle has had to come to terms, nevertheless, with inevitable realignments of power in the polity. The rise of new regional and caste elites, and the political dominance of Hindu religious fundamentalist groups, have made a dent in the traditional, secular, Anglicized ruling-class formation that shaped these writers. The consequences of electoral vote bank collectivization, lower-caste mobilization, competition for scarce resources, urban migration, women's changing roles, and the recent privatization of resources have combined to make inroads into traditional enclaves of privilege.[2] The old center no longer holds, weakening the inheritors' political and social claims on the nation. The Nawab Sahib of Baitar, a character in Vikram Seth's *A Suitable Boy* (1993), responds to the passage of the Zamindari Abolition Act that forms the novel's 1950s backdrop with the stoic diagnosis: "history is against our class" (758). And it is these generational changes that Kiran Desai conveys through the elegiac phrase "the inheritance of loss," in the title of her Booker prize-winning novel (*The Inheritance of Loss* 2005). A character in Sagarika Ghose's *The Gin Drinkers* (2000) mocks her own Oxford-educated class as the "Irrelevant Indians" (Ghose 2000: 256). The writing on the wall says that they must yield to the new, and newly relevant, Indians who are now the upwardly mobile Dalit intellectuals and the vulgar entrepreneurs. Both pique and pragmatism, such a way of thinking—in terms of one's loss of relevance in and to the nation—is itself revealing.

We must be cautious, however, of overstating the loss of power and influence of the English-educated "ruling" class, and of overestimating its extent. Though Sagarika Ghose's ironic reflections at the millennium record an awareness of changes in status, the novel refuses to indulge in lament for the passing of this class. In the central drama of the novel (the succession to the directorship of the elite Gandhi Foundation), not only is power ceded gracefully—and with more than a modicum of political correctness—it is also made clear that the members of this versatile educated class can reinvent themselves as the allies of the new meritocracy and find new uses for their seemingly anachronistic English education. The protagonist Uma's Oxford (English) boyfriend is quick with reassurance when she expresses desolation: "But that's far too harsh, sweetheart. There's so much for you to do here. If I were in your place, hey, I wouldn't have a minute to spare" (256). The changing fortunes of the nation may have made redundant the nation-building task assumed by this class in the immediate post-Independence years, but there has been no necessary diminution of its importance in the era of globalization. Satish Deshpande draws attention to the smooth transition the middle class and particularly its "upper (managerial-professional) segment" has made to the changed conditions of a liberalized economy marked by consumption. Its claims with regard to the nation, Deshpande suggests, have become even more grandiose: "From its position as a 'proxy' for the nation, this class has now graduated to thinking of itself as a 'portrait' of the nation." In other words, he adds, it no longer merely represents the people but is *itself* the nation (Deshpande 2003: 150).

An exhaustion with nationalist sentiments was in any case to be expected as the first exaltation of freedom subsided and the postcolonial nation settled into the bad habits of nationhood. When the nation was newly decolonized and still "developing," a member in good standing of the Third World community of nations, it could legitimately call forth high-minded patriotic commitment. But the nation that has begun to perceive itself as transforming into a military and economic superpower is a very different entity. It is now a big as well as bad nation. In contemporary India moreover, nationalism has been taken over by the Hindu right majority claiming it as its birthright, to the exclusion of all other claimants. *Opposing* this nation—or opposing *this* nation—is the new patriotism, even if it is expressed as secession as in Arundhati Roy's famous declaration: "I secede. I hereby declare myself an independent, mobile republic" (Roy 2001: 21). Amitava Kumar reads this as an instance of the "narrowly individualistic, even selfish" attitude that he diagnoses as characteristic of the tribe, because it leaves the people behind (Kumar 2006). But he misreads the rhetoric of the performative. Roy is guilty, if anything, of what we might call a *hyper*-identification with the nation rather than disidentification or abandonment. Coming as it does at the heart of her long argument opposing the nuclear bomb tests carried out in 1998, Roy's threat expresses her "desolation" at the passing of a world that is identifiably a certain India, a symbol she had idealized as a "real option" to the ills of the rest of the world (Roy 2001: 22).

But Amitava Kumar is correct all the same that the critique of nationalism tends to be expressed by the Indian-English writer in the language of individualism. And typically it is framed in terms of a refusal or rejection of compulsory national identity. What causes revulsion in the progressive-minded cosmopolitan young Indian is a new nationalism expressed in the language of "Indianness." Shuddhabrata Sengupta's eloquently articulated position piece, "Identity Card and India Ink," is subtitled "Confessions of an Anti-national." Sickened by the hype of media-tized nationalism during the fiftieth anniversary celebrations in 1997, Sengupta demystifies national identity. It is, he argues, simply the product of "a limited choice, a great deal of coercion, considerable indifference and some convenience." His response to this ascriptive identity is escape: "I want out"—and the fantasy of liberation:

> Columbus went sailing in search of India and found the New World instead. Perhaps I need to gather a band of foolhardy mariners, a bunch of time-passing exiles, refusees and refugees, stateless and rootless illegal immigrants of the imagination to continue his journey—a quest in the other direction. In losing what he sought we might find another new world. We could each take our own favourite India with us, not the excess baggage of India that is *Bharat*, that is *Aryavarta* multiplied by *Dravida Nadu*, that is *Punya, Pitri, Matri,*

Janma, Mrityu-Bhoomi, but the India that is the ink, the India that is the rubber, and the India that is the magazine—these we could still carry with us, provided we left our identity cards behind (Sengupta 1997: 13).

Note his preference for the plain English (secular) "India" to the indigenized versions of the nation's name, several of them Sanskritized and sacralized.[3]

In *English, August* (1988), Upamanyu Chatterjee's protagonist defines an Indian as "one who is born one and doesn't wish to change his citizenship," a sentiment Chatterjee repeats in a later article written in his own voice, insisting that "it is a valid enough definition to instill in us a lasting sense of identity, to provide for the future a sort of harmony—even better that it is low-key" (Chatterjee 2007). We might retort that to stay in one's nation if one chooses (if it behaves?) or leave it if one doesn't (to go to a place of one's choosing elsewhere in the world presumably), is a luxury available only to the privileged cosmopolitan even in a globalized world (particularly in a globalized world, where passports are only as strong or as weak as one's nationality). When placed alongside Shama Futehally's "Idea of India"—"all we thought about India was that we had to live in it"—we can understand this sentiment as expressing a historical fact about postcolonial elite citizenship: that it is not an ascriptive identity but a chosen one. "I repeat," Futehally carefully explains, "that there was nothing jingoistic or 'heroic' in our attitude. We just assumed that we were born here in order to remain here, and that remaining would do some sort of good to our surroundings (2006: 46-47)." These writers speak, I want to emphasize, from a location *within* the nation, articulating a position that is as tenuous (they could leave if they chose) as it is strong (they don't leave although they could).

It is undoubtedly important to claim the nation from the side of the excluded, to read its history as hybrid and impure, and to contest jingoism, as these writers do. Is it because it is articulated in the accents of the English "I" that their protest sounds lofty rather than partisan, impulsive rather than considered, elitist rather than populist, rhetorical rather than real, expressive of urban radical chic rather than grass-roots activism? When residence in one's country is a matter of choice rather than destiny, is it patriotism, privilege, or a unique combination of the two that underlies the decision to stay?

One final clarification. Although they tend to be conflated, it is important to distinguish this postcolonial critique of the nation from postwar European nation-weariness of the kind Michael Ondaatje so poignantly evoked in *The English Patient* (1992). The passage in the book in which Count Almásy, the Hungarian-English patient, passionately inveighs against nations, is justly famous:

> I came to hate nations. We are deformed by nation-states. Madox died because of nations.
>
> The desert could not be claimed or owned—it was a piece of cloth carried by winds, never held down by stones, and given a hundred shifting names before Canterbury existed, long before battles and treaties quilted Europe and the East. Its caravans, those strange and rambling feasts and cultures, left nothing behind, not an ember. All of us, even those with European homes and children in the distance, wished to remove the clothing of our countries. It was a place of faith. We disappeared into the landscape. Fire and sand. We left the harbours of oasis. The places water came to and touched...*Ain, Bir, Wadi, Foggara, Khottara, Shaduf.* I didn't want my name against such beautiful names. Erase the family name! Erase nations! I was taught such things by the desert (Ondaatje: 138-9).

For Almásy and his kind in the years between the wars in Europe, the desert is the landscape so poetically Orientalized in the description above, the soul's other space, the romantic escape from his own and all nations, and from civilization as he knows and loathes it.

But no such escape appears to be available to postcolonial writers from India. The significant difference between Amitav Ghosh's *The Shadow Lines* (1988) and Ondaatje's *The English Patient*, despite the revulsion from the violence of the nation that informs both novels, is that none of Ghosh's protagonists can easily call for the erasure of nations. The novel's ending is instead marked by an elegiac sense of the historical destiny that traps the postcolonial elite subject within the narrative of the nation. And even if Indian writers were to actually move away from the home country—and of course a great many do, to live in countries in the West—they are unable to conjure up the new country as the simple imaginative alternative to the place they left.[4] The(ir) nation still remains the burden of their fiction even after they have addressed their valediction to it.[5]

If postcolonial Indian intellectuals find it difficult to be ideologues of the nation, it is not only because *nationalism* has become so wholly corrupted as an ideal, but also because the nation-*state* has become a repressive structure. In *Midnight's Children* and the novels after it, the state is identified with particular governments or even specific figures of political authority. A bifurcation between the "nation" and its "fragments"—center and peripheries, state and people—is presupposed in this critique (Chatterjee 1993). Writers share in what is a pervasive, almost, we might say, universal discontent with the government. The idealism about nationalist politics began to wane very soon after Independence with the death of the generation of freedom-fighters whose selfless struggles had given them a mandate for ruling the nation. A new and different breed of men began to fill party organizations and parliamentary bodies. There was and continues to be considerable disillusionment about this later politics and its association with corruption and power-mongering, which contributes a rich vein of satire and angst to Indian literatures (in all the languages).

Rushdie's political critique in *Midnight's Children* was unprecedented in English fiction in India, however. *Midnight's Children* is itself not completely free of the ambivalence that is a consequence of the complicity, not to say identification, of writers in English with "their own" kind of people in power. The divided self of Saleem Sinai reflects this conflict. The contradictions of aspiring to dissent while at the same time occupying the political mainstream can become acute when a novel features a bureaucrat as protagonist and when, further, it casts him as the unlikely mouthpiece of anti-establishment sentiments, as in the case of Upamanyu Chatterjee's *English, August* (1988). Leela Gandhi bemusedly asks: "Where else [but in the new Indian novel in English] can we imagine the formation of the radically abusive artist as a young civil servant?"(Gandhi 2000: 156)

The Emergency (shorthand for the state of internal emergency declared by Prime Minister Indira Gandhi in 1975, leading to suspension of civil rights) offered an opportunity to change sides, whose advantages Rushdie was quick to see and seize. He was able to position himself as writer in adversarial relationship to the state, and to stage his protagonist as the *bête noire* of the dictator herself. No longer was the postcolonial writer limited to anticolonial resistance—he was now an adversary of his own government, no less. What such opposition actually amounts to in the case of Saleem is unclear. Lacking any political clout, endowed only with the symbolic capital of his birth date, Saleem is seemingly left without any clear sense of his options on the nation's political scene. He ends up as Emergency's opponent only in the role of its victim, denied any active oppositional role of the resistant kind that (*some*, at least, of) the intelligentsia played in India at the time. But this is emphatically not an admission that is made within the novel itself.

However meager his protagonist's capacity for meaningful political opposition, Rushdie himself joined the ranks of "postcolonial" writers through his exposure of the corruption and excesses of the ex-colonial nation's rulers in *Midnight's Children* and, again, in *Shame*. Robert Fraser, for instance, places Rushdie's work alongside Ngugi's and Wole Soyinka's as an example of the postcolonial novel that breaks away from the initial anticolonial and nation-building project toward the expression of "internal dissent." These writers find themselves "at loggerheads with government," writes Fraser. In the post-Independence period,

> As the *entente cordiale* between the political leadership and the intelligentsia breaks up, artistic and intellectual freedom, often written into the constitution of the state, are in practice interpreted in the light of overwhelming public priorities. . . . Within a few years political dignitaries and authors of fiction frequently discover themselves existing on opposite sides of a gulf, quarrelling through the medium of a lingua franca through which they express, no longer common aims and an agreed programme but abuse, recrimination and acrimony. . . . Functionally speaking, the novel is transformed into a laboratory in which the technology of national self-criticism is developed and tested (Fraser 2000: 33).

This is the received view of the generic "postcolonial novel." Anthony Appiah has pointed out how, in the context of Africa, "Far from being a celebration of the nation...the novels of the second, postcolonial, stage, are novels of delegitimation: they reject not only the Western *imperium* but also the nationalist project of the postcolonial national bourgeoisie."[6] Or as Rushdie himself declared in an essay written in 1997 for *Index of Censorship*, the "and" connecting the writer and the nation-state "for many of us... meant 'versus.'" In this oppositional mode he places himself in the company of Gordimer and Coetzee in their opposition to apartheid in South Africa and, elsewhere in the same essay, with writers from Eastern Europe and Latin America, all of them writers like himself "unable to deny the lure of the nation, its tide in our blood" (Rushdie 2003: 65-66).

Writing in a repressive state enjoins certain forms of writing—obliqueness, allegory, circumlocution, utopianism, or direct and populist forms of address that enter the fray—that are different from the kinds of cultural production we are likely to encounter in a democracy; and post-Emergency India does not lend itself easily to such modes of representation. Consider by way of contrast the role of literature in Latin America in the Cold War decade of the 1960s. This writing is described by Jean Franco as a "mirror" in which "the *antithesis* of the real state was reflected." Although writers in Latin America were "ambiguously situated, participating in state power and standing in opposition to it"—in this like intellectuals in India, we may add—"there also persists the topos of an antistate, a world turned upside down in which the excluded and marginalized move to the center" (Franco 2002: 123). It is *this* kind of anti-state imagination, one that figures in the "marginalized and excluded," that is conspicuously lacking, I would argue, in the new English novel in India, despite the resemblance and debt that Rushdie's writing, as the chief claimant to such an imagination, bears to this literary genealogy.

Not that political subjects are in short supply in India—corruption, nepotism, developmentalism, militarism, economic liberalization, religious fundamentalism, casteism, and gendered violence are obvious targets, among numerous others—and they are freely availed of by writers high and low, in all the languages. Writing in English in India, the intellectual is the bearer of liberal thought in relation mainly to certain issues like communalism, cultural nationalism, the fate of minorities, or gender. To these we can add the environment as a recent concern. It is not a negligible form of politics, but it must not be aggrandized as a writing that risks repression by the state.[7]

POSTCOLONIAL WRITING AND DIASPORA

The paradox of the postcolonial novel of nation lies typically in the deployment of nation as narrative material, in combination with a critique of nationalism. In my view, this essentially cosmopolitan perspective—rather than a more typically "postcolonial" anti-statist politics—defines the Anglophone Indian novel's critique of the nation. "Cosmopolitanism" is not adequately explained by an individual's access to English or by his diasporic location, but these are constituent historical elements in the formation of the postcolonial intellectual of a certain category to which the Anglophone novelist belongs. It is to an understanding of this formation that I now turn.

In effect, there are three categories of so-called Indian writers in English to consider: the immigrant, the "exilic," and the resident. These descriptive identities shade off into each other, though the first and the last are quite distinct in their implications for cultural production. By "exilic" writers I mean those who have made their residence outside India but have had or continue to have connections with India—they are Nonresident Indians, to use an Indian governmental (tax-paying) category.[8] An article in the *Guardian* also reports on a reverse trend, that of writers abroad returning to India from long-time residence or short stints abroad—Altaf Tyrewala, Tishani Doshi, Jeet Thayil, Rana Dasgupta are listed—mainly, it would seem, as a result of their perception of a more vibrant cultural scene in the country (McCaul 2007). While it would be disingenuous to pretend that the location, residence, or citizenship of a writer is entirely irrelevant in judging literary matters, neither is any one of these factors solely determining. Arundhati Roy made a point of stressing her resident Indian identity, self-deprecatingly representing it as a parochialism that is in contrast with the cosmopolitanism of her (mostly) male peers abroad:

I don't feel part of a pack. I grew up on the banks of a river in Kerala. I spent every day from the age of three fishing, walking, thinking, always alone. If you read other Indian writers most of them are very urban: they don't have much interest in, you know, air or water. They all went from the Doon School to St. Stephen's and then on to Cambridge. Most of those who are called Indian writers don't even live here: Rushdie, Seth, Amitav Ghosh, Mistry: they're all abroad, while I've never lived anywhere except India" (quoted in Dalrymple 2005).

We cannot miss her mockery of lives lacking (local, rural) air or water, subtle though it is—or the gender of her diaspora. Roy's residence in India would go a long way in explaining her involvement in local social movements. But contradicting the easy belief that residence in India is a precondition for social or political activism, there is for instance Indra Sinha's long-time involvement with the Bhopal gas victims' movement from his location in London. Eventually it resulted in the original, brilliant novel, *Animal's People* (2007). Sinha has studied, lived, and worked in Britain almost his entire adult life. Nor does residence in India automatically generate political commitments: resident writers in English are generally known for their political aloofness.

It is a question then of what writers themselves make of their residential status. Writers resident in India full-time have stressed their patriotism (their investment in the nation) or, like Roy, their parochialism (the sphere of their interests limited to not even the nation but the region, the small town, or the spaces of domesticity).[9] Nonresident writers—though of course we would have to stretch this term to include Naipaul and Rushdie—have similarly taken a range of positions with regard to their location. Naipaul has made the postcolonial subject's predicament as "mimic man" nothing less than central to the history of the twentieth century through his fiction. Rushdie builds reflexivity about the postcolonial writer's divided location into his novels, attending to questions of memory, its distortions, the double perspective of the writer in exile, and "translation" as mediation in ways that have come to define the genre of postcolonial writing itself.[10] Some writers of the diaspora assert that their living abroad makes no difference—that they are just as "local" or "regional" as their fellow-writers in India's dusty hinterlands (especially so when this assertion becomes a self-certification of their "authenticity").[11] Amitav Ghosh, as one whose writing career has been divided between India and the United States, focuses on the narrower but more immediately relevant issue of readership and its influence on what a writer writes about, and how. In reply to the question he was asked in an interview, "Who do you write for?" he thoughtfully replied: "My target audience when I was starting out used to be my group of friends in Delhi....I had a small group of friends and I would read to them as I wrote. So, I had a clear sense of who I was writing for." Later, living in New York and writing for American journals, it is different:

> One of the most interesting things that I have done over the past few years is that I have been writing for the *New Yorker*. The people who read it do not know anything about India. Literally nothing. They do not know where Calcutta is, they do not know where Delhi is, they do not know where Bombay is. And in some strange way, it has been a very challenging thing for me to write for them. Often when you are writing for your own sort of social circumstance, you begin to write in a kind of shorthand. You know that your readers know the references, you know the references. You start writing in a kind of shared shorthand. In this instance, what was really challenging for me was to discover exactly what was interesting, what was universal, what was communicable. The challenge was to write with a universal human interest (Ghosh 2000).

At a practical level and at several levels of consciousness, writers writing *in English* about a society or culture that is *not English* make decisions about their perceived readership—at a minimum as to how much to explain or disregard, what degree of glossing or translation to provide—considerations to which both native English writers and writers in the Indian vernaculars are likely to remain largely oblivious.

The distinction between resident and diasporic writers has been framed nevertheless as an absolute difference of kind rather than degree, and then turned into a contest of merit by the historian of India and critic William Dalrymple in a (no doubt deliberately) mischievous article he wrote in the British paper, the *Guardian*: "As far as writing in English is concerned, not one of the Indian literary A-list actually lives in India, except Roy, and she seems to have given up writing fiction. It is not just that the diaspora tail is wagging the Indian dog. As far as the A-list is concerned, the diaspora tail *is* the dog."[12] His challenge caused a mild flutter in Indian literary circles.[13] Marc Parent, an editor at the French publishing house Buchet Chastell, which has a significant Indian writers' list, has a different take on the relative merits of the two kinds of writing. He prefers the novel that "stems out of the flesh of India" (his examples are Tarun Tejpal and Kiran Nagarkar), finding diaspora novels "repetitive" since they "always have to do with acceptance or rejection of Indians as immigrants" and "can be applied to quite a few immigrants in the world you know. Africans, Turkish, Asians in general" (Chaudhury 2007). The foreign publisher's preference for an "indigenous" writing that he considers implicitly "more different," so to speak, is undeniably problematic; but it reveals some of the issues at stake in the debate. The real contest, if a contest must be staged, ought to be between mainstream British writers and minority, multicultural writers in Britain, not between the Indian dog and its so-called diasporic tail.

That there are differences between resident and nonresident Indian writers cannot be denied, but these are more significantly posed between those who write in the Indian vernaculars (so-called), and those (located anywhere) who write in English. It is the language and the place of publication—India, or Britain/the United States—that more substantially structure the hierarchies between writers in India. It was the publication and sales of Arundhati Roy's *God of Small Things* in Britain and the United States that made her internationally visible; her location in India did not affect the book's success (and may have added something to her cachet). The fact that the book is written in English made it an exportable commodity, a necessary (but not of course sufficient) condition of international critical and popular success. The complex politics of India's multilingualism is subject for another essay.[14] The point made here is the limited one about the implications of an *Indian* writing in *English*. Whether we define "Indian" in this context as a work written in/from India, or by a person of Indian origin living in the Western metropolis, the English "Indian" novel occupies the space of *difference*. In the case of the literature, it is the language (English) that is minor ("minor" as in spoken by a small percentage of the population: a second language, exclusive, privileged); in the case of authorial identity, it is the writer who belongs to a (racial) minority. Its minority status can either open this literature to charges of exoticism, alienation, or inauthenticity on the one hand, particularly in the case of English writing within India; or it can become the grounds for admiration for what it represents in terms of novelty, resistance, impurity, and hybridity as—on the other hand—has happened in the case of much immigrant South Asian writing.

NONFICTION PROSE

This anomalous status of English writing in India is, I believe, beginning to change; and it is changing mainly because of developments in *nonfiction* prose writing in English. Suddenly this large, loose, heterogeneous print phenomenon looks all set to explode. A mostly young generation of Indians—but with a notable ancestry going back at least to Nehru and his contemporaries, from the brilliant Cornelia Sorabji to the juristic framers of the constitution—are beginning to produce extremely competent writing in English.[15] In genres like investigative journalism, books on travel, cricket, popular science, or cinema, political commentary, memoirs, biographies, and autobiographies, and more belles-lettristic productions like essays, they are making their mark, if inconspicuously. This has been made possible by the spaces newly available for them in English-language journalism (prominently newsmagazines and Sunday newspaper magazines), through competitions like the annual prize sponsored by *Outlook-Picador* for nonfiction prose writing, the sporadic appearance of the *Granta*-type publication *Civil Lines* as well as new annual anthologies like Penguin's *First Proof* (both these publications showcasing "new writing from India" include substantial numbers of nonfiction prose entries). The success of two recent books, Suketu Mehta's *Maximum City* (2004) and Vikram Seth's *Two Lives* (2005), augurs well for nonfiction. These big books by established writers, based on years of documentary or historical research—therefore inimitable, one would have thought— represent nonetheless the kind of pioneering success that exhibits the potential of the genre and spurs imitations.

Placing this with two other notable phenomena—one, an increased volume of translations and other kinds of transactions between English and regional literary and cultural production, and two, more popular fiction in English written for a local market—it would be possible to come to this conclusion: that as prosaic writing gains in "literariness," English writing is becoming less merely "literary" in our milieu. As English percolates to a more general level of writerly usage, it makes itself more at home in India. And it is from this comfort level, I would predict, that paradoxically its future achievements in the literary field will grow.

A research team sponsored by Open University in the United Kingdom recently conducted one of the few systematic investigations of the Indian market for English writing. It was headed by Tapan Basu at Delhi University, who confirms the significance of nonfiction prose (he chooses to call it by a somewhat question-begging name, "nonliterary" writing): "If publishers are running head over heels to sign up Indian writing in English, the Indian writing in English that they are signing up is not always 'literary' writing in the narrow sense. As fallacious as the impression that Indian writing has little of worth except as Indian writing *in English*, is the impression that Indian writing in English has little of worth except as Indian *literature* in English" (emphasis added). Basu points out that it was Arvind Krishna Mehrotra's anthology of Indian writing in English, *An Illustrated History of Indian Literature in English* (2003), that first opened up the canon to nonfiction prose by including "translations of regional writings into English, nature treatises, dissertations on literature and art, political essays and tracts on social issues"; the editor had even envisaged commissioning chapters on history-writing and pulp journalism (Basu 2007).

Once we accept the existence of nonfiction prose writing in English as a significant autonomous genre in India, the next step is to ask whether it is a supplement to or radically disjunct from the conditions that have produced Anglophone prose fiction in India. In particular, I want to consider this question from the perspective of the present.

Let me begin by suggesting that writing in English in India has necessarily been an artificial production. I don't wish this to get derailed into the old tired argument about "authenticity." I mean "artificial" in the sense of "constructed" and deliberative, that which is not a given. Anglophone Indian literature is the only substantial body of creative writing in the world that is produced (written, published, read) in a second language from *within* a colonial/postcolonial nation-space. (African, Maghreb, or Caribbean Anglophone, Francophone, or Lusophone literatures by contrast are either largely diasporic, or they are first-language creolized productions.) However determined its usage might appear to be by the author's existential circumstances, English is a site of tension even if not choice, a tension produced by the vernaculars acting as a pull, as an option, as the road not chosen. The language of the text is never transparent, never simply a medium of expression; it is too saturated with its own history. The self-consciousness of literary English means that Anglophone fiction is and always has been an inescapable tour de force.

Nonfiction prose is prosaic ("prose is the language we speak without knowing it"),[16] instrumental, communicative, everyday: or at least this is the conceit by which it operates. The cumbersome identification "nonfiction" establishes fiction as the norm, relegating everything else written in prose to a vast and heterogeneous alterity. The economy of its regime is a tight one—from production to consumption the text is "used up," leaving no excess. It is local and topical, constrained by and limited to the place and time of its appearance. These generic differences are of course generalizable to any context, not just postcolonial India's. But in India it is a difference that identifies the politics of English differently in each case.

If I read contemporary nonfiction prose in English in terms of a break rather than a change from both fiction and earlier prose writing, it is because the changed conditions that have spawned it have dynamically altered the significance of English. Anglophone Indian fiction has a colonial genealogy it cannot disavow, but the new nonfiction is the product of a different formation, loosely called globalization, in which English has a more demotic dimension. Apart from the influence of television, advertising, glossy journalism, and the Internet, which bring "global culture" home (the old "US cultural imperialism"), and the phenomenon of call centers emerging as the new factories for global English language production, there is also the fact that for a large and growing yuppie population in India with something to say and the ability to say it in English, writing a blog is an easily available space of self-expression—and a means of finding the ideal responsive readership with shared interest in the specialist topic the blog promotes.

The sheer *quantity* and variety of such writing transforms the mode. Nonfictional English necessarily operates at a variety of levels, registers, and inflections as it is pressed into different roles and functions. In general, this is the sphere of public debate. Many of the contentious debates that have so enlivened the intellectual scene—whether on politics, cricket, the environment, nuclear policy, communalism, or a host of other subjects—are fought out either explicitly as debates in the print media, or implicitly through the ideological diversity of non-fiction book publications. In a bookshop you have a choice of Gurcharan Das's *India Unbound,* the suave bible of liberalization, or Arundhati Roy's radical polemics in *The Algebra of Infinite Justice.* By contrast, the quantity of fictional writing in English remains small, even if it is growing, making it look like a coterie production, and it tends to extreme homogeneity of style and matter. Not that there is no ideological continuity between fiction and serious nonfictional works in English: it is well known that Nehru's *The Discovery of India* served as a source book for *Midnight's Children,* and many of the novels that came after it are seamless with Sunil Khilnani's *The Idea of India.* The overlaps of style, meaning, and actual authorship between fiction and serious nonfiction is a matter that calls for more discussion, to which I shall now turn.

As a preliminary ground clearing, it is necessary to offer a rough-and-ready classification of nonfiction genres. Leaving aside the purely functional such as technical manuals and self-help books (although it is interesting that so many of these should be in English), and limiting ourselves to "serious" writing, I will identify four kinds of nonfiction writing.

The first is academic writing, a good part of it in India still written in English, which serves as the medium of higher education. This kind of writing also has the longest history, going back to the early nationalist history books like R. C. Dutt's *The Economic History of India* (1902). It is the medium, English, that has put academic discourse in India in conversation with the rest of the English-speaking world (Subaltern Studies being the most successful example in recent times). Oxford Univesity Press (OUP) India has been around as an independent university press for decades now and has been responsible for most of the quality academic publishing in English since Independence (much of it of course textbooks, but OUP maintains a sizable list of monographs), now diversified to other publishing companies with more specialist foci, like Permanent Black and Kali for Women. Academic writing does not generally get discussed in terms of literary attributes like style, but readers are quick to appreciate virtues of clarity and elegance in the writing. The magisterial periods and the memorable turns of phrase in Ranajit Guha's writing, for example, ("the law, as the state's emissary"), or the skilled rhetoric of Ashis Nandy's prose, which, together with the absence of jargon in his work, have made him something of a popular writer, are obvious to any reader.

Next is a broad general category of serious nonfiction writing. By "general" I signify a diversity that is not susceptible to subject classification, and by "serious" I indicate topics not entirely ephemeral in nature. The "general" list subsumes a range of politics and genres, reflecting a heterogeneous readership. A. P. J. Abdul Kalam's autobiography *Wings of Fire* and his inspirational teachings for children, *Ignited Minds,* the critic Nilanjana Roy tell us, are being sold in "bushels" at local cigarette-shops and on sidewalks in Indian cities (Roy 2007). It would be interesting to analyze what in the former president's rags-to-riches narrative—his fame as a scientist, or his faith in the simple virtues of hard work and sacrifice, or his patriotism—touches the pulse of a certain class of readership. Prominent in this general category are other autobiographies or memoirs by mostly out-of-power political figures (who choose to write in English). It includes also unacademic but popular sociologies and ethnographies of cinema, cricket, the environment, and urban histories. It is from this kind of writing that nonfiction in English gains its range and variety.

I will identify the third group of nonfiction books as "literary" nonfiction, and it is these that overlap most closely with the works of fiction, sometimes for the obvious reason that the same people write both: Vikram Seth, Amitav Ghosh, and Arundhati Roy have all produced substantial nonfiction writing. Roy has gained a different kind of stature, as a public intellectual, in the process. Amitava Kumar has moved the other way, from being a regular columnist to writing a novel. There was the intriguing almost-simultaneous appearance of two books, one a novel by Vikram Chandra (*Sacred Games*, 2006), and the other a blockbuster city-biography by Suketu Mehta (*Maximum City*, 2004), generated from very similar material on Mumbai. The aspiration to move from highly wrought literary prose to more ambitious writing (the novel is a step up in the literary hierarchy), is evident in several of the prize-winning entries in the *Outlook*-Picador contest in five successive years, from 2001 to 2005. One of these, for example, a long descriptive account of a 41-hour train journey from Shillong to Delhi by Ankush Saikia, ends with this paragraph after the journey is concluded and he is back in his Delhi flat, to come full circle to the article's opening sentence:

> Then, after hesitating for over a week, he finally sits down one morning and starts writing. The third person-present tense narrative he has in mind has been done before, most notably by a South African writer who has won the Booker twice. No matter. He will go ahead. The tense is not the problem; the problem is finding his own voice, and not imitating the South African's. The first line he writes is: "It is raining on the morning he leaves Shillong."

This, as we can see, is very self-conscious, very much a matter of life-experience becoming grist for the mill of "fine" writing.

It is not the criteria of literary aesthetics then, that divide fiction in English from nonfiction. It is rather the greater possibilities that the latter opens up in terms of who might write, where they might publish their writing and above all, what they might write about. It is this that leads me to the last of the kinds of nonfiction in my taxonomic survey: English language journalism. Open an English newsmagazine in India at random today, and you are as likely as not to come across a piece of writing describing a day in the life of a young surgeon at the Ram Manohar Lohia Hospital in New Delhi. He is trying to set up a surgical operation for a woman with a tumor in her stomach. The writer is Ambarish Satwik, a surgeon, who has also written a novel called *Perineum: The Nether Parts of Empire* (2007). The essay's burden is familiar to anyone who has grown up in India: nothing works, but people make do. An HIV-positive woman is brought in with a perforated ileum, and the surgical team sets about repairing her. They manage to remove a "bolus of roundworms" from her insides which caused the perforations, and then a portion of the ileum. There are only three Z-kits to go round (for protection from HIV infection), and these have to be paid for by the patient's husband. We see that the surgery is of necessity a very improvised affair, but the tone is matter of fact; one can read the piece as very funny or very grim. The account works as an exposé of the state of corruption, decrepitude, and poverty in the government hospital, but we realize—even though the author would downplay such claims—that what necessarily compensates is human dedication and skill, and the fortitude of both those who get sick and those who cure them. Satwik, writing in the first person, is self-deprecating: "that's about all it takes in the belly. Getting the plumbing right"; and the woman gets better against all odds.

This kind of writing inaugurates a new realism in Indian writing in English. Drawing on experience, observation, research, involvement, and investigation, and given the medium's voracious appetite for the sensational, journalistic writing has opened up a field of endless possibilities. The newsmagazine *Tehelka* (in which Satwik's piece appeared) has published long pieces of investigative journalism (Dilip D'Souza on Dharavi, Sonia Faleiro on Mumbai's sex-workers, Sankarshan Thakur on Bihar's politics). Some years ago P. Sainath wrote a series of searing pieces on poverty and caste in *The Times of India*, which have no equivalent in fiction in English. Many of these articles, like a comparable body of documentary films, are topical and interventionary. The nation has not disappeared from these writings, but—like the English language—it is worn more lightly than before. In its own laconic way,

Ambarish Satwik's article carries the same burden of nation as Gieve Patel's "Nargol," both translating into a responsibility toward the nation's poor. (Coincidentally, Patel too is a doctor by profession.)

One final example of these slow-changing ideas of nation in a changed register, from another nonfiction work. This is *Oona: Mountain Wind* (2001), a memoir of a young woman who died tragically young, written by Jasjit Mansingh, her mother. Oona Sharma (neé Mansingh) was the founder of Aarohi, an environmental NGO she set up in the small village of Satoli in the Kumaon hills in the Himalayas with her husband, a doctor. At the time of her death, Oona was deeply involved in a variety of projects involving the hill people and their livelihoods, which were just beginning to bear fruit. Oona's attitude and approach represent the point that has been reached with an ethics of postcolonial citizenship, one that is also gendered. Not unlike in the case of bourgeois women of an earlier generation, there is the felt pressure of "payback" for the privileges of education and affluence, reflected in Oona's own writing in journals, letters, and diaries (in English). But there are differences in the attitude toward the nation, even if it is similarly proprietorial and loyal. It has moved away from the earlier certitudes of state-led development, shifting instead to the people at the grass roots and necessitates *going to* them;[17] it is an investment that attends to the tangible problems of land, mountains, forests—the environment—rather than the abstraction of the "nation"; a pedagogy that eschews the interventions of so-called social reform; and a perspective that is bound up with *global* agendas (that are simultaneously *local*) that displace the national. These are my tentative tracings of the imperceptible ways in which discursive shifts have occurred in English-language writing, from the triumphant arrival of *Midnight's Children* over a quarter-century ago, into our contemporary present.

NOTES

1. I am indebted to Gayatri Spivak's use of "burden" in these two senses, "first, as the content of a song or account" and "secondly, a singular load to carry." See Spivak (1992), esp. p. 275. See also Josna Rege's invocation of Spivak's phrase in her book, *Colonial Karma* (2004: 165).

2. The political scientist Atul Kohli diagnoses a "crisis of governability" in India as a result of four related "variables": "the changing role of the political elite; weak political organizations; the mobilization of new groups for electoral reasons; and growing social unrest, including class conflict." See Kohli (1997), esp. p. 389.

3. It has become a common ploy of nationalists today to pit "Bharat" against "India" to suggest an authentic, populist, and Hindu idea of the nation, as opposed to its spurious, modernist, secularized version.

4. Compare Naipaul, who represents England in the very terms of Almasy's desert inverted: replete with the place names, the history, the tradition, the cathedral towns (Canterbury) that the other place is without.

5. Rushdie's valediction to his city in *The Ground Beneath Her Feet* is well known.

6. Appiah (1991: 353). For a nuanced understanding of African literature of the 1960s and 1970s, see Lazarus (1990). Lazarus diagnoses a utopianism in the writings of the early independence period that would quickly turn to disillusionment about the failure of the revolution. The African novel's case can be generalized to describe a broader postcolonial tendency, but its elaboration requires care.

7. If it is important to respect the degrees of difference between "sedition" and "criticism" in the legal and political context, equally one must distinguish between censorship and criticism in the cultural context. The novelist Vikram Chandra mistook his critics in India for "cultural commissars" in a complaint that appeared first in an American journal (Chandra 2000) and was subsequently reprinted in the Sunday supplement of the Indian national daily, *The Hindu*. In an imaginary confrontation staged as the climax of the article, he featured himself vanquishing the phantasmagoric figures of Hitler and Mao by being true to his art (Hitler and Mao jointly representing Meenakshi Mukherjee, at the time professor of English at Jawaharlal Nehru University, who had been critical of Chandra's writings).

8. This list, without being exhaustive, would include: Amitav Ghosh, Vikram Seth, Pankaj Mishra, Siddhartha Deb, Shashi Tharoor, Vikram Chandra, Anita Desai, Kiran Desai, and Rohinton Mistry.

9. Apart from Arundhati Roy (the most famous of the resident writers), the following are established resident novelists in English (not an exhaustive list): Upamanyu Chatterjee (a civil servant, member of the prestigious

Indian Adminstrative Service), Mukul Kesavan, Tarun Tejpal, Susan
Visvanathan, Githa Hariharan, Manju Kapur, and Shashi Deshpande.
In addition there is a growing number of India-based younger writers
(ages between 25 and 35), who are products of the new global India
but who are, observes the critic Claudia Kramatschek, "rooted in India
to an amazing degree." She notes in their work a "marked turn toward
localism... meaning toward the microcosms of one's own lived world,
to the history of the individual towns where these authors lead their
lives." "In literary terms," she goes on, "this return is associated with an
opening toward genre literature and toward what might be referred to as
the small form." The authors Kramatschek mentions are Altaf Tyrewala,
Sarnath Banerjee, Chetan Bhagat (a best-selling author of several books
now), Samit Basu, and Rana Dasgupta. To this list we might add Kalpana
Swaminathan, who writes detective fiction, and Kuzhali Manickavel,
author of an astonishing collection of short stories titled *Insects are
Just Like You and Me, Except Some of Them Have Wings* (2008), who is
identified on the book jacket only as resident of "a small temple town on
the coast of Southern India."

10. See, especially, Rushdie's "Imaginary Homelands," the title essay in the
collection (2003: 9-21).

11. See for instance, Chandra (2000), reprinted from a two-part article
in *The Hindu Literary Review:* "Indo-Anglican Writers: Nowhere and
Everywhere" (December 5, 1999), and "Indo-Anglican Writers: Where
the Mind Is without Fear" (December 19, 1999).

12. See Dalrymple (2005). He wrote a follow-up article in the Indian
newsmagazine *Tehelka* (2005: 24) entitled "India Cancelled," in which he
argued that Indian film and music in the British diaspora, like the books,
had overtaken their rivals in India. Responses by Rana Dasgupta and
Samit Basu are included in the same issue.

13. The novelist Nayantara Sahgal responded that when she hears it said
"with great authority," that "there is no Indian writing of worth except
diasporic writing," it sounds to her "like knowing there is an Athens
in Ohio, and having to be told there is also an Athens in Greece." Her
ordering of the cultures of nation and diaspora in terms of the real and the
fake, the original and the derivative, and the primary and the secondary,
is revealing. See Sahgal (2007).

14. Girish Karnad's play, *A Heap of Broken Images* (*Odakalu Bimba* in Kannada), stages the relationship between English and Kannada writing as sibling rivalry. The conceit represents the intimacy that exists between writing in English and the other Indian languages as inseparable from the enmity that pits them against each other. The entire play is staged within the divided self of the writer Manjula Nayak, the play's sole actor. Manjula is a Kannada short-story writer of small fame—until she publishes a novel in English (in Britain) and shoots to international celebrity-hood. It turns out that the novel had really been written by her handicapped younger sister, Malini, completed just before she died of a progressive illness, and slyly appropriated by Manjula, who had long borne a grudge against this talented and attractive sister. The play was first staged in Kannada in 2004 and in English in 2005.

15. See for instance *Indian Masters of English: An Anthology of English Prose by Indian Writers,* selected and edited by E. E. Speight, senior professor of English at Osmania University, Hyderabad, in 1934. In his introduction Speight describes the purpose of the book: "this little book...has been compiled to give Indian students a series of models of what can be done by elder students of their own nationality in the handling of so difficult a language as English." He includes speeches and writings by Gandhi, Syed Ross Masood, Sarojini Naidu, Srinivasa Sastri, J. C. Bose, and several others (but puzzlingly, not Nehru).

16. Molière, *Le Bourgeois Gentilhomme* (1670): "Good heavens! For more than forty years I have been speaking prose without knowing it" (Act II, sc. iv).

17. In Fanon's resonant call, "We must join (the people)...in that fluctuating movement which they are just giving a shape to, and which, as soon as it has started, will be the signal for everything to be called into question. Let there be no mistake about it; it is to this zone of occult instability where the people dwell that we must come; and it is there that our souls are crystallized and that our perceptions and our lives are transfused with light" (1963: 182-183). Fanon's revolutionary sentiments can be adapted without too much violence to other postcolonial reconstructive projects, I hope.

REFERENCES

Appiah, Kwame Anthony. "Is the Post- in Postmodernism the Post- in Postcolonial?" *Critical Inquiry* 17 (1991): 336-57.

Basu, Tapan. "Contemporary Indian Writing in English: Is There a Market in India for This Text?" *Contemporary Indian Literature in English and the Indian Market* (2007) <http://www.open.ac.uk/Arts/ferguson-centre/indian-lit/workshops/london-workshop2007-tapan-basu.htm>.

Chandra, Vikram. "The Cult of Authenticity." *Boston Review,* February/March 2000.

Chatterjee, Partha. *The Nation and Its Fragments: Colonial and Postcolonial Histories.* Princeton: Princeton University Press, 1993.

Chatterjee, Upamanyu. *English, August: An Indian Story.* London: Faber and Faber, 1988.

———. "Rambling at Fifty." *India Today,* August 18, 1997.

Dalrymple, William. "The Lost Sub-continent." *The Observer,* August 13, 2005.

Das, Gurcharan. *India Unbound.* Delhi: Penguin India, 2000.

Deshpande, Satish. *Contemporary India: A Sociological View.* Delhi: Penguin, 2003.

Desai, Kiran. *The Inheritance of Loss.* Boston: Atlantic Monthly Press, 2006.

Fanon, Frantz. "On National Culture." *The Wretched of the Earth.* Trans. Constance Farrington. New York: Grove, 1963.

Franco, Jean. *The Decline of the Lettered City: Latin America in the Cold War.* Cambridge: Harvard University Press, 2002.

Fraser, Robert. *Lifting the Sentence: A Poetics of Postcolonial Fiction.* Manchester: Manchester University Press, 2000.

Futehally, Shama. "The Idea of India." *The Right Words: Selected Essays, 1967-2004.* New Delhi: Penguin India, 2006.

Gandhi, Leela. "Some Notes on the Rise of the Stephanian Novel." *The Fiction of St. Stephen's.* Eds. Aditya Bhattacharjea and Lola Chatterji. New Delhi: Ravi Dayal Publisher, 2000: 151–158.

Ghose, Sagarika. *The Gin-Drinkers.* New Delhi: Harper Collins, 2000.

Ghosh, Amitav. *The Shadow Lines.* London: Bloomsbury, 1988.

———. "Writing Is Like Music." Interviewed by Banibrata Mahanta, Somdev Bani, and Namrata Rathore. *The Hindu,* May 21, 2000.

Karnad, Girish. *A Heap of Broken Images. Collected Plays.* Vol.II. Delhi: Oxford University Press, 2005.

Khilnani. Sunil. *The Idea of India.* New York: Farrar Straus Giroux, 1997.

Kohli, Atul. "Crisis of Governability." *Politics in India.* Ed. Sudipta Kaviraj. New Delhi: Oxford University Press, 1997: 383–95.

Kramatschek, Claudia. "Farewell to Spice and Curry" <www.signandsight. com/features/1117.html>.

Kumar, Amitava. "The Currency of Arundhati Roy." *Rediff on the Net.* August 30, 1999 <http://www.rediff.com/news/1999/aug/30us.htm>.

Manickavel, Kuzhali. *Insects Are Just Like You and Me Except Some of Them Have Wings: Short Fiction.* Chennai: Blaft Publications, 2008.

Mansingh, Jasjit. *Oona: Mountain Wind.* Delhi: Srishti/Bluejay, 2001.

McCaul, Kathleen. "Subcontinental Shift." *Guardian*, February 13, 2007.

Mehrotra, Arvind Krishna, ed. *An Illustrated History of Indian Literature in English.* New Delhi: Permanent Black, 2003.

Nehru, Jawaharlal. *The Discovery of India.* Delhi: Oxford University Press, 2002 (1946).

Ondaatje, Michael. *The English Patient.* London: Picador, 1992.

Parent, Marc. "Paris Can Be the New Centre." Interviewed by Shoma Chaudhury. *Tehelka,* February 3, 2007: 24–25.

Patel, Gieve. "Nargol." *Ten Twentieth-Century Indian Poets.* Ed. R. Pathasarathy, New Delhi: Oxford University Press, 1976: 88.

Rege, Josna Rege. *Colonial Karma.* New York: Palgrave Macmillan, 2004.

Roy, Arundhati. "The End of the Imagination." *The Algebra of Infinite Justice.* New Delhi: Penguin Viking Books, 2001: 1–41.

Roy, Nilanjana S. "Publishing in India." *Le Monde* (March 2007) <akhondofswat. blogspot.com/2007/.../publishing-in-india.html>.

Rushdie, Salman. "Imaginary Homelands." *Imaginary Homelands: Essays and Criticism, 1981-1991.* London: Granta Books, 1991: 9–21.

———. *The Ground beneath Her Feet.* New York: Henry Holt, 1999.

———. *Step Across This Line: Collected Non-fiction, 1992-2002.* London: Jonathan Cape, 2002.

Saikia, Ankush. "Spotting Veron." *Outlook India,* May 12, 2005.

Sahgal, Nayantara. "The Ink Is Soiled." *Outlook India,* March 5, 2007.

Sainath, P. *Everybody Loves a Good Drought.* Delhi: Penguin India, 1996.

Satwik, Ambarish. "Innards of the System." *Tehelka*, September 29, 2007.

Sengupta, Shuddhabrata. "Identity Card and India Ink." *India Magazine,* 1997: 12-14.

Seth, Vikram. *A Suitable Boy.* New York: HarperCollins, 1993.

Sinha, Indra. *Animal's People.* London: Simon and Schuster, 2007.

Speight, E. E. *Indian Masters of English: An Anthology of English Prose by Indian Writers.* Calcutta: Longmans, Green, 1934. Rpt. Davidson Press, 2007.

Spivak, Gayatri Chakravorty. "The Burden of English." *The Lie of the Land: English Literary Studies in India.* Ed. Rajeswari Sunder Rajan. New Delhi: Oxford University Press, 1992: 275–99.

Commonwealth Games 2010: The Index of a "New" India?

Boria Majumdar

The Commonwealth Games were Delhi's and India's biggest sporting event ever. As the shiny promise of hosting them enveloped Delhi, questions loomed—large, unasked, and ominous: Who would emerge the winner in the contest to present Delhi as a global city? Would Indian sports gain at all? How much was it costing the person on the street? Who would actually benefit from all the digging and window dressing? And did the average Indian, some forcibly resettled to facilitate Games construction, lose materially?

This paper sets out to analyze the story of the Games' legacy—their politics, economic impact, and to what extent they were successful in transforming Delhi into a global city and India into a sporting force to reckon with. It starts from the premise that the Commonwealth Games (CWG) had the potential to create conditions for the building of a "culture of winning" in India, measured in terms of gold medals won and state status earned in front of the international sports fraternity. This "'winning culture'" is fundamentally different from an already existent sports culture in the country in such sports as *kabaddi*, *gilli-danda*, and other street sports and games, which are alive and vibrant in spite of very little national or global recognition.

Thanks to all of the Indian athletes whom I could speak to in the course of my research, and to my team at *Times Now*, who made the Games coverage a fascinating experience.

It is essential to declare at the outset that two fundamental motives lie at the heart of this project. The first is the determination to contribute to the growing corpus of research on Indian sport, a subject area still somewhat underdeveloped. The second is to understand the Indian sporting story against the backdrop of what is happening inside a nation trying to establish its postcolonial identity in the world. The thread running through the paper is the politicized nature of India's Commonwealth Games experience. The CWG story, the paper demonstrates, is also a story of Indian politics, of power equations, and the failure to professionalize Olympic sports vis-à-vis cricket in India.

Having already documented the history and politics of the Commonwealth Games with a focus on Delhi (Majumdar and Mehta 2010), this paper instead tries to place Delhi 2010 in perspective, understand its long-term meaning, and explain its lasting legacy.

PRE-GAMES FEARS

While the Games organizing committee and the politicians continued to be hopeful with just days to go for the Games, the national media discourse on Delhi 2010, the world discourse, and indeed the mood in the city presented a rather gloomy picture.

In Canada, for instance, days before the athletes departed for the Games, they were issued strict instructions that India wasn't secure enough amid terror threats from the Lashkar-e-Toiba; Canadian athletes were asked not to stay on in Delhi following their events. While some were upset at the prospect of missing out on the cultural experience of India, others concurred that it was ultimately the responsibility of the Canadian Olympic Committee to ensure security concerns were given due importance.

At a Commonwealth Games conference in Glasgow in June 2010, organized by, among others, Louise Martin, vice-chair for the Glasgow Games in 2014, the discourse on Delhi could be symbolized in one word: apprehension. Most, if not all, of the speakers were critical and some were even scathing about Delhi's continued state of underpreparedness.

Similarly, while many dismissed the queen's decision to give Delhi a miss—her first nonattendance at the Games in years—as irrelevant to

India, it only underscored the negative undercurrent of the discussions in Britain. The BBC's airwaves may have been full of *Incredible India* advertisements, but the only news of the Games on the BBC's domestic networks between May and August were the damning reports alleging serious scandals about funds assigned for the poor being diverted toward Games organization (Morris 2010). (There were many similar reports in other news agencies of the world as well.) Human rights activists were concerned that the 40,000 families moved between June and September in the lead-up to the Games would not be offered necessary resettlement.

The global discourse, it must be acknowledged, was as negative as the domestic discourse in the country's newspapers and TV networks. If anything, the Indian press was even more scathing.

"NERVOUS BUT OPTIMISTIC": DELHI'S POLITICAL DISCOURSE ON THE EVE OF THE GAMES

What about the leaders who were driving the Games? In trying to gauge the thinking in Delhi's political circles in an ambience of growing global apprehension, I conducted a series of interviews with Games stakeholders, members of the Prime Ministerial Committee on the Commonwealth Games, and members of the Games organizing committee.

Three clear strands emerged in these interviews. First, many of those interviewed remained confident, but some of the confidence on display was clearly false bravado. Second, they underscored a growing sense of urgency in trying to wrap things up in time. It was this sense of desperation that explained the rapid pace of work in Delhi in the third quarter of 2010, a pace that stood out in sharp contrast with the agonizing apathy witnessed in the years 2003–2009. Suresh Kalmadi, the chairman of the organizing committee, now facing a series of charges for alleged misappropriation of funds, vehemently insisted that there "was no reason to panic." Sheila Dikshit, chief minister of Delhi, acknowledged that she was "nervous" but argued that this anxiety was par for the course before an event of this magnitude. And Kapil Sibal and Kumari Selja, two of India's leading cabinet ministers, broadly repeated the soft-power argument, akin to one made of South Africa as it played host to the soccer World Cup in June–July 2010. All asserted that India would ultimately pull it off, as the prime minister's report card to the nation after the United Progressive Alliance's first year in office also declared (personal interviews 2010).

In all the interviews, the one common strand was that the hosting of a sporting event at a scale such as the Commonwealth Games was a matter of international prestige for the country and was bound to boost "brand India." The same sentiment was expressed in the official website for the Delhi Games, which went on to add that the "Games will leave behind dramatically improved world-class sports facilities that generations of Indian sportspersons can use in the future. The establishment of an Olympic-size pool as well as a gym in the Delhi University will boost sports among the youth of Delhi."

Are such claims tenable? As the naysayers note only half in jest, the only thing that playing chess makes you better at is chess, and the only thing a successful sporting event proves is that country's ability to host it (Skapinker 2010: 11). Greece hosted a great Olympic Games in 2004, but see where it is now, says this school of thought. And the argument about the Games turning the host country into a sporting nation is seductive but facile.

Are the 101 medals, a first in India's sporting history, a mirage at best? Or have the Commonwealth Games finally paved the way for India to become a truly sporting nation? Is the dream of sport for all and sport for peace a dream that we can aspire to fulfilling, or will the Games' performance soon turn into a footnote as the euphoria recedes and the nation moves its focus to punishing the corrupt in the post-Games scenario and toward hosting the Cricket World Cup and the fourth season of the Indian Premier League (IPL) in mid-2011?[1]

As Hans Westerbeek (2010) has rightly argued, the key point to be made here is that "long-term urban and social planning for a destination needs to coincide with long-term planning and scheduling of capacity building. The key to success remains a long-term vision for the city of Delhi that also fits the plans the government has for India. Only then can events such as the Commonwealth Games be made into tools that assist in economic development, justifying the fast-tracking of construction of critical transport and building infrastructure, attract tourists and business investment, providing event spin-off programs for the local community leading to a range of socially beneficial outcomes, and so on."

As I write this paper, with only a few months having lapsed since the Games concluded amid much fanfare on October 14, 2010, because of its heuristic, practical, and political value, Delhi 2010 has become a highly sought-after commodity, the long-term impact of which hinges not only on what happened during the Games, but more appropriately on its legacy.

On the plus side of the ledger, to India's credit, Delhi offered the world's athletes a first-rate Games village, despite the initial hiccups, and very good stadiums for most sports competitions. Barring the Shivaji Stadium for hockey, which was meant to be a practice venue, most venues, despite initial concerns, were ready on time. But even if they were all ready, even if they were gleaming on the day with near-packed crowds, was that by itself enough? And was that what these Games were about? What after that? And at what cost to the city? Most important, what about our athletes?

LASTING LEGACIES

More than the venues or the Games village, our urban infrastructure, the issue of community integration, and, most important, the performance of our athletes—who have created the possibility of India finally embracing Olympic sport—are of paramount importance in the longer term. This belief was only strengthened after India's fantastic performance at the Asian Games at Guangzhou in November 2010. For the first time in India's history, the country won medals in 14 sports disciplines, including an unprecedented 13 gold medals. The key question to ask in the post-Games scenario is: Did these Games belong to the organizing committee or the government of India, or did the Games in fact belong to our athletes? To go a step further, should the success of the Games encourage our sports administrators and officials to mount a serious Olympic bid for 2020, or should they concentrate on creating more champions who can win medals for the country at the London Olympics in July and August 2012?

If it is the latter, as should be the case, little has been done yet to give our athletes the feeling that it was their event and that it was organized to benefit them in the long run. At the same time, while Delhi inhabitants never adopted the slogan, "We want bread not circuses," which was raised by Toronto's citizens in the 1990s and had derailed the city's Olympic bid in 1996, the average Delhiite, smarting under the impact of the entire city being dug up, was largely indifferent to the biggest event in India's sporting history. Unless the organizers are successful in winning over people's confidence in the post-Games scenario by allowing the average Indian the use of the Games facilities, the emotional connect, so very necessary in ensuring a successful legacy, will be extremely difficult to achieve.

Ethnography around Delhi and the National Capital Region in the build-up to the Games helped demonstrate that the ordinary taxpayer, whose money was being used to fund the Games, was in the dark about most things pertaining to the event. For the average Delhiite, it was an exercise in opulence with little or no benefit in the longer term. Most believed that the sports facilities created for the Games were destined to be white elephants, never to be within the reach of ordinary citizens. The problems facing them on a daily basis far outnumbered the gains promised.

Without bridging this gap, the long-term legacy of Delhi 2010 can at best be mixed, nothing more than a marketing slogan gone awry. And as every marketer worth his salt knows, there is nothing worse for a dodgy product than a good slogan.

Finally, can a mega-event of this nature really create a sports culture in India? Can CWG 2010 create a rallying cry for "sport for all"? Or will Indian sport continue to remain a lottery destined only for a few? These are questions that continue to animate experts in the post-Games scenario and are questions this paper will seek to answer in the following section. The notion of sport for all was certainly part of the Delhi 2010 legacy vision, which states that "More than all, the legacy of the XIX Commonwealth Games 2010 Delhi will be to boost the sports culture as a part of the daily life of every Indian, particularly the youth" (See the 2010 Commonwealth Games website). But how did the reality in fact turn out?

These questions are extremely relevant when studied against the legacy of the 1982 Asian Games in Delhi. While there is little doubt that Delhi was fundamentally transformed as a result of the event, it can definitively be asserted that the legacy of the Asian Games remains negative in terms of nurturing an all-pervasive sports culture in India, a drawback that helps explain why India has won one solitary individual Olympic gold medal after 88 years of competition.[2]

Knowing full well that the tremendous effort and cost of staging major games militates against the realization of a sustainable legacy for sport and physical activity, Delhi needs to step up and set an example. Only if this is done can Delhi serve as a perfect model of what the Commonwealth Games can do for a host city. This is especially pertinent in India because even to this day, among most Indian games organizers, sport is still too often phrased as somehow being separated from its cultural and historical context. To illustrate the point, the mainstream sports discourse in India on the 2010 Commonwealth Games tell us that it is all about medals won, records broken, or television rights sold as ends in themselves, or that it is about the idea of India's emergence as a sporting power, a dream the country has nurtured since Independence in 1947. However, as is documented more globally, the Commonwealth Games and their relevant records and statistics are important only insofar as they can affect societies surrounding them.

In fact, it would not be unfair to suggest that mega-events, such as the Olympics, or the Commonwealth Games on a lesser scale, are still not fully understood in all their dimensions. In recent years, such crusading journalists as Andrew Jennings have set out to expose the inner workings of the International Olympic Committee (IOC) and what he considers its corruption. The organizational clean-out that followed the Salt Lake City scandal in 2002 confirmed many of Jennings' assertions, even if his recent attacks on the IOC appear motivated rather than searching.

The Commonwealth Games Federation, too, has been subjected to serious criticism in recent times. Few works on the Olympics, like John Macaloon's biography of Pierre de Coubertin and the origins of the Olympic Games, are comprehensive and balanced. There is hardly anything on the history and politics of the Commonwealth Games.

For the most part, writing on mega-events has been sycophantic and idealized. This is why there is a significant disconnect, as Bruce Kidd argues, between the highly visible mega-sports spectacles and the ideal of sport for development:

> Governments, sponsors and the media reward and punish on the basis of the medal count, no matter how courageous, moving or ethical the performance, so the whole culture of high performance sport is increasingly preoccupied with the recruitment and training of champions. As a result, only a fraction of the public and private funds spent on sport goes to grass-roots development; even less for sport for development (Kidd 2010).

ATHLETIC ACHIEVEMENT AND THE FOUNDATIONS OF A SPORTS CULTURE

Had anyone suggested to me at the start of the Commonwealth Games that India would win 101 medals and come second in the medals' table, I would have laughed off the claim. This was simply unbelievable. But miracles do happen, and CWG 2010 is nothing short of a miracle as far as India's athletic achievement is concerned. It is India's best performance ever, by quite a distance. India can finally aspire to becoming a serious sporting nation. We had champions not in one sport but across disciplines and gender, in events that were hardly spoken about in the run-up to the Games. From the athletic standpoint, CWG 2010 is a watershed event that will forever have its place of pride in the Indian sporting pantheon.

Any assessment of India's CWG performance has to begin with Gagan Narang, India's ace shooter and best athlete at the Games. Winner of 4 gold medals, each with a Games record, India suddenly has an athlete capable of taking on the mighty Chinese at the Olympic stage. To go back to the moment when Gagan won his first gold at the Games in the 10 meter air-rifle event: he had just scored a 600 out of 600 to make the final. A commanding 5-point lead over second-placed compatriot Abhinav Bindra, India's only individual gold medal winner at the Olympics, Narang was the overwhelming favorite for gold. But there's a huge difference between a CWG gold and a world record. Once Gagan had scored 703.6 in the final, one expected him to be euphoric. But there he was, calm, composed, reserved, and focused. At the insistence of the media, the gun was picked, and slowly walked the champion to pose for photos. With both hands holding the gun aloft, Gagan Narang was making a statement to the world that India, finally, has an athlete capable of winning multiple gold medals at the London Olympics in 2012. Certainly a tall order, for CWG is not half the competition that London 2012 will be. But having won everything there is to win barring the Olympics, Narang now knows he needs to make the London podium his own to transform himself from being India's top athlete to India's most loved icon.

The important thing for India is that he is not alone. India already had Abhinav Bindra, but now we also have a slew of shooters who can make the world stage their own. Ranjan Sodhi and Manavjit Sandhu may not have had the best CWG, but they are both recognized world beaters in their respective events, double trap and trap shooting. Others, such as Omkar Singh (winner of 3 gold medals at the CWG) or Heena Sidhu, are shooters who have come of age in recent months, making India a shooting powerhouse to reckon with.

If shooting is currently India's number one Olympic sport, wrestling and boxing do not lag far behind. Three gold medals in boxing, with a bad decision preempting the favorite, Vijender Singh, from adding to the tally in the 75 kilogram category, mean that India now has a crop of boxers who can make the London podium in 2012. The wit and cockiness of Suranjoy Singh and the skill of Vijender don't come easy. Years of effort have finally resulted in India being labeled "Asia's Cuba," a tag India will proudly carry to London.

In wrestling, with Sushil Kumar justifying his billing as the best in the world and developing a cult following in the process,[3] it is only natural that corporations will start looking at wrestling with new eyes in the days ahead. Interestingly, the Indian challenge is no longer limited to our men. In fact, it wouldn't be a far cry to suggest that our women wrestlers were a revelation in Delhi. From Alka Tomar to Geeta and Babita, the skill and effort on display will go a long way to encouraging many more to take up the sport in days to come.

This is fascinating because wrestling continues to be regarded as a male domain, a taboo for respectable middle-class women. In contrast to other Asian nations, such as China and Korea, women wrestlers in India (despite having achieved considerable success in recent times) mostly try their hand at the game without hope of earning a livelihood from it. Wrestling associations continue to stagnate, and financial crisis is a permanent companion of the women's game. Leading wrestlers are hardly ever given due recognition, and the jobs on offer are never higher than the clerical grade. It is commonplace to see noted women wrestlers languishing in penury after retirement, only to be rescued from such a plight by welfare organizations and sports enthusiasts. When placed against this backdrop, the success of India's women wrestlers is a testament to their skill and determination, and stands tall as one of the lasting legacies of the Delhi Commonwealth Games.

And there are other more established stars who continue to amaze and startle at the same time. One such is Leander Paes, who continues to win laurels for the nation with amazing regularity even at age 37. Leander is often said to be an average tennis player who reaches another level when he wears the tricolor. While on the one hand this is meant as praise—he continues to remain patriotic after 20 years of the professional grind—on the other, it dwarfs all his other achievements: 12 grand slam titles, which, to remind us all, have helped reinstate India in the world tennis map.

So what if Leander's completing 20 years in international sport wasn't celebrated with half the fervor in comparison to that of Sachin Tendulkar;[4] so what if people don't throng the airports when Leander comes back to India after each tournament; so what if he continues to be hailed as a Davis Cup wonder. The truth—and his amazing track record of having won 44 career doubles titles—will demonstrate that Leander Paes, along with Vishwanathan Anand,[5] has been the best thing to happen to Indian sport, except cricket, over the last two decades. And when he finally retires, nothing, not even the frenzy associated with Indian cricket, can take this truth away from him. He will continue to be the most awe-inspiring Indian sporting icon of all time. For who else could say: "Most people see Davis Cup as pressure on their shoulders. For me Davis Cup puts pressure under my shoulders, pressure that lifts me up." Maybe the Commonwealth Games weren't as good as he may have expected, but as Leander said to the media soon after the Games, "Fingers crossed I will give it one more crack at London 2012. I have a singles medal already. It will be great to have one for doubles as well." With Somdev Devvarman stepping up to winning the men's singles gold at the CWG and Rohan Bopanna having the best year in his career and making the US Open doubles final in the process, Indian tennis looks to be healthier than it has been in the years gone by.

Speaking of Indian sporting icons, it is imperative this paper acknowledge the two young women from Hyderabad who have captured the nation's imagination, Saina Nehwal and Sania Mirza.

Sania Mirza has seen both the highs and the lows. From seeing 200,000-plus women buying nose rings in emulation of her after her fourth-round US Open appearance in 2005 and first WTA tournament win, to dropping out of the top 100 because of a recurring wrist injury, Sania Mirza at 23 is already a veteran who has seen it all. Unnecessary media glare on her personal life may have made her cynical, but it hasn't taken away the zeal to wear the tricolor.

While her brand value is facing stiff competition with the rise of Saina Nehwal, she seems unfazed. Watching her closely gives one an awkward feeling. Has she seen it all in too short a time? Has the hype followed by the slander in the media during her marriage, again totally unnecessary, made her a changed person? Will all of this result in her losing faith in her own people and will Sania Mirza, the quintessential icon for India's girl power, be reduced to a footnote in the Indian sporting pantheon?

From the evidence at hand in Delhi, the answer is negative. She appeared focused, determined, able, and confident. She knew Delhi was her platform and that she needed to make it count. Thankfully for India, she did.

Saina, on the other hand, is in the form of her life. From three super series wins in June and July 2010 and a fourth in December, when she triumphed at the Hong Kong super series, to a gold medal at the Commonwealth Games, she is justly India's sportswoman of the year. By winning the last gold at the Games and catapulting India to second spot, Saina Nehwal in 2010 can do no wrong. And in winning these titles and challenging the Chinese, she is continuously making a statement to the world that Indian Olympic sport is at a crossroads, and she is here to make a huge difference. We can, finally, dream of having a sports culture of our own, especially with the Commonwealth Games having successfully relegated cricket to a back burner. Even an India–Australia cricket series seemed colorless in comparison, drawing attention to the huge interest the Commonwealth Games had managed to create. Watched by 115 million viewers over 11 days, their viewership was 13 million more than the 102 million who watched the entire Indian Premier League (IPL) season one from April to May in 2008.

For the first time in Indian sporting history, the media appropriated the accomplishments at CWG in a manner associated commonly with cricket. Suddenly, CWG stars were flooded with interview requests and offers that had long since been reserved for over-pampered cricket stars alone. Multiple polls on news channels revealed that the national religion of cricket had slid in the popularity charts. According to one survey, 60 percent of sports fans in Delhi were glued to the Commonwealth Games. In contrast, 31 percent watched the Indian cricket team in action against the Australians. Needless to say, it is a historic moment and also perhaps a mark of our times that India is moving beyond its singular obsession for cricket and embracing Olympic sport as well.

With medals in athletics, especially the one, two, and three in women's discus and gold in the 4 x 400 women's relay, India eclipsed the 50-year-old jinx. Equally credible was the silver in gymnastics and the bronze in para-swimming won by Prasanta Karmakar. And in archery, with Mangal Champia watching from the sidelines, we can easily surmise how good Rahul Banerjee, Tarundeep Rai, and Jayanta Talkukdar are. A medal or two in archery at London 2012 will hardly be a surprise.

The success of the Commonwealth medal winners, it can be argued, is as much a testament to their own skills as it is a metaphor for the larger story of India. These men and women have arguably shattered the grand narrative of failure that has characterized Indian sport. As John MacAloon (2008) argues, the Olympics are a "crucible of symbolic force" into which the world pours its energies and a stage upon which every four years it plays "out its hopes and its terrors." For every Indian, that terror always came in the form of a question: A billion people and hardly any gold medals at mega-events. Why? CWG 2010 has finally provided that answer, and hence the nationalist frenzy that follows, a frenzy best borne out by the euphoria surrounding Indian hockey at the Games.

To see the 17,500-strong crowd at the Dhyan Chand stadium go berserk when Bharat Chetri saved the penalty stroke against England in the penalty shoot-out, and when Shivendra Singh converted his stroke to propel India to the final, it was truly a picture-postcard moment for Indian hockey. The final was an aberration, but the performance en route, a thrashing of Pakistan and a comeback against England from being 1-3 down, augurs well for Indian hockey. The sport is on an upswing and the crowd support only serves to point out that the passion for our national sport isn't dead after all.

In contrast to the euphoria surrounding hockey at the Commonwealth Games, the period since the late 1970s presents a rather dismal picture. The decline in the 1970s was such that India's eight consecutive Olympic gold medals between 1928 and 1956 seemed a distant memory. In 1976 a world hockey magazine, in an article analyzing this decline, decided to define it with the pathos-ridden headline, "The Fall of Rome."

India continued to perform miserably in the Olympics and the Champions' Trophy in the 1980s and 1990s. In the eight-nation tournament in Holland in August 2005, the Indian hockey team finished a dismal seventh. It was only in the 2007 Asia Cup that Indian hockey demonstrated possibilities of a resurgence, winning the competition by defeating archrival Korea 7–2 in the final.

That this was a mirage became clear when India, for the first time in history, failed to qualify for the Olympics, losing 0–2 to Great Britain in the finals of the Olympic qualifying match at Santiago, Chile, on March 9, 2008. This was its second consecutive loss to Britain in the tournament, having lost 2–3 at the group stage. Indian hockey had come full circle. From its halcyon days in the 1920s and 1930s, it had plummeted to its lowest ebb by not being able to make it to the Olympic Games.

India's performance was such that even if it had won, the victory wouldn't have done much to contest the fact that since the late 1970s, hockey has languished (bronze medals in Mexico in 1968 and Munich in 1972, a world championship win in Malaysia in 1975, and gold in Moscow in 1980 notwithstanding) and it is hardly comparable in popularity to cricket, which has gained in reputation since. With cricket reigning as the national passion, mass spectatorship in hockey in contemporary India is a rarity. Often, it is less than 5 percent of the spectator base for cricket in the country.

Hockey's failure to retain its earlier glory has been the primary reason for the game's decline. The Indian Olympic Association and the Indian Hockey Federation blame the corporate world and the media for stepmotherly treatment, but poor marketing strategies, internal politicking, and the myopic views of the officials who run these institutions are also accountable for the decline of the sport.

MOVING ON

Do the CWG victories mean the arrival of a national sporting culture? Or will Indians clap their hands in glee and return to their daily dose of cricket once the euphoria recedes? While the medals at CWG 2010 could certainly be the catalyst to help correct years of frustration at India's poor sporting performances, administrative inefficiency continues to be a major stumbling block, best borne out by comparing the organization of the Delhi CWG with the Cricket World Cup, played out to packed stadia in India in February and March 2011.

There is a perennial complaint in India's Olympic sporting circles that cricket has destroyed, or rather harmed, the Olympic sporting fraternity. Sponsors inevitably queue up to pay for the gentleman's game, television broadcasters give cricket a lot more airtime, and print publications publish cricket news as the lead sports item. These facts, more often than not, are correct. However, the reasons behind such treatment of Olympic sports have hardly been delved into by the administrators of these disciplines, for these would tend to expose their own deficiencies and amateurish work ethic. A comparison between the Delhi 2010 Commonwealth Games and the Cricket World Cup 2011 makes clear the fundamental differences in the governance structure of cricket and Olympic sports in India.

The best way to drum up interest before a mega-event is through sale of merchandise. For the Commonwealth Games, a full-scale merchandise program was never launched. There was no sale of Games merchandise at outlets throughout the country, no official agent appointed until the very end of the preparations, and the few samples produced were sold out within minutes of the start of the Games on October 3, 2010. The result: a huge revenue earning opportunity lost. In contrast, Cricket World Cup merchandise was on sale in India beginning in November 2010, four months before the tournament. The range was vast and the sales options easy to maneuver. One could buy official merchandise from the International Cricket Council (ICC) website and also from the kyazoonga.com website, official ticketing agents for the World Cup. By allowing Kyazoonga to sell merchandise, the ICC, in a smart marketing move, enabled customers who bought tickets also to pick up merchandise.

It is the professionalism associated with cricket that explained the tremendous interest in the event across sectors of the Indian economy and society. Interest in the Cup wasn't confined to just the sponsors and marketers. Unlike in the Commonwealth Games, where tourist interest had dwindled to minimal levels due to the disastrously poor buildup, tour operators from across the world used the World Cup to make a killing. Especially for Indian tour operators and planners, the World Cup was looked upon as their best opportunity to sell packages to nonresident Indians who made their way back home to catch World Cup action.

In the final analysis, the World Cup was much more than a cricket competition. It was a platform for rival brands to leverage the opportunity and for marketers to prosper because it was a professionally managed and run event—unlike the 2010 Commonwealth Games.

HOSTING THE OLYMPICS: LOGICAL COROLLARY OR UNWARRANTED GAMBLE?

A survey of international media reports in the aftermath of a successful CWG 2010 draws attention to one singular strand of argument: whether or not India is ready to mount a strong Olympic bid. These arguments are based on assumptions that a successful CWG is a stepping stone toward bidding for the 2020 Olympic Games.

Put bluntly, India is not ready to submit a serious Olympic bid. The Commonwealth Games came to India prematurely in 2003,[6] a decision that explains all of the problems in the lead-up to the Games and the clean-up act that is currently under way. An Olympic bid, which comes at a serious cost to a nation, will in fact divert attention from the athletic achievement at CWG 2010, which for the first time ever in our sporting history has given us hope of becoming a true sporting nation.

The Olympics, unlike the CWG, is a vastly complex and gargantuan exercise. If the CWG experience is taken as evidence, an Indian bid will only be a waste of time, energy, and money. In a scenario where the world's largest democracy has one solitary individual gold medal to show at the Olympics in 88 years of participation, it is imperative we concentrate on creating and nurturing champions, men and women who can do the country proud at London 2012. Trying to prepare an Olympic bid for 2020 amid competition from Madrid and Tokyo, cities which were in contention for 2016 but eventually lost out to Rio, will only result in large amounts of money spent on non-sporting activities at the cost of our athletes.

Taking stock of CWG 2010, the foremost gain from the sporting extravaganza, as documented earlier in the paper, is the success of our sporting icons. Having come in second at the medal table with 101 medals, holding England to third place, India can finally start talking of having a sports culture.

Moving focus to an Olympic bid will mean these victories do not mark the arrival of a national sports ethos. It will once again ensure that Indians move on to cricket. The Commonwealth medals will soon be subsumed under the pressures of preparing the Olympic bid and subsequently attempting to garner global support for India's candidature.

In fact, in an atmosphere of relative optimism, a note of caution is an urgent necessity. India's sporting culture needs an overhaul, and the CWG medals have indeed created a possibility for such a change to come about. Unless the government, sports administrators, the IOA, and, finally, the corporations come forward to embrace Olympic sport, CWG 2010 and the subsequent Asian Games performance will remain an aberration. Such private efforts as the Mittal Champions Trust and Olympic Gold Quest, already doing their bits, must contribute more toward Indian sport. Tough questions need to be asked. Is it time, for instance, to merge the Indian army's celebrated Mission Olympics with the larger national effort to mainstream sport in India's public imagination?[7]

While India celebrates CWG 2010 for what it has done to place Olympic sport on the national map, it is time to replicate such achievements across the country. Only if there is a systemic overhaul can India expect more medals at the 2012 Olympics. As Jacques Rogge, the IOC president, repeatedly emphasized during his recent visit to Delhi when asked about an Indian Olympic bid: "You have great athletes and you have one overriding sport, which is cricket. But we need more gold medals from the second most populous country in the world before you make a pitch for hosting the Olympics" (2010 interview).

THE UNDERBELLY OF SUCCESS

While CWG 2010 is a success and has encouraged a debate on India mounting a bid for the 2020 Olympics, the euphoria of success should not also mask the rotten run-up to the Games. In fact, it is nothing short of a miracle that the Games went off without a hitch. This, more than anything else, should preempt Indian sports administrators from trying to put together a bid for the Olympics in the immediate future.

In late 2006, when the Games organizing committee made a presentation to the prime minister, it listed six points on the impact of the Games. Only one referred to sport. The rest of the listed aims are revealing: "enhance the image and stature of India," "project Delhi as a global destination," "act as a catalyst for sustained development of infrastructure," "add to the prevailing upbeat mood in the Indian economy," and "create opportunities for trade, business and investment for Delhi and India." Judging by its own logic, the result has been a failure. Delhi was to have done a mini-Beijing; instead, it threatened to take the sheen off the India story.

According to government records, estimated Games-related costs shot up to more than $15 billion. This is 114 times the original calculation made in 2002. In running a company, such a phenomenal cost overrun would in most cases be seen as management failure. By comparison, Melbourne's total spending for the 2006 Games was $2.9 billion: just 0.6 percent above its estimate. (Majumdar and Mehta 2010).

Part of the problem has been skewed priorities. For example, to showcase Delhi 2010, its organizers flew in Bollywood stars to dance to the drumbeats at the closing ceremony of the 2006 Commonwealth Games. The 10-minute Bollywood trailer cost the Delhi government over $6 million. In contrast, the entire Indian sports contingent at the Melbourne Games cost the government less than $1 million. In a sense, this lopsided spending was symbolic of the Games effort. When they should have been focusing on the basics, the organizers seem to have concentrated on what Bollywood calls the "item number": the idea that getting a sexy starlet to do a slinky dance number will be enough to draw an audience, irrespective of the quality of the film itself.

To add to the misplaced priorities, Delhi got off the starting block rather late. Beijing 2008 and London 2012, for instance, followed a seven-year time cycle: two years for planning and approvals, four years for construction and development, and the last year for test events and trial runs. In Delhi's case, the first few years were utterly wasted. As per the contract with the Commonwealth Games Federation, Delhi's organizing committee was to be in place by May 2004, but it was not formed until February of the following year. In contrast, the organizing committee for the 2014 Commonwealth Games in Glasgow was formed even before the award of the Games.

This delay rendered most of the original timelines redundant. The bid document had four phases: 2004 to 2006 for planning, 2006 to 2008 for creating, 2008 to 2010 for delivering, and 2010 to 2011 for concluding. The government's own auditors found "no evidence of the four-phase approach being translated into action during the first phase years of 2004 to 2006." Planning only really commenced from late 2006. At least 21 major organizations and agencies were involved, each with different roles, budgets, and reporting lines. According to the comptroller and auditor general of India, "Many agencies were either unaware of their role or refuted the role expected of them." Many even had different timelines for the same project.

The managerial limbo translated into chaos on the ground. The Games' organization plan and Games' master schedule were to have been ready by May 2004; they were only finalized for approval in August 2007 and May 2008. Going by the official record alone, the Games' effort always had the appearance of watching an accident unfold in slow motion.

In the end, that India managed to stage a spectacular opening ceremony that stunned the world and that the Games went off without any major disaster is as much a testimony to the effort put in by the government of India in the last weeks leading up to the Games as it is to the many hundreds-strong volunteer force that manned the stadiums, the village, the Main Press Centre, the International Broadcast Centre, and other relevant areas with tremendous efficiency and resilience. Working tirelessly for days on end, these men and women made the Delhi games what they turned out to be: a showcasing of India's national pride and ability. That there weren't complaints at the airport, village, the Games hotels, and other sites was largely because of the efforts of these men and women.

THE FUTURE

What now of the future? There are many in India who look longingly across the border at China's awe-inspiring sporting machine. The Chinese too built their success by focusing on key sports initially— gymnastics, table tennis, badminton, and athletics. India, however, cannot hope to replicate the Chinese model blindly. The organization of Indian sport is far too complicated and far too political to allow for a unilinear approach like that of the Chinese or the East Europeans before them (Hong et al. 2008).

As with Indian democracy, Indian sport has evolved its own unique model. When Kapil Dev's unfancied team won the Cricket World Cup in 1983, no one could have predicted that the surprise victory, coinciding with the television revolution, would ignite deeper processes that would ultimately turn India into the spiritual and financial heart of the global game. Now the CWG success has created another opportunity that, if harnessed, could usher in a new era in Indian sport. As India grabbed gold after gold for the first time, a national television audience, led by a cheerleading media, focused on Olympic sports. The fact that many of the stars had emerged from relatively underprivileged backgrounds with few facilities provided irresistible stories of human triumph against all odds.

When K. D. Jadhav won India's last wrestling medal at the Helsinki Olympics in 1952, the celebrations at home were extremely muted, restricted to the sports pages of newspapers, unlike the mega-hype now around Sushil Kumar and the new phalanx of Indian boxers. To compound Jadhav's agony, the political class gave the victorious hockey team of 1952 a tumultuous welcome in ceremonies across the country, while Jadhav had to make do with a localized cavalcade of a hundred bullock carts from his native village. In 1952, hockey was a potent symbol of Indian nationalism but Jadhav, despite winning independent India's first individual Olympic medal, was left to ultimately die in poverty. He was forced to sell off his wife's jewels to build a modest cottage and won a posthumous Arjuna award only in 2001 (awarded by the Indian government for outstanding achievement in national sports). In sharp contrast, government coffers have already opened up for the CWG winners and much more corporate largesse is on the way. In fact, each state is honoring its medal winners, and corporate India is not lagging behind either. In a nation starved of sporting glory, the intense media focus on these stars has turned them into new national heroes.

If India fails to take advantage of the fertile conditions created by CWG 2010, its lasting legacy will have been confined to history books by the time of the next Olympics in London in 2012. In fact, if a fundamental transformation of the sporting infrastructure in India is not brought about in the coming months, the CWG medals will remain as moments of individual brilliance lost amid countless failures since Independence.

Moving beyond sport and going by the definition that soft power is the ability to get what you want by attracting others to your values, the government of India and the Commonwealth Games organizing committee have promoted the Games as a tool to attract the West to what they call a truly "modern India." At the same time, it is obvious to everyone that there remains a sizable section of India that had chosen to remain beyond the realm of this marketing effort, for whom the Commonwealth Games did not signify much more than opulent spending with little tangible gain in the long run.

Slum dwellers in Kolkata or Kerala, people ravaged by incessant cyclones along the Andhra coast in July 2010, or the thousands who were forcibly resettled because of the construction of the Games village, continue to be scathing in their condemnation of the Games—not to mention a great number of those in Delhi who are ostensibly meant to benefit from the infrastructure being created. As Ashis Nandy argued,

> Anybody who spends a few weeks here will know that there is another India which was rebelling and continues to be indifferent to the version of the official India, the ultra modern India being hammered home by the government. The slums of Delhi for example are in a different kind of dialogue with the mainstream discourse on the Commonwealth Games (quoted in Dodd 2010).

For Nandy, the contradiction between the official rhetoric on India championed by the government and the "dissent" that is so easily noticeable in the slums of Delhi are too obvious not to be taken note of by global commentators and policymakers interested in studying the legacy of the Games. Such comments will only gain in strength unless the athletic achievements are consolidated upon, once again drawing attention to the issue of sustainable legacy of the Games.

CONCLUSION

In the final analysis, despite all the contradictions surrounding the legacy rhetoric, the Commonwealth Games, even with their attendant corruption and scams, helped India make a statement to a sizable global audience. A failed Games experience, on the other hand, could have added serious force to the murmurs that there remains a serious disconnect between India's newfound modernity and the masses of Indians who still inhabit pitiable conditions of existence, a stereotype championed by commentators intrigued by India's growing economic might and political clout.

At its best, the experience of Delhi 2010 can surely herald the start of a new journey. At the time of writing, however, such a possibility appears uncertain, given that the official class is focusing more on the 2020 Olympics bid than on consolidating the athletic achievements emanating out of Delhi. Also, Delhi 2010 was meant to reorder the city but it is unclear whether such a reordering can be harnessed to the common good of Delhites in the months to come. Whether or not the Games are a spectacle to remember will depend on achieving these twin objectives, the most enduring legacies of the 2010 Commonwealth Games.

NOTES

1. World Cup 2011 was held in India, Sri Lanka, and Bangladesh between February 19 and April 2, 2011, and IPL season 4 was played from April to May in 2011.
2. Abhinav Bindra won India's only individual gold medal at the Olympics at Beijing 2008 at the 10 meter air-rifle event.
3. Sushil Kumar is the first Indian to win gold at the world wrestling championships. He won gold in Moscow in August 2010, just days before the Commonwealth Games.
4. Sachin Tendulkar, completing 20 years in international cricket, was celebrated at a national festival with week-long celebrations and felicitations organized to recognize his achievements in November 2009.
5. Winner of multiple world chess titles, Anand is considered only second to Garry Kasparov in the list of the best chess players of all time.
6. India won the bid to host the Commonwealth Games at Montego Bay, Jamaica, in November 2003, beating Hamilton, Canada, by 46 votes to 22.

REFERENCES

2010 Commonwealth Games <www.cwgdelhi2010.org>.

China Gold: China's Quest for Olympic and Global Glory. Eds. Hong, Fan, Duncan Mackay, and Karen Christensen. Great Barrington, Mass.: Berkshire, 2008.

Dikshit, Sheila. Interviewed by the author. August 29, 2010.

Dodd, Phillip. *The Monday Documentary: Soft Power India* (2010) <www.bbc. co.uk/iplayer/episode/p007qdkn/The_Monday_Documentary_Soft_ Power_India>.

Duenas, Crispin. Interviewed by the author. June 1, 2010. University of Toronto, Toronto.

Kalmadi, Suresh. Interviewed by the author. September 15, 2010.

Kidd, Bruce. "Sport for Development." *Biblio: A Review of Books* (September/ October 2010).

Lee, Vanessae. Interviewed by the author. June 1, 2010. University of Toronto, Toronto.

MacAloon, John J. *Pierre DeCoubertin and the Origins of the Modern Olympic Games*. London: Routledge, 2008.

Macdougall, Alana. Interviewed by the author. June 1, 2010. University of Toronto, Toronto.

Majumdar, Boria, and Nalin Mehta. *Sellotape Legacy: Delhi and the Commonwealth Games*. New Delhi: Harper Collins, 2010.

Morris, Chris. "'No Accountability' over Delhi Games Spending." BBC, May 24, 2010 <http://news.bbc.co.uk/today/hi/today/newsid_8700000/8700010. stm>.

Paes, Leander. Interviewed by the author. October 12, 2010.

Rogge, Jacques. Interviewed by the author. October 3, 2010.

Selja, Kumari. Interviewed by the author. August 30, 2010.

Sibal, Kapil. Interviewed by the author. August 30, 2010.

Skapinker, Michael. "A Thirst for Reality Eclipses the World Cup." *The Financial Times* (London), June 8, 2010.

Westerbeek, Hans. "Driving Away White Elephants." *Biblio: A Review of Books* (September/October 2010) <http://tinyurl.com/TimesOfIndia-Westerbeek>.

Indian Science Today: An Indigenously Crafted Crisis

Sabyasachi Bhattacharya

Science must think in terms of the few hundred million persons in India.

—Jawaharlal Nehru, Speech to the
Indian National Science Congress, Delhi, 1947

The Indian government's efforts to improve the quality of science education and scientific research in the country in the postcolonial era are reminiscent of an apocryphal story recounted in Rabindranath Tagore's childhood memoirs. "I was...highly amused to hear from my father for the first time the story of the milkman who was suspected of watering his milk, and the more men one of his customers detailed to look after his milking the bluer the fluid became," Tagore writes, "till, at last, when the customer himself interviewed him and asked for an explanation, the milkman avowed that if more superintendents had to be satisfied it would only make the milk fit to breed fish" (Tagore 1917).

During the seven decades since the great expansion of science in the country, the government of India has established many committees,

The author thanks Dipesh Chakrabarty and Kalpana Raina for a critical reading of the manuscript and acknowledges Arvind Kumar, M. G. K. Menon, Govind Swarup, Obaid Siddiqi, and B. M. Udgaonkar as well as many graduate students of the TIFR for useful discussions.

commissions, and learned panels to supervise and evaluate its status, only to see the average quality of both education and research in the basic sciences deteriorate steadily. The latest report on the subject, commissioned by the Indian National Science Academy (INSA) and authored by some of the best and the brightest mid-career scientists in India, paints a picture analogous to Tagore's story.

> In Indian science currently, a few islands of relative excellence and a small number of talented individuals stand out amid a vast and unremarkable background. Indian institutions that support the scientific enterprise, ranging from large universities to research institutes, government laboratories and undergraduate colleges, share no common clearly articulated purpose. The problems include an absence of scalability of individual efforts to meaningful levels; plain misgovernance and uninspired leadership; an overall lack of democratic functioning; and the withering away of academic independence in many of our institutions. These are exacerbated by a failure to recognize how deep-rooted the problems are, coupled with an overall reluctance to accept correction (INSA 2010).

The INSA report describes the problems correctly, albeit harshly, and provides a scenario for a sorely needed recovery. In fact, recent reports on India's higher education in general, and on science education in particular, are similarly outspoken, insightful, and critical (Yash Pal 2009; Rama Rao 2009). However, analysis of just how the decline has set in is rare both inside and outside the scientific community in India. India's relative position in the world of the sciences, by any reasonable measure, declined significantly over the last quarter of the twentieth century. It is often pointed out that India is the only country to have won a Nobel Prize in the natural sciences under colonial rule, but not as an independent nation. Members of the Indian diaspora, however, have won a few since India's independence, a fact not overlooked inside the country.

After 60 years of Independence, the prospect for such high achievement is bleaker today than at any time before. Although Indian science retains a place among the top 20 nations in total output of scientific research, its rank, on average, is very low, a result of the prevalence of mediocre work. Attempts to explain the situation using metrics—such as the ratio of India's gross domestic product (GDP) allocated to research and development (R&D) to its scientific output—are not insightful, nor can they explain the decline as a result of lower investment. The surprise, as frequently noted, is the colonial period, which, with its infrastructural deficiencies and absence of investments, ought to have prevented high intellectual achievements in science. However, achievements did indeed occur, providing a powerful reminder of the freedom movement's impact on all aspects of India's intellectual life, including the sciences.

That kind of a head start during the colonial era naturally led to expectations that India's scientists, supported by an independent nation-state, would allow India to leapfrog over its competitors and emerge as a major scientific power and economic force on the world stage. These expectations were not fulfilled; worse yet, the crisis of science education and scientific research has grown too deep to be easily addressed. The half-hearted corrective measures over the decades have been grossly inadequate. The inability to act effectively, born out of a stubborn "reluctance to accept correction" has its genesis in a) Indian society's high level of comfort with "feudal" forms of governance, b) the tendency to convert all social organizations, including scientific ones, into caste-type hierarchical structures, and c) an enduring culture of hero worship that actively opposes attempts to correct the mistakes of the heroes of the past. This article attempts to explore possible modes of evolution of the current crisis.

At the heart of the problem lies the colossal blunder made during India's "nation-building phase" in the immediate aftermath of Independence in 1947, which institutionally separated research from higher education in science, two fundamentally interlinked activities. This created, in effect, a three-tiered caste-structure of institutions: at the top, research institutions with few students; in the middle, universities with postgraduates, teaching a large number of students, where research is increasingly endangered; and, at the bottom, undergraduate colleges, where research, for all practical purposes, is impossible (Ramakrishnan and Sondhi 2009). Early critiques of the system focused on the need to strengthen the universities by emulating the research institute model and finding ways to liberate universities from a paralyzing lack of autonomy and resources (Yash Pal and Udgaonkar 1967). It was correctly surmised that university-level teaching without research opportunities creates a disheartening environment that discourages scientific research as a career option for young people. However, it was not apparent then that without teaching, research institutions, too, could become sterile and mediocre.

Within the country, the decline of the top-tier, the elite research institutes, once called islands of excellence, was overshadowed by an even sharper decline of the middle-tier, the universities, but a global comparison clearly reveals the former trend (King 2004). In this context, the recently adopted National Knowledge Commission's (NKC) mandate to provide a road map to transform India's still dominantly agrarian economy to a knowledge economy (NKC 2008) appears unrealistic as India continues to fall further behind its global peers in the areas of science and technology. The absence of India's foresight to plan for the necessary intellectual infrastructure is qualitatively similar to other areas of development. However, unlike roads and bridges, intellectual infrastructure takes decades, not months and years.

Within the community of scientists, the response to the state of affairs has been, by and large, one of disinterest, denial, and diversion. They question the metrics of scientific achievements, blame the bureaucratic machinations of the government, complain about a perennial lack of financial and other resources, and even bemoan an erosion of noble sentiments of an earlier time in the globalized and commercialized economy of the modern era. The community continues to avoid recognizing the connection between science and technology, the importance of a historical perspective in creating a meaningful social consensus on the role of science, the critical significance of communicating the epistemology of science in the classroom and in the laboratory, and, finally, the essential duty of the practitioners of publicly supported science to deliver some form of social good, utilitarian or otherwise. Their Brahminical worldview of the community of scientists has instead helped to preserve a hierarchical division of labor and a sense of entitlement without accountability. Over the years, it has nurtured dichotomies between research and teaching, head and hands, theory and experiment, fundamental and applied, and the beautiful and the useful. These attitudes have contributed, in no small measure, to the crisis described in the INSA report.

THE EARLY YEARS (1850–1947)

A historical account is useful in establishing a context for the crisis. Modern science entered India during the colonial times through the spread of Western education in general. "But colonial rule was more than imperialism and exploitation," M. G. K. Menon writes in an enlightening summary of Indian science through the ages, "it also had the components of a cultural encounter" (Menon 2004: 8). The famous Wood's Dispatch of 1854 led to the establishment of Western-style colleges and universities. The year of 1857, which also included the Sepoy Mutiny, saw the establishment of three universities in Calcutta (Kolkata), Bombay (Mumbai), and Madras (Chennai) in the three Presidencies (the regions under direct British rule). The pioneering endeavor of science teaching started in the 1860s at St. Xavier's College in Calcutta, run by the Society of Jesus—the Jesuits—and most famously by Father Eugene Lafont (1837–1908), the physics teacher and mentor of Jagadish Chandra Bose, India's first modern scientist (Nandy 1972).

The establishment of the Indian Association for the Cultivation of Science (IACS, affectionately called "Cultivation" in the city of Kolkata) in 1876 was a watershed event. The founders, Dr. Mahendralal Sircar (1833–1904), the second medical graduate of the university, and Father Lafont of St. Xavier's College, patterned "Cultivation" after the Royal Institution in London, made famous for the research of member Michael Faraday (Biswas 2001). The very public discourse surrounding the establishment of the IACS was reformist, modern, cosmopolitan, sophisticated, idealist yet informed by realism, and, uncharacteristically for India, focused on substance rather than rituals. Sircar writes about the philosophy underlying the new institution: "Until men learn to respect each other's honest convictions, and until they are free from all prejudices, in other words, until they are fearless of the consequences of discoveries in the fields of knowledge, they cannot be said to have become civilized men. The one thing that can secure this blessing, the toleration, and freedom from prejudice is knowledge" (Sircar 1874; quoted in Menon 2007: 19). The orientalist Rajendralal Mitra defended a more holistic approach to science in the IACS, appealing for strategic development of Indian science with an eye toward the longer haul, and arguing against a more narrowly defined utilitarian approach:

> Science...was the more powerful lever for progress, for the advancement of civilization, for ennobling the mind of man....*Let every step of science education be explained by experiments, for science to be effectually learnt should be learnt in the laboratory: but do not attempt to make your institution a school of technical education in the industrial arts under the misnomer of practical science* (IACS 1976; quoted in Menon 2007: 22; emphasis added).

Lafont further remarked that the agents of the colonial power "wanted to transform the Hindus into a number of mechanics requiring for ever[sic] European supervision, whereas Sircar's object was to emancipate, in the long run, his countrymen from this humiliating bondage" (Menon 2007: 22). Although these remarks may seem to denigrate technical education today, they were meant to argue "for higher education for the natives" and not simply a technical education or training that the colonial masters were happy to dispense with. In other words, the educated elite were engaged in a public debate about the role of science and its applications as an indispensable part of the long-term intellectual aspirations of the country (Palit 2001; Menon 2004).

C. V. Raman's discovery of the phenomenon bearing his name in the IACS, Calcutta, in 1928 and being honored with a Nobel Prize in physics in 1930, was the crowning moment of Indian science in the colonial era. (The Raman Effect was an early experimental verification of quantum mechanics by an optical method and currently a standard method of molecular spectroscopy.) At the same time, equally significant discoveries by Jagadish Chandra Bose, Satyendranath Bose, and Meghnad Saha established India as a major force in modern science. Calcutta University, under the leadership of Asutosh Mukherjee, offered a chair to Raman, who taught at the university and conducted research at the IACS. The other three found homes in colleges and universities where they both taught and conducted research. Despite the small number of people actually engaged in teaching and research during the early years, the quality of the science was high, supplemented by synergistic institutional connections. Research institutions founded later include the Indian Institute of Science (IISc), which became Raman's home institution in Bangalore after his departure from Calcutta; the Indian Statistical Institute (ISI) in Calcutta; and the Tata Institute of Fundamental Research (TIFR) in Bombay; all of which retain considerable international stature. In the early stages of their development, they, too, would remain committed to a holistic development of science in the country.

But all was clearly not well during those early days. Warning signs of the rough times ahead were also emerging in the early 1930s, which was otherwise the golden age of Indian science. It took the form of personal discord among the great scientists of the time. A scathing indictment of this trend by the eminent physicist Max Born, an émigré to India from the Nazi Germany, was plainly expressed in his letter of 1936 to Lord Rutherford in Cambridge. Born wrote:

> Nothing can be easier in India than to rouse discord and to stir it. Once you allow and encourage people to speak, they will never end because they want an outlet. There is always latent jealousy and dissatisfaction which would be directed against almost anybody or anything. Take Professor Saha. I know the following from [him]. Saha is one of the greatest enemies of Raman. I do not know whether he also had hoped to become the successor of Raman in Calcutta, and Raman may not have helped him get this post. A very clever pupil of Raman—Krishnan—got it. Since then Saha attacks Raman when he can (Anderson 1975: 109).

Raman ultimately left Calcutta for the greener pastures of Bangalore (Bengaluru) and the opportunity for these two towering figures to cooperate in order to create a world-class scientific enterprise was lost. The feud also created an enduring rift among the more formal fraternities, such as the academies. Born continues in the same letter:

> They have another object of quarrel; Saha intended to found an all-India academy, but things went too slowly for Raman's temperament

and he founded his own academy (Indian Academy of Science) in Bangalore, with his own Proceedings. Now there are two academies in India, not too many for such an enormous country, but they are bitter adversaries. All the north Indians joined Saha's party, and the south Indians that of Raman. These parties have their delegates in the Council of the Institute, but the north Indians, and particularly the Bengali, have the majority"(Anderson 1975: 109).

Sustained by these feuds, a structure based on kinship, provincialism, personal loyalty, patronage, and entitlement began to form within the institutions of higher education. In the process, the scientific institutions would sacrifice the excellence and merit necessary to earn and protect a functional autonomy. The ultimate effect of tolerating mediocrity was to paralyze the intellectual vitality of the scientific enterprise as a whole. The academies themselves became vehicles of a culture of patronage for the scientific communities rather than a significant source of wisdom in the service of the country. The recent well-publicized "Bt Brinjal" fiasco (caused by a report on genetically modified crops, issued jointly by several scientific and professional academies, which was rejected by the government because of its poor quality and accusations of plagiarism) is evidence that little has changed over the years (Menon and Siddharthan 2010).

THE MIDDLE YEARS (1947–2000)

The decades immediately preceding and following India's independence laid the foundation of what was to happen in Indian science for the next half century, until the economic reforms of the 1990s. Jawaharlal Nehru, the first prime minister of independent India, was a strong believer in the role of science in modern times. His policy statement of 1958, a document of rare wisdom, insight and understanding, appears in its entirety in Appendix I. It is just the kind of a pronouncement of purpose called for in the INSA document, remarkable for a developing country emerging from a poverty-stricken, riot-torn, and all-round bleak colonial experience. It is well documented that Indian scientists of international stature—Saha, Bhatnagar, Mahalanobis, Bhabha, and their compatriots, well connected to the influential global fraternity of scientists—participated in the great 'expansion of science. New institutions were formed in rapid succession outside the ambit of colleges and universities in order to hasten India's progress in science and technology. Perhaps the most widespread in its impact was the complex of laboratories under the auspices of the Council of Scientific and Industrial Research (CSIR, built along the lines of the Department of Scientific and Industrial Research [DSIR] in the United Kingdom), led by Bhatnagar in 1942, just prior to India's independence. Such a large-scale and rapid expansion of science is perhaps unique in the history of developing nations. An expectation that such a beginning would propel India rapidly forward was widely shared. As late as 1984, John Maddox, one-time editor of *Nature*, remarked exasperatedly and insightfully on India's continual inability to deliver on this promise, despite notable success in agriculture, nuclear energy, and space (Maddox 1984). Similar frustrations were expressed also in the writings of the biologist J. B. S. Haldane (Haldane 1964).

During these middle years, from the mid-1940s until nearly the end of the century, Indian science by and large lost the momentum of a vigorous early start due to a variety of self-inflicted injuries, some doubtless a legacy of the colonial days, but others clearly "indigenous refinements," as Maddox called them. Important among them is a self-fulfilling Brahminical notion that activities involving only the brain are superior to those that require the use of one's hands, and that theory is superior to experiment, notwithstanding the achievements of J. C. Bose and Raman. There is also no denying that theory is cheaper, needs less investment in infrastructure, and thus creates a more even playing field in poorer countries such as India. Indeed, the semiconductor revolution, the forerunner of the IT revolution, was simply too expensive at the time for India to participate in. Bright young people thus flocked disproportionately to theory for both cultural and material reasons. An examination of physics departments globally, with which this author is more familiar, shows a striking inversion of emphasis on theory—at the cost of experiment—in India as compared to most countries in the West. Since much of scientific progress depends on experimental investigations, India was at a clear disadvantage. This situation, too, has changed little over the years.

It is tempting to speculate that India's protectionist industrial policy, a legacy of the country's freedom movement that was meant to promote self-reliance, also contributed to the decline of Indian science. India's independence came soon after the end of World War II and coincided with the beginnings of the Cold War. India's industry was in a primitive state; the Industrial Revolution in the West had affected India mostly through colonial exploitation. When Raman discovered the effect named after him, India did not even manufacture paper clips; those, too, had to be imported. India had also endured a partition that displaced millions, creating unspeakable misery that would continue for decades on both sides of the border. India's policy of industrial protectionism was born in those hard times.

However, during the years of protection from foreign competition, Indian industry did not develop as hoped. Instead, it limped along and exploited a captive domestic market. A version of *swadeshi* patriotism implied that the nation supported this policy of industrial protectionism for the national good. To the Indian, the label of "Made in India" on its products was meant to mean more than whether those products were made well or not. The phrase "indigenous" became code for a waiver of inquiry into a product's quality, a plausible explanation that addresses John Maddox's astonishment about India's obsession with self-reliance and penchant "for doing everything a little less than excellently." (Maddox 1984: 584).

The impact of the "self-reliant" protectionism coupled with weak governance systems was disastrous for Indian science. At the time, India had inherited two forms of governance, one colonial and the other "traditional." The latter was indigenous—resembling what is known in classical learning and classical music as the *gurukul* or the *gharana* system. This was the obvious choice because the patronage culture at the heart of the *gharana* system dovetailed perfectly with the spirit of protectionism. (The *gharana* system is a combination of a school, a clan, and a "religious" order; the disciples are expected to show extreme obedience and loyalty toward the teacher's authority, which, in return, guarantees the teacher's lifelong commitment to aid the well-being of the disciples.) While the policy adversely affected all areas of education and research, the situation with the sciences was particularly severe. Scientific truths are often more than global, they are sometimes universal, and there is nothing very indigenous about them. Protected backwaters are the natural habitat of sterile, mediocre, and "me too" science that, unlike "reverse-engineering" or "import-substitution technology," has no use whatsoever, not even temporary or tactical. The protected community guards its privileges jealously and habitually opposes new initiatives for fear of competition and having to share resources. When leaders of institutions eventually depart, the torch often passes on to trusted underlings as a reward for obedience and loyalty, not originality and independence. This is a kind of "Yayati Syndrome"—following the tale in the *Mahabharata* of the king who usurped his son's youth for himself and, in the end, rewarded his son with the kingdom in exchange for his lost youth. In such a demoralizing environment, institutions become easy prey to all kinds of influences. An uninspired leadership that INSA report mentions is a likely outcome of this system of governance.

The concept of indigenous development was not restricted to projects or products; it extended to people as well. Among the eminent scientists of the time, some were trained abroad and some were homegrown. J. C. Bose (physicist, inventor of millimeter wave transmission, later a biologist), P. C. Ray (chemist and successful entrepreneur), P. C. Mahalanobis (physicist-turned-statistician, founder of the Indian Statistical Institute), S. S. Bhatnagar (chemist, founder of the CSIR chain of laboratories to aid industrial research), Homi Bhabha (physicist, founder of the TIFR and the atomic energy program), and Vikram Sarabhai (physicist, founder of the space program) belonged to the former group, while Meghnad Saha (nuclear-astrophysicist, inventor of the Saha Ionization Equation, founder of the Institute of Nuclear Physics in Kolkata and later a member of Parliament), S. N. Bose (physicist, co-discoverer of the Bose–Einstein statistics), and C. V. Raman (Nobel Prize winner in physics in 1930 for the discovery of the Raman effect, later director of the Institute of Science, Bangalore and then founder of the Raman Research Institute) were in the latter.

This difference in academic pedigree appeared to make little difference in their professional outlook or purpose. In the middle years, as the community grew in size and the academic bureaucracy grew in complexity, the strain between the two groups grew as well, similar to the personality clashes of the earlier times. Yet another community, a scientific diaspora in the West, notably in the United States during the post-Sputnik era in the 1960s, also grew significantly in number, international stature, and achievements. The process of migration, pointedly referred to as "brain drain," did little to ameliorate a contentious, uncomfortable, and resentful relationship among these communities. Consequently, the diaspora residing outside the indigenous *gharanas* had neither credibility nor influence to affect domestic practices, especially for India's educational institutions.

The breakdown between scientific institutions within the country during this time is well illustrated by the evolution of the views of Homi J. Bhabha, the most successful of the institution builders of modern Indian science. In the early stages of his career in the 1940s, Bhabha remarked, "long-range research would appear, in general, best carried out in the universities or in special institutes attached to the universities, since while the research is in progress, its development and trend should be entirely unhampered by any thought of immediate utility" (Bhabha 1944: 29). Echoes of Rajendralal Mitra from an earlier time are unmistakable. Creating close ties between teaching and research was the right way to progress. Bhabha observed, "but, such a programme would need a very widespread revision of our university system in India, where...research facilities are very inadequate and the staff overburdened with teaching duties" (Bhabha 1944: 29). On another occasion a decade later, he astutely observed that "contact with students is a revitalizing factor for the research worker and conversely we feel that the presence of the Institute here [TIFR] will be of some advantage to the university" (1955).

In a later decade, however, Bhabha's frustration begins to show: "Above all, scientific teaching and research at the universities must be strengthened and expanded. The universities are, however, autonomous organizations, jealous of outside interference and the process must be slow and time-consuming" (Bhabha 1966 in Anderson 1975: 84). He is even more critical in his terse observation that "in universities people tend to stagnate. In science, stagnation should be avoided at all costs" (Bhabha 1965 in Anderson 1975: 84). From these remarks emerges the evidence of a vicious cycle: the decline of the universities led able researchers to abandon them, which naturally led to a further decline. An effect, intentional or not, of creating these newer institutes and laboratories and allocating resources disproportionately to them was indeed to relegate the universities to a lower status in the larger society. The concerns voiced about this outcome can be clearly inferred from the writings of those defending the institutes and national laboratories (Yash Pal and Udgaonkar 1964). But the policy of favoring the institutes, led by the Nehru–Bhabha alliance, held firm. The University Grants Commission (UGC), one of the much-criticized bureaucracies set in motion during this period, was left to look after the hapless universities.

Ironically, and to India's great misfortune, this was the time when the major research universities of the West, especially in the United States, were creating a formidable assembly of global talents for scientific research—including many from India. It is unclear if this phenomenal enterprise, which assured America's global leadership in the sciences for the rest of the century and beyond, remained largely unknown in India due to more restricted contacts with the West caused by exigencies of the Cold War and India's foreign policy choices. The educationist and physicist, B. M. Udgaonkar (1996), has written extensively and incisively about the struggles of this period. His comments will not be repeated here except to note that India's science establishment seemed to have little interest in the fate of the doomed institutions. Even Saha, whose heart was in the universities and who spoke forcefully against the top-down agenda of Bhabha and his colleagues (Anderson 1974), was unable to force reform. In other words, the massive expansion of science by the great heroes paradoxically sowed the seeds for the crisis the country faces today. Their miscalculation is typical of the times. Many of the research institutions placed their faith in the economy of shortages, whereby the student market would remain captive, the inflow of resources would remain protected, and neither competition nor accountability would pose challenges. When the markets finally began to change in the 1990s, they were left unprepared.

Table 1: Number and Types of Universities (as of July 15, 2009)

Category*	Total Number	Percentage
Central Universities	40	8
State Universities	236	49
Deemed to be Universities	127	26
Private Universities	42	9
Institutions of National Importance	33	7
Institutions Established under State Legislation	5	1
Total University Level Institutions	483	
Total Number of Colleges	20,918	

*Source: University Grants Commission (UGC) in Rama Rao (2010: 76).

NOW AND THE YEARS AHEAD

Some quantitative estimates available in the numerous recent reports on the state of India's educational system highlight the depth of the crisis. They can also explain why a substantial increase in the number of higher education institutions, made over the years, remains grossly inadequate. (See Table 1 for a summary of the number and types of institutions of higher education in India today.)

For example, India had 17 universities at Independence in 1947; in 2009, that number was 483, an impressive 30-fold increase in six decades. But on a per capita basis, India needs to have 2,900; 3,600; and 4,000 universities to equal South Korea, the United Kingdom, and the United States, respectively. India's numbers, when analyzed in terms of the country's R&D expenditure in academia, are even more telling. In a recent article, Rama Rao writes:

It is interesting to infer from the data...that academic R&D, expressed as a percentage of a nation's total R&D expenditure, correlates with a nation's wealth intensity, per capita income adjusted to purchase price parity (PPP).... India invests about 4% of its total R&D in academic R&D while [the] US, nearly 15 times more prosperous than India, invests 20% of its total R&D expenditure in academic R&D. Given that US R&D expenditure is 30 to 40 times that of India, the actual investment in academic R&D by the two countries differs by more than a factor of 200 (2010: 80).

The same article notes that the United States produces about 27,000 PhDs annually in science and engineering, while India produces a total of 6,600: 5,500 in the basic sciences and 1,100 in engineering. The latter number needs to be viewed in the context of a current shortfall of about 80,000 in engineering colleges. In other words, given the number of PhDs awarded in engineering annually, today's shortage can be made up in a staggering 80 years at today's pace. These mind-numbing numbers, however, do not even begin to address the quality of the PhDs produced. For a comparative estimate, TIFR, India's premier research institute in the basic sciences, with a faculty of 240, produces about 30 PhDs in a year; its world-renowned school of pure mathematics, with a faculty of 40, has produced between 1 and 2 PhDs per year on average in recent years. These astoundingly small numbers make no difference to the bottom line, but raise few eyebrows.

A comparison across the globe, in an influential article by David King (2004), titled the "Scientific Impact of Nations"—with a wink and a nod to Adam Smith—showed that as of 2002, India ranked thirty-first among the 32 nations included in the study. (The countries are: Australia, Austria, Belgium, Brazil, Canada, China, Denmark, Finland, France, Germany, Greece, India, Iran, Ireland, Israel, Italy, Japan, Luxembourg, the Netherlands, Poland, Portugal, Russia, Singapore, Spain, South Africa, South Korea, Sweden, Switzerland, Taiwan, the United Kingdom, and the United States.) The initial skepticism in India concerning the metrics faded rapidly as many came to realize that the report's conclusions were indeed correct. The report spawned a great deal of self-criticism, an example of which is quoted below:

> While the universities accounted for 60 percent of research output in the country in the 1950s, their share in the country's research output has dropped to less than 10 percent today. It is this reality that underlies the reported differential in the growth of research articles

between China and India. In 1998, China's output of research articles (~20,500) was not very different from that of India (17,500): by 2008, China's (~1,12,000) was 2.7 times that of India (~41,000) (Source: *Science Citation Index*). India's share of world S&T citation is less than 1 percent and is still lower in the world's top 1 percent of the most cited publications. Consequently, in the Shanghai Jiao Tong University Research Intensive Ranking of World Universities, India neither figures among the top 250 universities nor among the top 25 universities in the Asia-Pacific region (Rama Rao 2009: 81).

The undergraduate situation is even worse. A recent study summarizes the observations, cited in the same article by Rama Rao:

▸ The majority of students studying toward a BSc degree across the country do so only because they are unable to secure admission into professional courses.

▸ The rigid bifurcation into fixed combinations (Physics, Chemistry, Mathematics or Chemistry, Botany, Zoology) insisted upon at the BSc level severely limits the competence of science graduates for interdisciplinary advanced courses.

▸ Colleges are generally ill-equipped, overcrowded, and poorly staffed. The infrastructures found in most colleges are pathetic. Due to lack of experimental facilities, science is taught unimaginatively. Quality and excellence in teaching go unrecognized and unrewarded. Generally, teaching has remained divorced from research. As a result there is little training of students in methods of scientific inquiry (Rama Rao 2009: 81).

Appendix II contains a summary of recommendations made recently by the National Knowledge Commission for colleges and universities, from which it is easy to gauge the severity of the broader crisis in higher education. A recent newspaper article reports on one of the many attempts by the government of India to get a grip on the situation, an attempt that would have been unimaginable only a few years back:

[The] Human resource development (HRD) minister...called for "collaboration" [with] the Indian Diaspora in building the education sector and invited them back to the land of "new opportunities … the government plans to increase the gross enrollment ratio of children reaching college from 12 to 30 percent by 2020. To accommodate the increasing number of children reaching higher educational institutes, 1,000 more universities and 45,000 more colleges will be needed. "This is a mind boggling challenge," the minister said ("Kapil Sibal" 2011).

The numbers imply, in plain terms, that India needs to set up about 10 universities every month for the next decade. This scale of expansion is more than mind-boggling: it is impossible by any conventional methods. It takes about a decade for a teenaged undergraduate student to become a qualified teacher and researcher, and no alternative shortcut is known. The current pace of expansion of institutions already places enormous burdens on the institutions due to the severe shortage of high-quality teachers and researchers, and dooms them to a future of mediocrity from day one (Bhattacharya 2009). It is sadly obvious that even with the best of efforts, India will not be able to achieve this rate of growth, nor will it be able to prevent a decline in the short term, when compared to its peer nations.

The best India can hope for is to slow the rate of decline. This is particularly tragic since the country has recently made a turn toward a measurable, albeit highly inequitable, economic prosperity. "In the old days we had no money but we had the people. Today, we have the money but not the people," remarked the noted biologist Obaid Siddiqui in a recent academic forum (2009). The government today is more aware of the seriousness of the crisis than ever before. It is willing and able to provide meaningful support to both education and research without having to choose one or the other. Moreover, immensely powerful modern information technology, if used creatively, has the capacity to vastly improve the lots of Nehru's "few hundred million people in India" in ways unimaginable just a few decades ago.

Broadly speaking, India has long passed the point where throwing money at the problem can do much good. It desperately needs to create a workforce capable of teaching in high-quality higher education institutions, or risk serious social and political unrest stemming from unfulfilled aspirations of 100 million youngsters in the very near future. Through all these years, overseers of India's higher education have failed, utterly and consistently, like the milk-watchers in Tagore's story. They refused to recognize what others in the knowledge business have known for a long time: that knowledge is best acquired where knowledge is created, not only for those who receive the knowledge, but also for those who create it.

In the area of science education, the recent creation of the Indian Institutes of Science Education and Research (IISERs) and the decision by the Indian Institute of Science to start undergraduate programs are, at long last, steps in the right direction. It would be important to acknowledge that a premier research university in the West—not focused narrowly on science and engineering alone—has delivered, perhaps not perfect, but the best higher education in modern times. In fact, emulating the West in creating tried and true universities of the postwar era (which also face critical challenges today) is obviously among the wiser choices to make. Along the way, it would be liberating to assign the responsibility for the monumental policy mistakes where it belongs, namely, at the feet of some of India's heroes and their disciples, so that effective action can be taken without worrying about whose legacy is imperiled.

In view of Joan Robinson's famous comment that in India, everything and its opposite are simultaneously true, it needs to be remembered that India is rapidly growing into more than one country. Staggering disparities exist in the state of higher education between different groups of states, not to mention the socially and financially underprivileged—"the other India"—which has no realistic access to higher education, now or in the near future. One solution cannot suit all, but some solutions will suit some. The INSA report indicates that the depth of the problems and the urgent need to find solutions are at last finding space in the national discourse on the broader education crisis. Sixty years after Independence, India needs a fresh mutiny today, perhaps thousands of mutinies all over the country, aimed at overcoming the status quo and finding local solutions. One hopes India's scientists—teachers and researchers—will choose to become a part of the many possible solutions.

APPENDIX I

Scientific Policy Resolution, 1958. Jawaharlal Nehru
New Delhi, March 4,1958/13th Phalguna, 1879

1. No. 131/CF/57 The key to national prosperity, apart from the spirit of the people, lies, in the modern age, in the effective combination of three factors: technology, raw materials and capital, of which the first is perhaps the most important, since the creation and adoption of new scientific techniques can, in fact, make up for a deficiency in natural resources, and reduce demands on capital. But technology can only grow out of the study of science and its applications.

2. The dominating feature of the contemporary world is the intense cultivation of science on a large scale, and its application to meet a country's requirements. It is this, which, for the first time in man's history, has given to the common man in countries advanced in science, a standard of living and social and cultural amenities, which were once confined to a very small privileged minority of the population. Science has led to the growth and diffusion of culture to an extent never possible before. It has not only radically altered man's material environment, but, what is of still deeper significance, it has provided new tools of thought and has extended man's mental horizon. It has thus influenced even the basic values of life, and given to civilization a new vitality and a new dynamism.

3. It is only through the scientific approach and method and the use of scientific knowledge that reasonable material and cultural amenities and services can be provided for every member of the community, and it is out of recognition of this possibility that the idea of a welfare state has grown. It is characteristic of the present world that the progress towards the practical realisation of a welfare state differs widely from country to country in direct relation to the extent of industrialisation and the effort and resources applied in the pursuit of science.

4. The wealth and prosperity of a nation depend on the effective utilisation of its human and material resources through industrialisation. The use of human material for industrialisation

demands its education in science and training in technical skills. Industry opens up possibilities of greater fulfilment for the individual. India's enormous resources of man-power can only become an asset in the modern world when trained and educated.

5. Science and technology can make up for deficiencies in raw materials by providing substitutes, or, indeed, by providing skills which can be exported in return for raw materials. In industrializing a country, [a] heavy price has to be paid in importing science and technology in the form of plant and machinery, highly paid personnel and technical consultants. An early and large scale development of science and technology in the country could therefore greatly reduce the drain on capital during the early and critical stages of industrialisation.

6. Science has developed at an ever-increasing pace since the beginning of the century, so that the gap between the advanced and backward countries has widened more and more. It is only by adopting the most vigorous measures and by putting forward our utmost effort into the development of science that we can bridge the gap. It is an inherent obligation of a great country like India, with its traditions of scholarship and original thinking and its great cultural heritage, to participate fully in the march of science, which is probably mankind's greatest enterprise today.

7. The Government of India have accordingly decided that the aims of their scientific policy will be:

    ▸ to foster, promote, and sustain, by all appropriate means, the cultivation of science, and scientific research in all its aspects— pure, applied, and educational;

    ▸ to ensure an adequate supply, within the country, of research scientists of the highest quality, and to recognize their work as an important component of the strength of the nation;

    ▸ to encourage, and initiate, with all possible speed, programmes for the training of scientific and technical personnel, on a scale adequate to fulfil the country's needs in science and education, agriculture and industry, and defence;

    ▸ to ensure that the creative talent of men and women is encouraged and finds full scope in scientific activity;

> ▸ to encourage individual initiative for the acquisition and dissemination of knowledge, and for the discovery of new knowledge, in an atmosphere of academic freedom;
> ▸ and, in general, to secure for the people of the country all the benefits that can accrue from the acquisition and application of scientific knowledge.

The Government of India have decided to pursue and accomplish these aims by offering good conditions of service to scientists and according them an honoured position, by associating scientists with the formulation of policies, and by taking such other measures as may be deemed necessary from time to time.

APPENDIX II: RECOMMENDATIONS BY THE NATIONAL KNOWLEDGE COMMISSION (NKC 2007)

Reform Existing Universities

The endeavor to transform higher education must include reforming existing institutions. Some essential steps are:

▸ Universities should be required to revise or restructure curriculum at least once every three years.

▸ Annual examinations that test memory rather than understanding should be supplemented with continuous internal assessment, which could begin with a weight of 25 percent in the total, to be raised to 50 percent over a stipulated period.

▸ NKC proposes a transition to a course credit system in which degrees are granted on the basis of completing a requisite number of credits from different courses, which will provide students with a variety of choices.

▸ Universities must become hubs of research once again to capture synergies between teaching and research. This requires not only policy measures but also changes in resource allocation, reward systems and mindsets.

▸ There must be a conscious effort to attract and retain talented faculty members through better working conditions combined with incentives for performance.

▶ The criteria for resource allocation to universities should seek to strike a much better balance between providing for salaries and/or pensions and providing for maintenance, development and/or investment. It should also recognize the importance of a critical minimum to ensure standards and strategic preferences to promote excellence.

▶ The infrastructures that support the teaching—learning process, such as libraries, laboratories and connectivity, need to be monitored and upgraded on a regular basis.

▶ There is an acute need to reform those structures of university governance that do not preserve autonomy or promote accountability. Much work needs to be done, but two important points deserve mention. The appointments of vice-chancellors must be freed from direct or indirect intervention on the part of governments, for these should be based on search processes and peer judgment alone. The review of the size and composition of university courts, academic councils and executive councils, which slow down decisionmaking processes and sometimes constitute an impediment to change, needs to be made a priority.

▶ The need is for smaller universities that are responsive to change and easier to manage, and these should be created.

Restructure Undergraduate Colleges

The system of university-affiliated colleges for undergraduate education, which may have been appropriate 50 years ago, is no longer adequate or appropriate, and there is an urgent need for its reform.

▶ The most obvious solution is to provide autonomy to colleges either as individual colleges or as clusters of colleges, on the basis of criteria that have been stipulated. However, this would provide a solution for a limited number of undergraduate colleges.

▶ Some of these affiliated colleges could be remodeled as community colleges, which could provide both vocational education and formal education.

▶ A central board of undergraduate education should be established, along with a state board of undergraduate education, which would state curricula and conduct examinations for undergraduate colleges that choose to be affiliated with them. These boards would separate the academic functions from the administrative functions and, at the same time, provide quality benchmarks.

▸ New undergraduate colleges could be established as community colleges and be affiliated with the central board of undergraduate education or state boards of undergraduate education, or with some of the new universities that are established.

REFERENCES

Anderson, Robert S. "Building Scientific Institutions in India: Saha and Bhabha." Occasional Paper Series 11. Centre for Developing Area Studies, McGill University, Montreal, 1975.

Bhabha, H. J. "The Allocation of Scientific Research in the Universities." *Proceedings of the National Institute of Science: India* 10 (1944).

———. Reported in *The Hindu* (Madras), December 14, 1965. Quoted in Anderson (1975: 84).

———. Remarks at the Foundation Laying Ceremony of the Tata Institute of Fundamental Research. January 1, 1954. Quoted in "Scientific Research: Autonomous Institutions and Universities." B. M. Udgaonkar. *History and Development of Higher Education in India*. Vol. 2. Ed. S. Sharma. New Delhi: Saroop and Sons, 1954.

———. "Science and Problems of Development." *Science,* February 4, 1966: 547.

Bhattacharya, Sabyasachi. "India's Education Experiment in Basic Sciences: The IISER Solution." India in Transition, Center for the Advanced Study of India, University of Pennsylvania, 2009.

Biswas, Arun Kumar, ed. *Collected Works of Mahendralal Sircar, Eugene Lafont and the Science Movement, 1860-1910.* Kolkata: Asiatic Society, 2001.

Haldane, J. B. S. *Science and Indian Culture.* Calcutta: New Age Publishers, 1964.

Indian Association for the Cultivation of Science. *A Century.* Calcutta: Indian Association of the Cultivation of Science, 1976.

———. *INSA 2010: A Vision Document for Indian Science.* New Delhi: Indian National Science Academy, 2010.

King, David. "Scientific Impact of Nations." *Nature* 430 (2004): 311-316.

Maddox, John. "Excellence in the Midst of Poverty. *Nature* 308 (1984): 581.

Menon, Gautam I., and Siddharthan, Rahul, "What We Can Learn From the Inter-academy Report." *Current Science* 99 (2010): 1011-1012.

Menon, M. G. K. "Science in India: Past and Present: A Sociological Perspective." *Science in India: Past and Present.* Ed. B. V. Subbarayappa. New Delhi: Popular Prakashan, 2004: 1-48.

Nandy, Ashis. "Defiance and Conformity in Science: The Identity of Jagadis Chandra Bose." *Science Studies* 2 (1972): 31-85.

National Knowledge Commission. "Report to the Nation, 2007" <http://www.knowledgecommission.gov.in/>.

———. "Report to the Nation, 2006-2009." February 2010 <http://www.knowledgecommission.gov.in/reports/report09.asp]>.

Palit, Chittabrata. First Meeting of Subscribers at the Senate Hall, Calcutta University, 1875. Cited in "Mahendralal Sircar, 1833-1904: The Quest for National Science." *Science and Empire: Essays in the Indian Context.* D. Kumar. New Delhi: Anamika Prakashan, 1991: 156-157.

Rama Rao, P. *Higher Science Education in Science in India: Achievements and Aspirations.* New Delhi: Indian National Science Academy, 2010.

Ramakrishnan, T. V., and Sondhi, S. "Challenges in Indian Higher Education: A View from Physics." India in Transition, Center for the Advanced Study of India, University of Pennsylvania, 2009.

Siddiqui, O. Comments Made on the Occasion of the Homi Bhabha Fellowship Conclave at the Tata Institute of Fundamental Research, Mumbai, November 2009.

Sircar, Mahendralal, "On the Desirability of a National Institution for the Cultivation of the Sciences by the Natives of India." *Calcutta Journal of Medicine* 2 (August 1869): 286-306.

Tagore, Rabindranath. *My Reminiscences.* New Delhi: Rupa & Co., 2002.

"Kapil Sibal Invites Indian Diaspora Back Home." *The Times of India,* January 7, 2011.

Udgaonkar, B. M. *Complete Works of B. M. Udgaonkar.* Vol. 2. Mumbai: Homi Bhabha Centre for Science Education, 1996.

Yash Pal. *Report by the Committee to Advise on Renovation and Rejuvenation of Higher Education.* New Delhi: Department of Human Resources, Government of India, 2009 <http://www.education.nic.in/HigherEdu/YPC-Report.pdf>.

Yash Pal, and Udgaonkar, B. M. "Development of the Interface between the National Laboratories and the Universities, Vigyan Karmee." *Journal of the Association of the Scientific Workers in India* 109:90 (October 1967): 1-3.

Contributors

Ajit Balakrishnan, an entrepreneur in the IT and media industries, is Chairman of the board of the Indian Institute of Management–Calcutta, and presently chairs the Indian Ministry of IT committee on Internet governance.

Boria Majumdar, Senior Research Fellow at the University of Central Lancashire, is the author of *Sellotape Legacy: Delhi and the Commonwealth Games* (with Nalin Mehta 2010), Executive Academic Editor of *Sport in Society*, and General Editor of the series *Sport in the Global Society*. He covered the Delhi Commonwealth Games for Times Now Television, India's leading news channel.

Gopal Guru is a Professor of Social and Political Theory in the Center of Political Science at Jawaharlal Nehru University. He is the author of numerous articles on Dalits, women, politics, and philosophy and the editor of *Humiliation: Claims and Context* (2009).

Lawrence Cohen is Professor of Anthropology and of South and Southeast Asian Studies at the University of California, Berkeley. His current research projects include *The Other Kidney*, a study of the intertwined histories of surgery and of governance in modern India.

Mukulika Banerjee, author of *The Pathan Unarmed* (2000) and *Why India Votes* (forthcoming), is Reader in Social Anthropology at the London School of Economics. Her current research is on popular perceptions of democracy in India and she is preparing a monograph on the subject.

Rajeswari Sunder Rajan is Global Distinguished Professor at New York University, in the Department of English. She has been Senior Fellow at the Nehru Memorial Museum and Library, New Delhi, and was Reader in the English faculty and Professorial Fellow of Wolfson College at the University of Oxford. Her publications include *Real and Imagined Women: Gender, Culture and Postcolonialism* (1993), *The Scandal of the State: Women, Law and Citizenship in Postcolonial India* (2003), and most recently, the co-edited volume *Crisis of Secularism in India* (2007).

Ranjani Mazumdar is Associate Professor of Cinema Studies at the School of Arts and Aesthetics, Jawaharlal Nehru University, New Delhi. An author and documentary filmmaker, her publications include *Bombay Cinema: An Archive of the City* (2007).

Sabyasachi Bhattacharya, a condensed matter physicist and the former director of the Tata Institute of Fundamental Research (TIFR) in Mumbai, is currently a distinguished professor at TIFR.

Sheldon Pollock is Ransford Professor of Sanskrit and Indian Studies at Columbia University. He is the author of *The Language of the Gods in the World of Men* (2006) and founding editor of the *Murty Classical Library of India* (Harvard). In 2010 he was awarded the Padma Shri by the government of India.

Suvir Kaul is A. M. Rosenthal Professor of English at the University of Pennsylvania. He is the author of *Poems of Nation, Anthems of Empire: English Verse in the Long Eighteenth Century* (2000). His edited and co-edited volumes include *The Partitions of Memory: the Afterlife of the Division of India* (2001).

Wendy Doniger is the Mircea Eliade Distinguished Service Professor of the History of Religions at the University of Chicago Divinity School. Her current projects include Hinduism for the *Norton Anthology of World Religions* (2013), *Faking It: Narratives of Circular Jewelry and Clever Women*, and *Horses for Lovers, Dogs for Husbands* (a novel).